RISK PERCEPTION, C
AND LEGAL CH

Alla mia famiglia
per l'amore e il supporto
che non mi hanno mai fatto mancare

Risk Perception, Culture, and Legal Change

A Comparative Study on Food Safety in the Wake of the Mad Cow Crisis

MATTEO FERRARI

University of Trento, Italy

Routledge
Taylor & Francis Group

LONDON AND NEW YORK

First published 2009 by Ashgate Publishing

Published 2016 by Routledge
2 Park Square, Milton Park, Abingdon, Oxfordshire OX14 4RN
711 Third Avenue, New York, NY 10017, USA

First issued in paperback 2016

Routledge is an imprint of the Taylor & Francis Group, an informa business

British Library Cataloguing in Publication Data
Ferrari, Matteo.
 Risk perception, culture, and legal change : a comparative
 study on food safety in the wake of the mad cow crisis.
 1. Bovine spongiform encephalopathy--Prevention--
 Government policy--Europe. 2. Bovine spongiform
 encephalopathy--Prevention--Government policy--Japan.
 3. Bovine spongiform encephalopathy--Prevention--
 Government policy--United States. 4. Food law and
 legislation--Europe. 5. Food law and legislation--Japan.
 6. Food law and legislation--United States. 7. Culture and
 law.
 I. Title
 344'.04232-dc22

Library of Congress Cataloging-in-Publication Data
Ferrari, Matteo.
 Risk perception, culture, and legal change : a comparative study on food
safety in the wake of the mad cow crisis / by Matteo Ferrari.
    p. cm.
 Includes bibliographical references and index.
 ISBN 978-0-7546-7811-3 (hardback) -- ISBN 978-0-7546-9604-9 (e-book)
1. Food law and legislation. 2. Food--Safety measures--Public
opinion. 3. Bovine spongiform encephalopathy--Law and legislation. I. Title.

 K3626.F47 2009
 344.04'232--dc22
                                                                              2009030154

 ISBN 13: 978-1-138-25113-7 (pbk)
 ISBN 13: 978-0-7546-7811-3 (hbk)

Contents

List of Tables

Foreword

In this provocative and persuasive book, Matteo Ferrari asks us to consider the complex social, political and legal issues that arise in industrial democracies as governments seek to ensure that citizens are nourished rather than sickened by their daily meals. For centuries, there was little need for government involvement in ensuring the viability of the food supply. But as hunters and gatherers yielded to cultivators and then to merchants, the consumption of food became increasingly distant from its source. Along with the gap dividing consumption from source came a rise in the danger that food, the most basic and essential component of life, could carry with it the seeds of illness and death.

A scholar of comparative law whose primary interest is the regulation of risk, Ferrari offers us a multi-course meal of legal analysis that is sure to satisfy a wide range of appetites. His starting-point is the seminal work of Mary Douglas and Aaron Wildavsky, who famously framed risk in cultural terms. Using a carefully crafted and nuanced case study of a food-borne threat to public health – the emergence of bovine spongiform encephalopathy (BSE), more commonly known as mad cow disease – Ferrari argues that the very notion of risk, as well as the understanding and evaluation of particular risks, reflects and shapes the values, preferences and prejudices of society.

Legal scholars have long been interested in the link between law and its social context, but they have made little progress in articulating a theory of legal change that takes into account the role of culture. Ferrari clearly acknowledges the difficulty of using culture as an explanation for legal change, but he does not shrink from the challenge. Instead, he offers an analytically sophisticated approach to the study of law and culture, and a compelling account of the role of culture in the perception of risk and the construction of regulatory and tort regimes that are designed to manage it.

Ferrari's keen comparative eye provides readers with a rich understanding of the similarities and differences in how the European Union, the United States and Japan reacted to the emergence of a potentially grave threat to the food supply. He is attentive to the many large and small differences between the EU, the US and Japan in the realms of regulatory structure, administrative action, legal doctrine, and more. At the same time, his exploration of food safety in those three regions directly confronts the relationship between underlying cultural configurations and national/regional approaches to the risks inherent in the food supply. Why, he asks, was Japan's response to BSE so rapid and far-reaching while the US was complacent and unmoved? Why did the willingness to rely on the tort system to compensate victims of BSE vary so significantly between jurisdictions? Ferrari never shrinks from the hard questions, and his answers are theoretically satisfying and analytically precise.

What readers will find in the pages that follow is an unusually powerful example of comparative interdisciplinary legal scholarship. Deftly blending doctrinal analysis, historical inquiry, cultural studies and an investigation of the regulatory process, Matteo Ferrari has brought to life the issue of food safety while challenging and refining a variety of academic orthodoxies. This is a book to be savored, for it helps us to better understand our most important legal institutions, how they shape our lives, and the way they reflect our deepest sensibilities.

Eric A. Feldman
University of Pennsylvania Law School

Preface

The book is presented as a case study of the transformations which legal systems have experienced in the years following the so-called "mad cow" crisis. The analysis will deal with three specific legal systems. The European Union (EU) system was the first choice. Bovine spongiform encephalopathy (BSE) originated in the old continent; furthermore, member states have surrendered most of their regulatory powers in the field of food safety to the EU and this process has accelerated in the wake of the mad cow crisis. For this reason, I have focused primarily on European food safety norms, integrating the analysis, where necessary, with references to national legislation (in particular, in England, France and Italy). The US's legal system was the second one selected. While this country has a long-standing tradition in the regulation of foodstuffs, BSE seems to have raised scant alarm. The US's leading role in the regulation and trade of foodstuffs ensures that its reactions to the mad cow crisis are interesting to explore. Finally, I have chosen to study the Japanese system. Japan has recently reformed its food safety framework. The BSE crisis, which has also affected this country, has played a major role in shaping the reforms, especially those concerning the administrative system of controls. The three legal systems considered are furthermore characterized by different socio-cultural environments. The analysis of such environments will permit some considerations to be drawn on the role that socio-cultural variables play in the process of legal change.

This study is divided into four chapters. Chapter 1 has a twofold goal. First, it outlines the distinct food cultures that are peculiar to Europe, the US and Japan; second, it sketches a theoretical model stressing the importance that socio-cultural variables can have in molding legal reforms. Chapter 2 deals with the administrative regulation of foodstuffs. Attention is devoted both to the general framework governing food safety and to the specific measures adopted to combat the spread of BSE. In addition, it takes the international dimension of food regulation into account as well, with reference to the increasing importance of the World Trade Organization and of food safety standards in the private sector. Chapter 3 focuses on liability for defective foodstuffs. The first part describes the evolution of the liability regimes, with particular regard to food products, adopting a historical perspective. The second part surveys the applicability of these regimes, with regard to the recovery of damages for the victims of variant Creutzfeldt-Jakob Disease (vCJD, the human variant of the BSE). In addition, further, alternative routes to compensation will be explored. The final chapter draws some conclusions on the interaction between risk, regulation and compensation, and on the importance of cultural analysis in comparative law studies.

The research periods I spent at the University of Pennsylvania Law School and at the Boston University School of Law have been essential in writing this work. In particular, for the suggestions I have received, I wish to thank professors Matthew Adler, Michael Baram, Daniela Caruso, Keith Hylton, Nicola Lugaresi, Patricia Maclachlan, Kristin Madison, Frances Miller, David Nelken, Theodore Ruger, and the two referees for Ashgate. I am particularly grateful to Professor Eric Feldman for having warmly supported me during all the stages of my research and for having agreed to write the Foreword.

I would also like to thank the editor of this book and all the staff who assisted me during the stages of the publication with great competence, Lesley Orme for her precious and patient work of review, and the Department of Legal Sciences of the University of Trento for having offered me the opportunity to carry out my research in a stimulating environment.

The preparation of the book would have not been possible without the suggestions, criticism and help I have received over the years by the members of the Trento research group on law and technology, led by Professor Giovanni Pascuzzi. Warm thanks to Giovanni Pascuzzi, Roberto Caso, Giuseppe Bellantuono, Andrea Rossato and to all the other fellows who, like me, are part of the group. I owe a particular mention and thanks to Umberto Izzo, who has introduced me to academic research and perseveres in spurring me forward on this path. Credit for the valuable suggestions and support I have received goes to all those mentioned; responsibility for any errors in the book is mine alone.

Matteo Ferrari
Trento, June 15, 2009

Chapter 1

Risk Perception, Culture, and Legal Change

... toute société se construit d'elle-même et du monde visible et invisible une vision qui lui est spécifique, et de cette vision dépend le tracé des limites de la juridicité, dont le champ se confond partout avec ce qu'une société estime vital pour sa cohésion et sa reproduction.

N. Rouland, *Anthropologie juridique*, Paris, 1988, 400

The emergence in the 1990s of Bovine Spongiform Encephalopathy (BSE), also known as mad cow disease, has triggered a host of reactions worldwide. Far from being homogeneous, the responses have varied greatly, depending on which legal system is examined. Europe, Japan and the United States can be considered, among the industrialized nations, paradigms of the different approaches followed across the world. As we shall see in detail in the following chapters, the European Union and Japan have adopted a strong precautionary approach in coping with the crisis, not only implementing severe *ad hoc* measures to curb the spread of the epidemic, but also reforming the general framework governing food safety. This does not seem to be the case for the US, which has adopted less restrictive anti-BSE measures and no general food safety reform.

These heterogeneous reactions might appear strange. BSE represented in many respects the typical food safety crisis. The scientific uncertainties regarding the origin and consequences of the disease, the difficulties in singling out the agents responsible for the diffusion of the epidemic, the interaction between risk and media, are all elements to be found in most of food safety cases. Given these features and their homogeneity across the world, we might expect to have similar responses in the different countries. But, as noted, these expectations are frustrated. My goal is to investigate why the legal responses have varied so markedly across the legal systems of a host of industrialized countries. In doing so, different explanations will be examined, ranging from statistical evidence to economic considerations. But all these accounts fail in some respects to provide a complete picture. The impression is that a factor is missing from the overall picture: in my view, this factor is culture (Echols 2001: 13). Culture plays a pivotal role in shaping legal changes, but it is a paradigm often neglected in comparative legal analysis. This is the reason why, among possible, concurrent justifications, I chose to focus my attention on the role that culture occupies in the process of legal change. My goal is not limited to illustrating how culture molded the legal reforms which occurred in the aftermath of the mad cow crisis: I will also seek to underline the methodological importance that the study of the cultural context has in analyzing any process of legal change.

Before describing the role that culture played in the BSE case, other possible explanations must be analyzed. The first (and most obvious) explanation concerns the number of BSE cases which occurred in the three legal systems. BSE has been mainly a European affair. Most of the cases occurred in Europe, while only a tiny fraction were identified in the rest of the world. It seems natural that, in the geographical areas where the number of infected animals was particularly high, the BSE risk has been perceived as high. No wonder, then, that Europe has implemented far-reaching legal reforms to counteract the spread of mad cow disease. On the other hand, in a country such as the US, where only three cases of BSE have occurred up to now, the disease has not triggered the same reactions of fear that the Europeans have experienced.[1] The lack of social alarm surrounding BSE did not generate the conditions for promoting legal reform of the food safety framework. Stated in general terms, reform would have occurred only in those countries where real problems in relation to BSE were present.

Despite the simple attractiveness of such an explanation, it seems to fail in many respects. First, it fails with regard to Japan, which has implemented comprehensive reform of its food safety framework in the wake of the mad cow crisis; nonetheless, in the years between 1987 and 2006, only 31 cases of BSE occurred in the country. The link between incidence of cases and legal reforms appears to be, therefore, particularly weak. Second, the link also seems dubious with regard to Europe. It should, indeed, be specified that most BSE cases occurred in one of the member states that form the European Union, namely, the United Kingdom. If we compare the number of BSE-infected animals in the years between 1987 and 2006 in the UK (184,508) with those in France (989) and Italy (139), we can note the huge gap in the incidence of cases (see Table 1.1).

BSE, thus, has been mainly a British affair, while the risk of infection in the other European countries has been limited, if not extremely low.[2] This remark does not completely invalidate the link between statistical incidence and legal reforms, but poses some further doubts on its validity. It is true that the epidemic happening in one of the member states may have played some role in moving the European institutions to reform the supranational framework governing food safety. This might be particularly true in the agricultural sector, where integration is strong and the European Union plays a central role. But, on the other hand, there are plenty of cases where national crises have not triggered general reforms, such as occurred

---

1   The low number of BSE cases detected in the US could also derive from the testing policy implemented in the country. As we will see in the chapter dedicated to the administrative food safety framework, only a tiny percentage of the animals slaughtered in the US are tested for BSE: this might imply that some infected animals go unreported in the statistics. In Europe and, above all, in Japan, a much more severe testing policy has been implemented, with the consequence that statistical data at this regard appear to be more accurate than the American ones.

2   Regarding this aspect, see the UK BSE Inquiry Report, *Findings and Conclusion*, vol. I, 2.

Table 1.1   Comparison of BSE and variant Creutzfeldt-Jakob Disease (vCJD) cases in five countries

	UK	Italy	France	Japan	US
BSE cases (1987–2006)	184,508	139	989	31	3
Cattle population (millions)	10,400,000	6,250,000	19,400,000	4,390,000	104,800,000
vCJD cases (September 2008)	164	1	23	1	3

Note: For statistics related to the BSE and vCJD see http://www.cjd.ed.ac.uk/index.htm.

in the aftermath of the mad cow crisis. *Ad hoc* measures would probably have been sufficient to halt the spread of the disease from the UK to the other European countries. Therefore, the question regarding the reasons why BSE has triggered such reactions in Europe remains. It is evident that BSE has not been considered simply a national crisis, but something more. This points to the conclusion that the incidence of BSE cases played some role in the European context, and to a lesser extent also in the Japanese case: this is particularly true in the case of the UK, where the high number of BSE cases may have constituted an important engine for legal change. Nonetheless, the incidence factor cannot, *per se*, explain the quantity and quality of the reforms enacted.

The second possible explanation concerns the ability of business operators and other pressure groups to influence the legal arena. Reference is made here to phenomena such as lobbying and agency capture. By lobbying, I mean the ability of pressure groups to influence political circuits in order to obtain legislation whose content is in line with the interests of the groups. "Agency capture" refers to the capacity of the industry to manipulate the decisions taken by the regulatory authorities, again with the aim of steering them towards the desired goals. In other words, the regulated capture the regulator. Theoretical analysis predicts that small, well-organized groups, with high stakes and enough resources will be highly effective in the lobbying or capture process (Stiglitz 2001; von Wangenheim 1999; Epstein, Halloran 1995; Niskanen 1994). It should be borne in mind, indeed, that both lobbying and agency capture are the products of a dynamic and competitive process, in which different interest groups struggle in order to influence the political or regulatory circuit (Becker 1983). The stronger the group (that is, with the features mentioned above), the higher the probability that it will be able to dominate in the competition with the other groups.

In the context of BSE, we might imagine that strong pressure groups have been able to influence the political arena, determining the enactment or the absence of legal reforms, depending on the legal system considered. More specifically, if this theoretical model were applied to the mad cow crisis, in the US we should find strong agricultural lobbies preventing any attempt to reform the food safety framework. Conversely, in Europe and Japan, consumer lobbies would have gained centre stage in the political arena, determining the wave of reforms I will describe in the next chapters. But there is only slim support for such an explanatory model.

With regard to the US, agricultural lobbies have been traditionally very important, both in Congress and at Agency level (Wolpe 1990; Wittenberg, Wittenberg 1989). Agricultural lobbies are among the major contributors in the fund-raising campaigns of many candidates in Congress, being at the same time able to gather many votes during elections (Browne 1988; Hansen 1991; Heinz et al. 1993; de Gorter, Swinnen 2002; Gawande 2005). This may explain why such lobbies are able to bring strong pressure to bear on the committees dealing with agricultural affairs, contributing to directing their political agendas.[3] Similar comments can be made with regard to the influence that the farming industry, and the cattle lobbies in particular, have in the US Department of Agriculture (USDA; Nestle 2007, 2003; Schlosser 2005; Justice 2004; Rampton, Stauber 2004). Here we are more properly speaking of agency capture than of lobbying, even if there are many points of contact between the two phenomena. In both cases, indeed, the core feature is revealed by the ability of the pressure group to drive the political action of a public body, by molding the choices of the latter. In addition to the factors previously mentioned, another important element explaining the occurrence of agency capture relates to the closeness between the regulator and the regulated. The more an agency specializes in regulating a particular production sector, the closer will be the ties it has with the operators of that sector. This is particularly true in the case of the USDA (Casey 1998; Nestle 2003: 62 ff.). In this it differs, for example, from the Food and Drug Administration (FDA), which oversees different economic areas, whereas the USDA regulates a very specific field of the national economy, its competence being limited to the agriculture sector. Moreover, with regard to food safety, it has even more specific competences, since it is responsible only for the production and marketing of meat and poultry.

In such an environment, farm industries and the meat business are facilitated in advancing their requests, since they largely appear as the only counterparts in the regulatory process.[4] It is not surprising that the USDA has been often criticized

---

3   The ability of agricultural lobbies to influence the activities of the committees is particularly evident in the Senate. Indeed, any state elects two senators, regardless of its population size. This implies that states with strong agricultural economies but with low populations can play on an equal footing with other, more populous, states. In such a system, the interests of the agricultural sector, and of the lobbies connected to it, are better represented in the Senate than in the House.

4   As we will see in Chapter 2, the mission of the USDA has been business-oriented since the very beginning, that is, aimed at the promotion of US agriculture. The protection of consumer interests is something that was added on later and which has not as yet gained the same importance as the pro-business goal. The pro-business attitude is further reinforced by

for being too sensitive to the interests of the industry. This remark finds support in the many delays and "softening" to which food safety reforms have been subjected in the history of the agency (Casey 1998: 150 ff.; McGarity 2005: 389–90). Thus, at first glance, the initial assertion that powerful lobbies could have prevented the enactment of legal reforms seems to find some support.

Nonetheless, the accuracy of this assertion is called into question if we compare the strength of the American agricultural lobbies to those existing in Europe and Japan. Europe also has strong pressure groups in this area (van Schendelen 1994; Pedler 2002). The so-called Common Agricultural Policy (CAP), an (anticompetitive) system of subsidies aimed at protecting the European agricultural market, is a good example of how lobbies have been able to shape public interventions in a way which conforms to their interests (Fennell 1997; Ritson, Harvey 1997; Ingersent, Rayner, Hine 1998; Howart 2000; Rickard 2000; Whetstone 2000; Baldwin, Wyplosz 2004: 229–30). In more recent times, the same lobbies have defeated most of the attempts to reform the CAP (Elliott, Heath 2000; Swinbank, Daugbjerg 2006). The very fact that the risks deriving from the BSE epidemic have been long downplayed within the European institutions depended, among other things, on the influence that interest groups had in the committees dealing with food safety and animal health matters.

Given the strength of the European lobbies, we should expect an outcome similar to the American one. But, as noted before, the amount and quality of the reforms enacted in the wake of the mad cow crisis show the industry groups' inability to counteract the demand for changes. This remark also holds true in the light of the statistical evidence previously reported. An objection to our conclusion, indeed, would stress the fact that most of the BSE cases occurred in Europe, while in the US only three cases were reported. Hence it is natural that the European lobbies, faced with the vast scale of the epidemic, did not succeed in curbing the demand for reforms. But this contention does not take account of the fact that BSE has mostly been a British affair. Why were agricultural lobbies of countries other than the UK unable to counteract the reforms? Such reforms can be considered a burdensome onus for the food industry, imposing huge economic costs upon it.[5] Indeed, in the first years following the appearance of mad cow disease, there was a tendency, supported both by the British government and by the competent

---

the so-called "revolving door" practice, under which former USDA managers, once retired, are hired by the industry as consultants. In this way, the regulated, through these consultants, have a privileged channel by which to express their views and requests (McGarity 2005: 390–92). The phenomenon is not limited to the US: in Japan, for example, bureaucracy and industry are strictly intertwined.

5   The principle of traceability, the adoption of HACCP procedures, the extension of product liability also to primary agricultural products are all examples of new requirements imposed on food operators which entail the need to reorganize their structures and to adopt new precautions that, on their own, imply economic costs.

European committees, to consider BSE exclusively as a British problem (Medina Ortega 1997; Krapohl, Zurek 2006).

In this way, lobbies have been able for some years to block attempts to reform the food safety system. The turning-point, after which pressure groups failed to counteract the demand for reforms, came when the BSE epidemic changed status, becoming a scandal.[6]

Similar considerations can be expressed with regard to Japan. In the Land of the Rising Sun, agricultural and cattle lobbies are also influential and have determined, over the years, the enactment by the government of protectionist policies in favor of the farmers (Bullock 1997; Mulgan 2005). Such an attitude has often triggered trade wars with other countries, which on several occasions have resulted in Japan being accused of distorting international competition (Davis 2003). The strong power which agricultural lobbies possess in the Japanese political arena is explained by their electoral weight. Farmers can be considered the main reserve of votes for the Liberal Democratic Party (LDP), the electoral formation which has dominated in Japan almost without interruption since the end of World War II.[7] But the strength of the agricultural lobbies also depends on the financial power that especially the main agricultural cooperative, Nokyo, was able to create over the years (Bullock 1997).

With specific regard to the cattle industry, there has traditionally been scant production of beef in Japan. The reasons for such meager production are due not only to the scarcity of land available for grazing, but also to historical and cultural reasons (Longworth 1983: 54 ff.; Cwiertka 2006: 24 ff.). The handling of meat was considered impure and those who carried out this activity were discriminated against. The discrimination they suffered, conversely, gave rise to the strong sense of community that in recent times still characterized the so-called "butchers' guild" (Longworth 1983: 74). The closeness and isolation of the guild, on its own, have fostered the development of powers of control over the entire meat industry, with regard both to domestic production and the import of beef.

Thus, despite the economic marginality of meat production in Japan, the beef lobby has gained a major role in the political arena, at least with regard to the decisions regarding meat interests. This role has concerned not only the Japanese Parliament, but also the Ministry of Agriculture, Forestry and Fisheries, which largely regulates the agricultural sector. In a system in which bureaucratic ranks

---

6 The representative date of this turning-point can be considered as March 20, 1996, when the British Minister of Health announced a link between BSE and the variant Creutzelfdt-Jakob Disease (vCJD).

7 Mulgan (2005: 263) points to the fact that a poorly balanced electoral system and a single, powerful farmers' cooperative (Nokyo) have given rise to the great influence that agricultural lobbies have been able to exercise in the policy-making process. Although reforms have been introduced in the recent years to counteract the disproportionate power enjoyed by agricultural lobbies, their influence is still important.

are strictly intertwined with the industries, it is natural that public functionaries are particularly sensitive to the interests of the regulated.[8]

As in the European case, pressure groups in Japan have also had to surrender when confronted with the magnitude of the scandal triggered by the mad cow disease. The idea that the scandal has driven the reforms enacted in the wake of the BSE crisis, therefore, emerges further reinforced by the analysis of the Japanese experience. The only country where BSE has not become a scandal, that is, the US, also coincides, significantly, with a legal system where no noteworthy reforms have been made in the realm of food safety.

Agricultural lobbies are not the only pressure groups able to influence the enactment of reforms. Some consideration must also be given to the role that consumer associations could have had in this regard. If the industry lobbies might have hindered the path of the reforms, conversely, consumer groups may have speeded up reform. It is evident that, by fostering the drama and stressing the consequences connected to mad cow disease, such groups may have gained importance and prestige within the political circuits, using these factors for other, future battles as well. But also in this context there are features which do not fit such a picture. If the hypothesis is correct, indeed, we should expect strong consumer groups in Europe and Japan, and weak ones in the US.

This, however, is not the case if one looks at the real world. American consumer groups do not play a marginal role in the political arena (Maney, Bykerk 1994; Harris, Milkis 1996; Maclachlan 2006: 244–5). Starting at least in the 1970s, they have raised their voices on many occasions, counteracting the lobbying efforts of the industry within Congress and the regulatory agencies.[9] The very creation of the Environmental Protection Agency (EPA), established in 1970 by President Nixon, witnesses a more pro-consumer attitude taken by the federal government, especially when its mission is compared to that of other federal agencies (Harris, Milkis 1996: 225 ff.). In the same vein, activists such as Ralph Nader have built their political fortunes on the campaigns they have conducted on behalf of consumers (Martin 2002).

---

8   The links between industries and ministries are numerous. One of the most well-known aspects of such intricacies is given by the so-called *amakudari*, a practice consisting in the hiring of former public managers by the industry they once supervised. Another important element able to influence the relationship between industries and bureaucracies, fostering an environment of cooperation between the two, consists in the so-called "administrative guidance." This expression refers to the practice of ministries of releasing informal "guidelines" to those regulated, in order to direct their conduct in relation to specific problems. Despite the lack of coercive force of these guidelines, they are almost uniformly followed by the operators, at least in order to avoid the ostracism associated with the failure to respect the guidance (Young 1984).

9   Vogel (2003: 575 ff.) notes that, since the 1960s and up to the beginning of the 1980s, many sectors of American society were very sharply risk averse and sustained strict regulations protecting the environment and consumers' interests.

Europe and Japan do not have such a dynamic tradition of consumer movements as there is in the US. With regard to Europe, it was during the years when the mad cow crisis occurred that consumer lobbies began to participate actively in the political debate at European level. But BSE was not the first emergency in which consumer groups were able to exercise their influence on European institutions. Rather, it has been used as a blueprint by consumer movements in their struggle to gain a more institutional role in the political process of the European institutions. In fact, consumer groups have only marginally been able to influence the regulatory process set in train by the BSE crisis. Nonetheless, their inability to participate in such a process, together with the infamous consequences associated with the mad cow crisis, was later depicted as the proof that their exclusion can have deleterious effects on the protection of consumers' interests. Nowadays, consumer lobbies have a strong influence on other sensitive food safety issues: for example, in the case of genetically modified organisms, these groups seem able to effectively influence the final choices. But such influence cannot be explained if we do not consider that the BSE scandal has been used by such lobbies as a means of gaining political weight within the European regulatory process (Jasanoff 2005: 121 ff.).[10] The strategy followed by the consumer movements is part of a wider problem which is still affecting the European Union, often portrayed as democratic deficit (Boyce 1993; Abromeit 1998; Goodhart 2007). It is not by chance, for example, that the European Parliament has also exploited the opportunity presented by the mad cow crisis to attack the Commission (and the "comitology," as it has been called, behind it[11]), claiming that a more active role should be conferred on the Parliament, in the case of issues relating to the health of the European citizens.[12]

---

10   Ansell, Maxwell, Sicurelli (2006: 99) write: "The anti-GMO movement could capitalize on the issue salience of the mad cow crisis because it was able to effectively mobilize at each of these levels and to some extent mobilize one against the other." It should be further noted that, along with consumer lobbies acting directly within the European institutions, there are also lobbies that influence the politics of the single Member States which, on their own, "reverse" indirectly such influence on the European institutions. For example, France is one of the Member States most fiercely opposed to genetically modified organisms at the European level. Such opposition cannot be fully explained if we do not consider the influence that French consumer groups (along with traditionalist agricultural lobbies) have on the choices concerning this kind of products (Ansell, Maxwell, Sicurelli 2006: 106 ff.; Bonny 2003).

11   Comitology refers to the role played by the committees in the European law-making process. The committees are groups which provide assistance to the European Commission in preparing the various pieces of legislation. Member States appoint the members of the committees: in such a way the states are able to maintain direct control over the law-making process (Joerges, Vos 1999; Bergström 2005). For further details on the role of the committees, see Chapter 2.

12   The Report prepared by Medina Ortega (1997) denounces the maladministration of the crisis, repeatedly pointing to the lack of cooperation between the Commission and the Parliament. In replying to the findings of the report, Jacques Santer, at that time president

As for Japan, here consumer movements probably suffer the weakest position with respect to the other two legal systems considered. Consumerism is not a long-standing tradition in this country, although over recent years its importance has been steadily increasing (Vogel 1999; Maclachlan 2002; Hirata 2004b). Traditionally the notion of "public interest" has played a pivotal role in the Japanese political context: a notion closer to the interests of national productivity than to the protection of the consumers' rights. Even the recent reforms, which have introduced new pieces of legislation aimed at protecting consumers, seem to conform to the public interest paradigm, in the sense that the rights of the individuals are more muted than in the European and American consumer laws, by considerations relating to the protection of the national economy and of the producers' interests.[13] The role itself of the consumers' associations is to some extent confined by the presence of the consumer centers, which are semi-governmental bodies. Many of the issues that in the US and Europe are managed by (private) consumers' associations, in Japan are channeled through these centers, which provide services and assistance to the citizens (Ramseyer 1996; Nottage 2004). It is clear that, to some extent at least, in such a way the government is able to monitor consumerism, channeling the demand for social change in the desired direction (Upham 1987; Vogel 1999: 198).

To recapitulate, therefore, lobbying, both by agricultural producers and consumer associations, does not seem to have been the main cause of the divergent approach to the mad cow crisis adopted in the US, Europe and Japan. It may have contributed, to some extent, to magnifying or downplaying the risks associated with BSE, but does not in itself provide a decisive explanation for the differences between the three legal systems. It is necessary to have regard to other possible causes which may have determined this variance. I intend to introduce a third explanatory model that can function as a general background against which other causes interact, making their own contribution. The core idea is that phenomena, such as the lobbying, or data, such as statistical evidence, cannot be read without making reference to the context in which they emerge. This context is characterized, first and foremost, by cognitive and cultural features. These aspects largely determine the distinct approaches which can be observed in different countries. Moreover, focusing on the cognitive and cultural aspects will allow us a sharper appreciation of the role that the notion of scandal has played in determining the legal responses adopted in the three legal systems considered.

---

of the Commission, stressed the importance of a closer involvement of the Parliament in the decision-making process.

13   Maclachlan (1999: 263–4), speaking of the public interest paradigm in Japan in relation to the product liability law enacted in 1994, points to the fact that public interest means mainly producers' interests and that the paradigm has heavily influenced the enactment and implementation of the new law.

Law and Cognitive Sciences

The Human Mind and Bounded Rationality

The relationship between law and cognitive sciences is a relatively new field of inquiry. Research into the relationship between economics and behavioral sciences goes back much further, in which cognitivism plays a fundamental role (Simon 1955, 1982). The starting-point can be traced back to the mounting dissatisfaction economists felt with regard to the rational actor model of decision-making (also known as rational choice theory). A plurality of rational choice theories have been elaborated, ranging from the model in which the actor maximizes her own ends (whatever they are) to the model in which she maximizes her self-interest or her wealth (Korobkin, Ulen 2000). Despite the variance in the models, the core of all the theories consists in the prediction that individuals will act rationally, following patterns of decision maximizing their expected utility. These patterns of decision-making, moreover, allow the use of mathematical formulae aimed at predicting the conduct of the actors. This is true not only in the sense that it is possible to describe the future behavior of the individuals. Such behavior, indeed, can also be guided in the desired direction, by imposing incentives and disincentives on the actors, which can force them to adopt a specific line of conduct.

The problem with the mathematical precision of such predictive power is that it can be easily falsified by empirical evidence. Critics stress that it ends up being merely a theoretical model, without the possibility of being verified in the real world. There are countless examples in which the actor decides in sub-optimal ways, departing from the rational model (Kahneman, Slovic, Tversky 1986; Gilovich, Griffin, Kahneman 2002). First, individuals seem to respond not only to considerations maximizing utility, but also to fairness. Second, and more importantly from a cognitive point of view, they appear to take "simplified" decisions in contexts of uncertainty and/or complexity. The focus of attention rapidly centered on the routines our minds use in reaching decisions. Within such a context, part of the literature has considered the cognitive appreciation of the risks and the mental routines individuals adopt to cope with these risks. And nowadays, it is in this field that the liveliest debates occur.[14]

Drawing on the results achieved by the behavioral economists, law scholars in the second half of the 1990s began to focus their attention systematically on the implications that cognitive studies may have in the realm of the law. In particular, cognitive sciences have captured the attention of a particular group in

---

14   Some of the much-debated issues related to risk management and the role of cognitive processes and emotions concern: 1) the relation between cost benefit analysis procedures and cognitive/emotive considerations (Adler 2004); 2) the role of the government in protecting citizens from risks (Sunstein, Thaler 2003; Mitchell 2005), and 3) the relation between cognitive processes and cultural values, which I will analyze in further details in the following pages.

legal academic circles, namely law and economics scholars (Sunstein 1997, 2000; Jolls, Sunstein, Thaler 1998; Korobkin, Ulen 2000).[15] Given its interdisciplinary approach, it is no surprise that this group has shown itself to be the most sensitive to the suggestions coming from behavioral economics. On the other hand, the same (empirical) difficulties which made the economic models based on rational choice theories implausible are also evident in the context of law. This provides a further reason for enriching the legal discourse with the inspirations from the cognitive paradigm (Hanson, Kysar 1999a, 1999b).

The basic contention of this new academic movement lies in the idea that, given the complexity of the choices the actors face in almost any situation, they prefer using various mental shortcuts in order to simplify the decision-making process. The use of these routines creates a situation in which the human mind is unable to process the entire amount of information needed to take a (fully) rational decision, a condition which is often referred as of "bounded rationality."[16] The fact that the rationality is bounded does not have to be considered as a negative element. It can, indeed, be conceived as an evolutionary response, rendering our decision-making process more efficient. Given the huge amount of data that any situation entails and the myriad of interactions (both among themselves and with the surrounding context) that such data imply, assessing all the information connected to a particular choice would have paralyzing effects on our mind. Nonetheless, even if bounded rationality is the bright evolutionary solution we have created to minimize the risks of these paralyzing effects, it also presents some drawbacks which may have a negative impact on the quality of our choices. This is the reason why such disadvantages are often referred as cognitive biases, to indicate their ability to influence negatively the final outcome of our choice. In order to facilitate their description, I will group such biases in five types.

The first group of biases concerns the so-called *representativeness* heuristic. According to this bias, people tend to overemphasize specific features of an event/ person and use such features to "represent" that event/person. The bias finds its origin in the propensity to ignore base rates, that is, to neglect the statistical evidence concerning a fact in lieu of a particular characteristic of it able to attract the attention of the observer.[17] The problem with the representativeness heuristic is that

---

15   Already in the 1980s and early 1990s, a few authors had anticipated some of the themes belonging to the behavioral analysis of law: Edwards, von Winterfeldt 1986; Ellickson 1989; Eisenberg 1995. For an early critique of the law and economics movement on a behavioral basis, see Leff 1974. In Italy, the debate about the relation between law and cognitive sciences developed later: Bellantuono 2000; Caterina 2005, 2008.

16   Hanson, Yosifon (2003: 155) offer a radical and all-encompassing critique not only of the rational actor model, but also of what they call "its chief competitors," that is, the behavioral actor and the rationally bounded actor, advancing the idea that it is more appropriate to focus on the situation in which choices are taken rather than on the agents' behavior.

17   Korobkin, Ulen (2000: 1086–7) report the example of the US Federal Rules of Evidence, providing that evidence about the criminal precedents of a defendant cannot

we categorize people and events on the basis of the salience of one of their features, thus downplaying the probability that they also partake of other categories.

A second bias whose dynamics are close to those of the representativeness heuristic is given by the *availability* heuristic. In this case, too, there is an incorrect use of base rates. But, in contradistinction to the first bias described, here the problem consists in the overestimation of the frequency of an event depending on the recent occurrence of similar events. It is the well-known heuristic of *memorable incidents*, often used by people for events such as airplane crashes or nuclear accidents.[18] In the context of risk regulation, the availability heuristic plays a pivotal role. A mixture of over-reactions to catastrophic risks by the population and populism by the governments (unable to counteract the pressure for reforms coming from their citizens) determines the outcome of regulations which appear too sensitive toward risks whose occurrence is not so probable. There are numerous cases in which regulatory responses have been driven by the heuristic of memorable incidents. The case of the restrictive regulations concerning atomic energy is one of the most vivid examples in this regard.[19] But another example in the realm of food safety concerns the recent avian flu emergency. Many countries, including Italy, the US, the UK, Japan, and France, have ordered great quantities of vaccine to deal with the threat posed by the new virus.

The problem, of course, is not only limited to regulations biased in favor of determined risks. Indeed, the main trouble concerns the inefficient distribution of resources following the decision to spend part of these resources on risks which are inexistent or, at least, negligible. It is evident that such resources are subtracted from more efficient uses, such as reducing other risks which are potentially more dangerous. To use terminology belonging to cost benefit analysis, the problem is the cost-effectiveness of the measures adopted, meaning their capacity to have cost-saving effects with respect to the risks they minimize.[20] As will emerge more clearly when dealing with the social amplification of risk, the availability

---

be used, unless in a series of exceptions. The rule is aimed at preventing the jurors being misled by previous convictions and finding the defendant guilty, representing her on the basis of one of her features (that is, the fact of having been previously convicted).

18   The expression "memorable incidents" is contained in Korobkin, Ulen (2000: 1087 ff.).

19   In Italy, the use of atomic energy was abandoned in 1987 when, in the aftermath of the Chernobyl disaster, an abrogative referendum was passed. But tight new regulations were also enacted in the United States in the months following the accident occurred at the Three Mile Island nuclear power plant in 1979. In both cases, incidents have played a major role in determining regulatory actions.

20   For a comparison of the cost-effectiveness of different regulatory interventions aimed at reducing various types of risk, see Morrall 1986, 2003; the author points to the fact that there are regulatory interventions which are very costly but not so effective in saving human lives. An example is the 1978 regulation concerning arsenic levels, aimed at reducing the risk of cancer, which turns out to be one of the most inefficient regulations in terms of cost per life saved.

heuristic is prone to manipulation by the so-called "fear entrepreneurs," parties who can obtain benefit from emphasizing certain risks. The natural propensity to overestimate the occurrence of memorable incidents can, thus, be reinforced by external actions.

Connected to the availability heuristic is another phenomenon, the so-called *availability cascades* (Kuran, Sunstein 1999). The cascade mechanism helps explain the rapid spread of alarming information about a particular risk within a society, but also the cross-national differences in risk perception. The basic idea is that, when a piece of information about a risk begins to spread, it creates a sort of exponential exposure of the risk, which is, therefore, magnified. The mechanism mimics that of the children's game known in the US as "Telephone." The fact that more and more individuals are aware of the risk, passing the information on, reinforces the idea that the risk deserves attention. The differences in cross-national perceptions of risk become clearer, according to the advocates of the availability cascades, since they can be seen as the by-products of a random diffusion of the risk information.[21]

A further group of biases affecting our cognitive abilities relates to *self-serving feelings*. The mind tends, indeed, to overestimate our capacity to control the events happening to us or to interpret their meaning in a self-serving way. In the first case, we speak of *overconfidence* bias, while in the second of *confirmatory* bias. The overconfidence bias concerns the feeling that "good things are more likely than average to happen to us and bad things are less likely than average to happen to us" (Korobkin, Ulen 2000: 1091). In other words, it consists in the belief that we are able to keep under control risks which depend on our activities (such as driving a car, skiing, and so on). Conversely, we tend to magnify risks we perceive as independent from our activities and, therefore, out of our control (for example, flying on an airplane, living close to a nuclear power plant, and so on).

On the other hand, the confirmatory bias relates to our capacity to interpret the information we receive in a way which conforms to our self-serving interests. We tend, indeed, to attribute a meaning to the information supporting our pre-conceived ideas. The point of contact with the overconfidence bias consists in the fact we interpret the information conforming to our interests in a positive light, downplaying the importance of the other. The final result is that, in the case of both forms of bias, we have a distorted perception of the risks we face and, consequently, we may adopt regulatory solutions which are not tuned to the real importance of the threat.

---

21   An important role is played by the media, which can reinforce the cascade mechanism, by increasing the salience of a given fact or activity. Sunstein (2005: 96), referring to the spread of a risk through the availability cascades, notes: "Because different social influences can be found in different communities, local variations are inevitable, with different examples becoming salient in each. Hence such variations – between, say, New York and Ohio, or England and the United States, or between Germany and France – might involve coincidence or small or random factors, rather than large-scale cultural differences."

The last kind of cognitive bias which is relevant for our analysis is the so-called *hindsight* bias. According to this, people tend to make univocal correlations between the information they had before knowing the outcome of an event and the actual outcome of that event. In other terms, they reinterpret the data they had in order to adapt them to the already known outcome of a specific event. It is the logic fallacy represented by the Latin expression *post hoc ergo propter hoc*. Together with the availability heuristic, this kind of bias is also often present in the context of risk regulation. It is, indeed, easy to make causal connections between some facts (the presence of radio antennae in a neighborhood, for example, or of genetically modified organisms in grain) and some events (the insurgence of brain cancer in that neighborhood or, correspondingly, of food allergies).

Although easily made, such connections can nonetheless be erroneous. Not only may a causal link between facts and events be quite nonexistent, but there might be a concurrence of different causes in which the assumed causal link plays only a minimal role. The promptness with which people make connections based on the hindsight bias, along with the willingness of governments to listen to the requests of their citizens, can lead to inefficient regulations in which public money is used to reduce risks which are only the by-products of this fallacy. The problem is the same as in the case of the availability bias: money is diverted from more efficient regulations in order to minimize threats which are, in most cases, negligible. There is also another point of parallelism between the two biases: as in the case of the availability heuristic, the hindsight fallacy can also be manipulated by fear entrepreneurs, stressing the presupposed link between facts and final outcomes.

Something more should be added here. The cognitive amplification of risk can occur in the local dimension, when dynamics within a given society can give rise to the occurrence of cognitive biases which, on their own, can lead to a distorted cognitive perception of the risks. But this phenomenon has also an international dimension. Not only can local conditions[22] influence the perception of risk, but also the fears and pressures experienced by other societies can produce the same effect. This occurred in the case of mad cow disease. If we look at how the US and Japan handled the BSE testing of cattle to be exported, we can clearly see that the fears of a country (Japan) influenced the regulatory responses of another country (the US). The case began with the Japanese request that all American cattle to be exported be tested for BSE regardless of their age. Indeed, in Japan, all cows slaughtered for human consumption are tested for BSE: accordingly, the authorities of that country requested that the same apply to American exporters. The problem was that BSE testing was not required in the US. The American authorities brought pressure to bear on the Japanese government to ease the requirement, which would have implied additional costs for the firms willing to export their meat products. The pressure rapidly became a struggle between the two governments, concluding in the Japanese decision to ban the import of all

---

22 For example, the strength of the media or the power of consumer groups and of the industry lobbies.

American beef (Wijers-Hasegawa 2006). After long negotiations,[23] the USDA finally decided to introduce a stricter testing policy for BSE with regard to the beef to be exported to Japan; as a consequence, the ban was lifted in August 2006. The episode shows that a legal system can modify its regulations in order to conform to the fears expressed by another country. It is true that such modification is partial, since it concerns only the testing of beef to be exported to Japan: but still it is significant, since it has been able indirectly to influence the policy implemented by the USDA in this regard.[24]

Cognitive Biases and the BSE Crisis

After this brief description of the main cognitive biases affecting the human mind, it is possible to see if and how they worked in the case of the mad cow crisis. To what extent have the cognitive biases affected the perception of the risk posed by BSE and the regulatory responses implemented to reduce it? From the statistics cited in the previous pages, it is clear that something else must have occurred to magnify the reality of the BSE crisis. Statistical data are, indeed, unable to explain fully why the spread of mad cow disease gained such momentum among consumers to the extent of becoming a scandal. The problem, of course, lies in identifying this unknown factor. In this sense, cognitive dynamics can offer a preliminary answer to the question, by highlighting how the human mind may have amplified a few facts, building a much more troublesome representation of reality than was in fact the case.

First, the characteristics of the disease are likely to have played a role, leading to an overestimation of the probability of negative facts occurring. The mysterious ways in which the pathology spreads and the difficulties in eliminating the infective agent (which cannot be rendered harmless by washing, cooking, or other normal methods of disinfection) may have cognitively reinforced the idea that it is impossible to control the risk of getting the disease. As we have previously seen, the overconfidence bias brings us to think that negative events are more probable when we are unable to control the source of the risk. This might be the case with the BSE/vCJD.

---

23 The first lifting of the ban was agreed on December, 2005, but it proved to have short life. After having discovered that the first shipment of beef from the US was contaminated with spinal cord (a potentially very infective part of the animal, with regard to BSE), the Japanese authorities decided to reinstate the ban.

24 The fears of the Japanese consumers about BSE-contaminated meat have had another effect which has involved the USDA's position on the BSE threat. Some beef producers, indeed, requested the USDA to authorize them to carry out private tests for BSE, in order to comply with the stricter testing requirements provided in another countries, such as Japan. The USDA, fearing that such authorization would force all the beef producers to adopt the BSE tests, refused permission. One of the firms making the request, Creekstone, petitioned the District Court of Columbia, asking to declare that the USDA does not have the authority to ban private testing for BSE. In March 2007, the court found for Creekstone, thus allowing the testing for BSE on a private basis. For further details, see Chapter 2.

Second, the hindsight bias may have played some role in the BSE case. The generic clues that a link might exist between BSE and vCJD may have been interpreted *ex post* as proofs, once the link had effectively been ascertained. This of itself may have reinforced the idea that public institutions did not react properly and promptly when the first signs of the risk emerged. In other words, people may have blamed public institutions more than necessary, misinterpreting the few clues existing in the first phases of the BSE crisis and magnifying their importance *ex post*.

The third bias which may have influenced the magnitude of the mad cow crisis is the availability heuristic. As a preliminary, it should be noted that the BSE is one of a series of food safety scandals which have occurred in Europe in the last twenty years. Starting from the beef raised with growth hormones and continuing with the chicken feed contaminated with dioxin and, more recently, the fears about the threats posed by genetically modified organisms (GMOs), the environment into which mad cow disease fits can be considered particularly sensitive to food risks. The fact that "memorable incidents" have occurred in the past (or, as for the GMOs and chicken feed examples, contemporaneously) may have led to the overestimation of BSE and vCJD threats. As shown in Table 1.1, the total quantity of BSE cases cannot be considered as large, except in the case of the UK, while with regard to vCJD, the number of cases is very limited in all the countries considered. Statistical evidence, therefore, does not explain the alarm existing among consumers. But the fact that BSE may have remind people of similar food emergencies, along with the high media profile given to it, has distorted the assessment of the disease, exaggerating its incidence. The last remark acquires particular significance if we think that the salience of the BSE risk may have been magnified because of availability cascades triggered, among others, by the media.

The last bias which might have contributed to shape the contours of the BSE emergency is the confirmatory bias. The fact that the BSE has spread through the use of a technique for producing feed (so-called Meat and Bone Meal: MBM) may have been interpreted as a signal confirming pre-conceived ideas, such as that the employment of technologies in food manufacture can be dangerous. In other words, the meaning attributed to the use of MBM is negative because it confirms ideas we already had about the relation between food and technology. The formation of these pre-conceived ideas, and in particular of the idea that the relation between technology and food may be negative, will be the subject of the next section.

Risk and Cultures

The Cultural Perception of Risk

The fact that we have pre-conceived ideas which can relate to our perception of risk opens a new field of investigation. How are these ideas formed? What is their content? How are they able to influence the process of risk perception? This is the core of the risk perception dilemma and, most importantly, the fundamental reason behind the variance in legal responses that legal systems offer when facing a new risk. Focusing the attention on the cognitive model behind the occurrence of the risk amplification explains only in part why such a phenomenon took place in Europe and Japan, and not in the US. It may help to explain the process leading to magnification of the risk, but not the reasons why it occurred in some countries and not in others. The question, thus, becomes: what can account for the differences behind social amplifications of risk?

Before answering such questions, it is appropriate to analyze whether the cognitive mechanisms we have mentioned before are able, by themselves, to explain the discrepancies in regulatory responses present in Europe, the US and Japan. To be clear, it is evident that in Europe and Japan we had a cognitive amplification of risk not to be found in the US. But this simple consideration does not explain why Europe and Japan witnessed such amplification, while the US did not.

First, Europe, Japan and the US have similar amplification conditions,[25] such as media circuits, institutions and consumer groups.[26] There must, therefore, be an underlying element which can explain why the amplification conditions became operative in some legal systems (Europe and Japan), while remaining quiescent in others (the US).

Second, the problem must be analyzed not only with regard to a single episode, the mad cow crisis, but in a larger context. The mad cow crisis is, indeed, only one of numerous food safety emergencies which have occurred in the last 25 years. The alarm triggered by beef raised with growth hormones in the 1980s can be considered the first important scandal to occur in the food industry. After that, other crises have given rise to social alarm, such as mercury-poisoned fish, chicken raised with dioxin-contaminated feed, concerns about long-term effects of GMOs or the use of pesticides, and so on.

It is worth noting that only in some legal systems can we detect a trend in magnifying the risks related to the safety of the food supply, while in others a more

---

25   By "amplification conditions," I mean the institutional and operational conditions necessary to amplify a risk. In this sense, the main amplification conditions can be considered to be the media, consumer groups and public institutions, with particular reference to those charged with the tasks of risk management and risk communication.

26   For example, we have noted that consumer groups are well developed in the US, more so than in Japan. We should, therefore, imagine a higher capacity to magnify a new risk by US consumer groups.

episodic approach is in play. Some experiences (namely, in our case, Europe and Japan) systematically highlight the risks posed by the foodstuffs, and this occurs over a long period of time. Other countries, like the US, tend to select the risks arising from food production in a more erratic way. While Europe and Japan have reacted to almost all the crises we have mentioned, the US has been much more selective in this regard. Only pesticide use has provoked some social alarm in recent times,[27] while other risks have passed almost unnoticed. These risk perception trends cannot be explained uniquely by cognitive dynamics. If everything could be understood in terms of cognitive mechanisms, it would be impossible to explain any trend in risk perception: there would be an extreme variance in the perception of risk, each month presenting the "risk of the month." Even the interpretations based on availability cascades are eventually unconvincing. They can offer some explanation as to the formation of risk trends, but are unable to provide an answer to the fundamental question as to why some societies are more prone than others to form such trends, at least with regard to the food sector.[28]

To return to the questions posed at the beginning of this section, in my view the missing element I have mentioned several times relates to the cultural context in which the cognitive mechanisms operate (Henrich 2002).[29] Culture forms the background which not only allows these mechanisms to work, but also guides the risk selection process in the first place. The idea is not new. The seminal work in this field is one on the cultural selection of risks, *Risk and Culture*, co-authored by anthropologist Mary Douglas and political scientist Aaron Wildavsky (Douglas, Wildavsky 1982). Their core idea is that individuals, but also societies, select risks according "to clusters of values that form competing cultural worldviews – egalitarian, individualistic, and hierarchical" (Kahan et al. 2006: 1083).[30]

According to this view, rather than being a creation of the cognitive processes, risk is a product of the social and cultural structures within which it is placed. Some dangers, which are objective and real, are elected as risks by societies according to the values and interests that are threatened by those dangers.[31] The passage from

---

27   I refer to the so-called "Alar case," which occurred in 1989. Alar is a pesticide used on apples, which contains UDMH, a carcinogenic chemical. The use of this product, and the negative consequences associated with it, have sparked social alarm, which is also due to the media campaign which has contributed to magnifying the risks posed by Alar (Kuran, Sunstein 1999: 698 ff.).

28   Sunstein (2005: 96) who strongly supports the use of availability cascades to explain the formation of trends and cross-national differences in risk perception, seems then to make reference to further, unspecified socio-cultural factors to justify the discrepancies in the selection of risks between societies.

29   Hanson, Yosifon (2003) use the notion of situation in a way which is similar to the idea of cultural context which I adopt.

30   For a case study on the cultural selection of risk in the case of nanotechnologies, see Kahan et al. 2007.

31   On the distinction between risk and danger, see Luhmann 1993; Sofsky 2005. In *Alpharma Inc.* v. *Council of European Union*, September 11, 2002 (T-70/99), *European*

danger to risk is determined, therefore, by the cultural representation we have of the threat. The more the threat is perceived as endangering values and interests which are considered fundamental for the survival of the society's cultural identity, the more that threat will be construed as a risk (Douglas 1992, 1986).

Another point of view which can help us to understand the cultural selection of the risks is centered on the notion of risk acceptability. Any society must deal with a number of risks posed by technology. A particular society may consider some of these risks as acceptable, while judging others as too burdensome to be tolerated. The point is that the line dividing risks into acceptable and unacceptable is traced according to cultural evaluations. It is the degree to which that society's fundamental cultural values are endangered which determines whether the risk can be considered acceptable.

The discourse is much more complex than the simple reference to cultural values seems to imply. First, the degree of acceptability of a risk also depends on the confidence a society has with regard to a given activity or product. In its turn, such confidence is the product of the level of experience and trust a society has in that activity or product (Frewer 2003; Kjærnes, Dulsrud, Poppe 2006). The experience and trust we are referring to are well known both to economists and psychologists, even if different terms are used. Status quo bias (Korobkin 1998; Scharff, Parisi 2006), patterns of consumption (Haines, Guilkey, Popkin 1988), endowment effect (Korobkin 2003; Sunstein 2002b) and consumption habits (Grignon 1988; Dynan 2000) are all expressions alluding to the repeated behavior of a subject (or a group) toward a given activity or product. The core idea behind them is the reluctance to move from a situation which is perceived to be a status of equilibrium and with regard to which the subject/group feels a sentiment of trust and confidence. It is a sort of inertia, by which a change from the equilibrium requires a higher than usual amount of (psychological, financial, and so on) energy. In this regard, experience plays the pivotal role. Experience is the key element allowing human beings, and societies, to acquire their knowledge; but it is also the means by which our representations of the world are filtered. Experience generates trust and confidence and, therefore, makes a risk acceptable. But experience, and this is the second point, interacts also with the cognitive mechanisms, by reinforcing them. The case of the availability heuristic is symptomatic in this regard. The fact that we have positive memories of a given fact or product (that is, we are confident with it) implies that, when we encounter it again, we will tend to overestimate the probability that positive effects will derive from that fact or product. In a similar vein, the overconfidence bias, that is, the idea we can control the risks coming

---

Court Reports 2002, II-3495, the European Court of First Instance distinguishes between risk and danger, adopting the following definition (point 160): "... 'risk' thus constitutes a function of the probability that use of a product or a procedure will adversely affect the interests safeguarded by the legal order. 'Hazard' ('danger') is, in this context, commonly used in a broader sense and describes any product or procedure capable of having an adverse effect on human health."

from a given activity, is strictly correlated to the degree of confidence we have with that activity: the higher the confidence, the greater the overconfidence.

The strict interconnections existing between cognitive dynamics and cultural values lead us to ask if it makes sense to distinguish between cultural perception and cognitive perception. The answer, in my view, should be positive. In the first place, culture is something different from cognition, because it refers to values, meaning "the worth, usefulness, or importance of a thing; relative merit or status according to the estimated desirability or utility of a thing."[32] In this sense, values and culture come before cognitive appreciation. Second, even if the distinction between the two is clearer at the theoretical than at the operational level, being difficult indeed to distinguish where one starts and the other ends, nevertheless the notion of culture fulfills an operational role which is distinct from that of cognitive mechanisms. As we have noted before, if everything could be traced back to cognitive dynamics, it would be impossible to conceive any trend in risk perception. On the other hand, we should not overemphasize the role that culture plays *vis-à-vis* the cognitive process. In other words, culture cannot be considered as a paradigm able to explain everything related to risk perception. Cultural perception and cognitive perception cannot be conceived as two distinct elements, but they coexist in symbiosis. This means that the two cannot exist without one another, but one (culture) cannot be absorbed by the other (cognition).

Risk and Emotions

A further element to be taken into consideration when we speak of risk perception concerns emotions (Finucane et al. 2000; Kahan 2008). When we face a threat or when we are in a risky position, our first reactions are emotional. The stress affecting our minds when facing a dangerous situation triggers a host of feelings which deeply influence the ways we perceive the risk. Experience is the main catalyst behind the association between these feelings and the risks we face: the result is the presence of mental shortcuts that, in this case, are emotionally (and not cognitively) driven.[33]

---

32   *The New Shorter Oxford English Dictionary*, Oxford, 1993, 3542. Chase (1997: 863) adopts a definition of culture similar to the one I use: "… I define culture for the instant project primarily by reference to collective values, not institutions."

33   Epstein (1994: 710) maintains that two different systems of information processing cohabit in the human mind: a rational system and an emotionally driven experiential system. According to the author: "people apprehend reality in two fundamentally different ways, one variously labeled intuitive, automatic, natural, nonverbal, narrative and experiential, and the other analytical, deliberative, verbal, and rational."

The so-called "affect heuristic" refers exactly to the role that emotions play in the process the human mind follows when it must assess a given situation or risk in terms of goodness or badness.[34] As Slovic and colleagues write:

> The basic tenet if this paper is that images, marked by positive and negative affective feelings, guide judgment and decision making. Specifically, it is proposed that people use an affect heuristic to make judgments. That is, representations of objects and events in people's minds are tagged to varying degrees with affect. In the process of making a judgment or decision, people consult or refer to an "affect pool" containing all the positive and negative tags consciously or unconsciously associated with the representations. (Slovic et al. 2002: 5)

Thus, in a way similar to the cognitive biases, emotions too can be conceived of as the responses that evolution has created to provide a type of routine to deal with stressful or dangerous situations. For example, people tend to label certain activities and/or products as safe/unsafe, a classification which is not based on the probability that a risk from that activity will occur, but it is mostly emotionally driven (Sunstein 2002a: 74 ff.). As in the case of cultural values, emotions, too, cannot be treated as independent from cognition. Authors point to the fact that emotions are mostly driven by cognitive processes and, in this sense, cannot be considered as operating at a pre-cognitive level.[35] The fact that emotions play a role in the way we perceive risks also has important consequences in the realm of the law. It has been demonstrated that when strong emotions are triggered by a given risk, we tend to focus on the worst-case scenario (that is, the realization of the risk), regardless of the probability that such a scenario will occur. It is what one author calls "probability neglect" (Sunstein 2002a). The most important implication for the law is that people will tend to ask for (overly) strict regulations when such neglect takes place, taking away resources from more efficient uses.

Social Amplification of Risk Framework

One of the first attempts to sketch a comprehensive picture of the many interactions between culture, cognition and emotions is given by the so-called "social

---

34   For a study showing how emotions play a fundamental role in explaining cross-national differences in risk perception, see Feigenson, Bailis, Klein (2004). Similarly to our contention, the authors discard the statistical and psychometric explanations regarding the differences in the perception of terrorism and SARS risks among Americans and Canadians. The affect heuristic, that is, the heuristic centered on the role of emotions, appears to them as the one capable to provide a more robust explanation in this regard. The importance of emotions in the perception of the BSE/vCJD risk is stressed by Setbon et al. 2005.

35   Some neurological studies have tried to map the brain areas which are activated when we feel emotions; see Elster 1999; Nussbaum 2003; Damasio 2003.

amplification of risk framework" (Pidgeon, Kasperson, Slovic 2003).[36] According to the researchers who explored this research field in the 1990s:

> ... the idea arose out of an attempt to overcome the fragmented nature of risk perception and risk communication research by developing an integrative theoretical framework capable of accounting for findings from a wide range of studies, including: from media research; from the psychometric and cultural school of risk perception research; and from studies of organizational responses to risk. The framework also serves, more narrowly, to describe the various *dynamic* social processes underlying risk perception and response. (Kasperson et al. 2003)

The goal is ambitious and the framework is far from being fully developed; nonetheless, the recent findings concerning risk perception indicate the need for a research project capable of integrating the advances made in different scientific fields. As we have noted previously in several instances, it is inconceivable to contemplate dealing with the intricacies of risk perception by relying solely on an explanatory model which is, by its very nature, partial. Cognitive and the cultural factors, as well as emotions and the rational actor model, all play some role in the process of risk perception. If we want to draw a picture which seeks to take into account all these elements, we must also illustrate the way they interact. The social amplification of risk framework attempts to offer a preliminary answer.

How does the framework represent the different components of risk perception and their interactions? The idea is that a "risk event" must first be communicated to others in order to be considered real.[37] Once the report of the existence of the risk begins to spread, this passes through a series of amplification/attenuation stations which magnify or downplay the risk. Such stations consist in psychological, heuristic, cultural, social and institutional processes which filter the information about the risk, in some way transforming it (Kasperson et al. 2003: 15–16). The transformation, as mentioned, can increase the initial level of alarm triggered by the risk or, on the contrary, can attenuate it. It is important to underline that the amplification/attenuation stations interpret the risk signals, selecting the ones deserving attention and disregarding the others. Moreover, "these interpretations provide rules of how to select, order, and explain signals emanating from the physical world" (Kasperson et al. 2003: 15). In this sense, the hope is that at some stage it will become possible to predict the transformations the risk signals

---

36 For an attempt to apply the social amplification of risk framework to a series of case studies (HIV, BSE, contraceptive pill, and so on) in the UK, see Breakwell, Barnett 2001. The study by the two authors has highlighted the potentialities, but also the limits that the social amplification of risk framework presents, especially with regard to its predictive power.

37 Risk event is meant to be "actual or hypothesized accidents and incidents": Kasperson et al. (2003: 15).

undergo, passing through the different stations. To further complicate the picture, such stations can be individual (for example, in the case of the heuristic or the emotional stations), or social (for example, the institutional or the cultural stations).

One of these stations deserves particular mention, namely the one in which those whom I have called "fear entrepreneurs" operate. These are subjects and institutions which have an interest in magnifying or downsizing a given risk because in such a way they are able to gain some profit from their actions. Lobbyists can be considered the typical example of fear entrepreneurs who, in order to protect the interests of their groups, manipulate the extent or the salience of a risk. Focusing attention on the role of fear entrepreneurs allows the importance that economic and political interests have in the dynamics of risk amplification/attenuation to be taken into account. For example, economic actors, such as producers and retailers, have a strong interest in directing consumers' consumption choices. Stimulating fear of goods produced by competitors can be a winning strategy, permitting the fear entrepreneur to gain a new market share. But the same strategy can be used by political groups which, by magnifying fear in relation to activities they oppose, aspire to win new voters. An interesting observation is provided by the fact that fear entrepreneurs often stress that a risk constitutes a menace for some important values of their society, thereby simultaneously activating the cultural stations in the amplification process.

A final point related to social amplification concerns the so-called "ripple effects" (Kasperson et al. 2003: 16). Here the processes which have led to the intensification (or attenuation) of a risk have indirect effects on the perception of other risks, in some way connected to the first. This is clearly the case for risks pertaining to foodstuffs. The risk connected to the consumption of a particular food (for example, beef) can have indirect effects on the perception of the risk belonging to another type of food (for example, food produced using genetically modified organisms). The fears concerning one product, therefore, are passed in some measure onto a different product, which has, nonetheless, some connection with the first.

Social Constructionism of Risk

The importance of culture in the process of risk perception can be appreciated also by reference to another perspective. We are referring to the wide array of anthropological and sociological studies focusing their attention on the role that culture plays in defining what is risky or safe. Here I can only sketch some suggestions that these branches of human studies have offered us. It is significant, nonetheless, that psychologists, sociologists and anthropologists converge on the importance of culture in explaining the processes of social change and the reactions to the perceived risks. This convergence has resulted in what is called the "social constructionism of risk" (Lupton 1999: 28 ff.).

According to this group of theories:

> ... all knowledge about risk is bound to the sociocultural contexts in which this knowledge is generated, whether in relation to scientists' and other experts' knowledge or law people's knowledge. Scientific knowledge, or any other knowledge, is never value-free but rather is always the product of a way of seeing. (Lupton 1999: 29)

There are, of course, differences between the different theories which are within the social constructionism paradigm. In particular, it is possible to distinguish between weak and strong social constructionist positions (Lupton 1999: 30).

The first positions assert that risk exists as something both real and objective, that is, it is measurable (Beck 1992, 1995). But at the same time, the perception of the risk is altered by cognitive and sociocultural filters. The strong constructionist positions, on the contrary, contend the existence of real and objective risks, sustaining that risk is entirely a construction of the human mind. Within this line of thought, some authors stress the fact that the notion of risk, as well as that of taboo, is designed to protect values and traditions embedded in a society (Burchell, Gordon, Miller 1991). Others focus their attention on the function that the notion of risk performs within modern societies: risk is a social construct brought into existence through a series of institutions, strategies, discourses and practices and used to govern societies.[38]

Why should all these theories matter for legal discourse?[39] As will be seen in further detail in the final section of this chapter, cultural cognition can shed additional light on the processes of legal change and enrich the methodology of comparative law by focusing on an element – culture – which is often neglected. Another point worth exploring in this context concerns information. Information is often invoked as the panacea capable of solving most problems: simply stated, the imperative is to provide more information, either to consumers or to regulators,

---

38   According to Foucault (1991: 87), modern states create risks through institutions and practices such as medical research, sociological studies, statistics, and so on. Once a risk is created, the same states can recommend or impose to individuals behaviors to avoid that risk. In this way, that is, through the imposition of conducts to escape risks, states are able to govern societies.

39   Simon (2005: 122), speaking of the importance of a socio-legal analysis, notes: "Rather than striving to produce a general theory of risk to locate all the ways risk is articulated in contemporary law, a socio-legal approach focuses on the plurality of different ways that risk choices are ordered by actual institutions, belief systems, and identities." The interaction between culture and law emerges also with regard to branches of law different from food safety. For example, with regard to criminal law, scholars write more and more about cultural defenses, which should shield the defendant from criminal charges or, alternatively, mitigate sanctions. On the cultural defense in the US, see Levine 2003; in the UK, Phillips 2003; in Italy, Bernardi 2006. Another example of a possible interaction between law and culture can be found in water law: Klein, Huang 2008.

in order to prevent hysterical fears and expensive reactions (Maclachlan 2006). The critique offered by cultural cognition is that providing more information does not necessarily entail a lower degree of conflict (Setbon et al. 2005: 825). Being cultural evaluators, consumers and regulators will select the information they get in a way which conforms to their cultural biases. This means that the same problems existing before implementing the information solution will persist even after the implementation. An alternative and more effective solution, according to this line of thinking, could be to frame the information we disseminate in a way that renders them culturally acceptable to the largest number of people possible: information, in other words, both cognitive and culturally oriented (Kahan et al. 2006).

Problematic Aspects in Using the Notion of Culture

In this book, I am proposing the idea that the notion of culture can be used as an explanatory device to improve investigation of the mechanisms conditioning the process of legal change. But the same notion of culture, and the use of it within the legal context, must be scrutinized more closely.[40]

First, we must not conceive of culture as something coherent or unchanging (Nelken 2007: 120 ff.; Cotterrell 2006: 81 ff.). As will become clear, we will speak of *cultures*, meaning that food culture (but culture in general) can be seen as a mosaic in which contradictory eating habits coexist. We are referring here not to divergences between different nations, but to discrepancies at the sub-national level. It is within the same nation state, in other words, that competing local cultures coexist, determining that lack of coherence we have underlined before. This is the case, for example, of groups which follow different culinary practices in accordance with their religious prescriptions. Along with these differences at a synchronic level, cultures also change in a diachronic perspective. Tastes shift not only depending on geographical areas, but also on the historic context to which we refer. Ancient Romans enjoyed dishes which nowadays we would probably decline, having found them appalling.

Second, cultures cannot be categorized on a national basis (Nelken 2007: 117 ff.). Interaction between cultures located in different geographical areas, accelerated by recent phenomena such as globalization, makes drawing a clear-cut line between nation states' culinary practices difficult. Examples are countless. The hamburger culture has rapidly expanded out of its place of origin and is now common both in Europe and Japan. Sushi restaurants are becoming popular in Europe, having been a long-established presence in the US. Pasta consumption is widespread in many Western countries.

Third, culture is not something existing "out there," which can be viewed objectively. Not only risk, but culture too, is in part the product of a social

---

40 I wish to thank Prof. David Nelken for the challenging suggestions he has offered me on the use of the notion of culture as an explanation rather than an explanandum.

construction, an imaginary vision we have of a society and of the values and traditions that society should embody. A good example can be seen in the "creation" of modern Japanese cuisine. Within a general effort to modernize the country along the lines of Western standards, and due also to the increasing contact with foreign eating habits, Japanese cuisine has been developed to convey a vision of modern cooking practices which nonetheless still defer to tradition. As Katarzyna Cwiertka writes:

> Japanese cuisine as it is projected and valued today is a modern construct conceived in the midst of the twentieth-century historical dynamics. Even the term *washoku* ("Japanese cuisine"), nowadays saturated with a sense of timeless continuity and authenticity, is a modern invention. It emerged in the late nineteenth century in response to the growing prominence of foreign cuisines in the Japanese culinary discourse. (Cwiertka 2007: 175)

The direct consequence of these problems is that culture cannot be conceived merely as an explanation, but also as something which must be explained (Nelken 2007: 123 ff.; Cotterrell 2006: 88). The intricacies of competing cultural clusters, their historical evolution, the influences they experience both at the local and supranational level are all, in themselves, factors requiring careful analysis. These difficulties, nonetheless, do not make culture an ineffective means of analysis.

In the first place, the concept of culture must be employed as a *tool*, without crediting it with a pervasive ability to explain everything. In addition, the same fact of using culture as a tool to explore the mechanisms of legal change helps us also to understand the intricacies behind the notion of culture itself. Law is an important component of the culture characterizing a given society. Studying the interactions between legal change and the broader cultural background within which it operates also implies, in a sort of circular pattern of analysis, knowledge of something more about culture in the sense of an *explanandum* rather an explanation.

Second, the fact that culture can be conceived of as a projection does not mean that it is totally detached from tradition. Again, as Katarzyna Cwiertka (2007: 175) notes with regard to Japanese cuisine:

> This by no means implies, however, that Japanese cuisine is a twentieth-century fabrication; that it does not rest upon time-honored foundations ... The construction of Japanese national cuisine was deeply embedded in the existing environment and relied on knowledge, skills and values that the Japanese people had accumulated over time. (Cwiertka 2007: 175)

National Cultures and Food Safety

What role does culture play in the field of food safety (Henrich 2002: 353; Jussaume, Judson 1992)? We should talk here, and not incidentally, of national *cultures*. The way societies relate to food consumption and food safety varies greatly, mirroring the existence of a plurality of food cultures, each one with its own preferences in terms of tastes and safety.

A first group of divergences among food cultures concerns cross-national differences in the preferences related to foodstuffs. The expressions "American food culture" or "European food culture" can be nonetheless misleading, as it is hard to imagine a monolithic food culture in the US, Europe or Japan. Such a high degree of homogeneity is unthinkable in large societies. Therefore, the second group of differences in food cultures can be discerned at the national level. Within each society, a plurality of food cultures coexists: their number can be considered a variable, depending on the degree of homogeneity in that society. In societies which are large, multiethnic and have different historical backgrounds, such as the American and European ones, it is possible to imagine the coexistence of a number of food cultures which is greater than in a society like the Japan's, which is more homogeneous.

Moreover, each society not only has different food cultures, but such cultures are also competing with one another. Notwithstanding this, I can speak of an American food *culture* or of a European food *culture*, because the competition between the various sub-national cultures leads, in fact, to the predominance of one of them. Such a selection is probably the by-product of those same mechanisms we have underlined with regard to the perception of risk. Availability cascades, cultural values, economic and political interests, and so on, are all factors contributing to the creation of a predominant food culture. Second, the process leading to the emergence of a predominant food culture must be thought of as dynamic. The implication is that supporters of the other competing food cultures will try to subvert the predominant one, replacing it. Historic evolution shows shifts in the food culture considered predominant: any historical phase has its own tastes and safety concerns. It would be erroneous, therefore, to attribute a static character to the cultural paradigm predominant in a given frame of time and in a given society.

Clues to such an evolution emerge clearly if we look at the experiences of the legal systems considered in the study. In the US, for example, food production has long been characterized by heavy industrialization. Typical features of the American food culture are considered to be the mass production of foodstuffs and their marketing on a large scale. But recent times have witnessed a partial change in this regard.[41] The success of organic food may indicate a transformation in the attitude American consumers have towards their food choices. Also the recent initiatives that some states have taken against obesity can be viewed as the sign of a new approach to the problems that (wrong) food styles can pose for human health.[42] Even with regard to the specific field of food safety, the last decade has

---

41   The change in attitude is more intense in some geographical areas of the US, such as in the cities located on the east and west coasts of the country.

42   Huehnergarth (2005) reports initiatives taken in New Jersey to block the sale of soda and junk food in schools. As to the initiatives taken by the New York State to reduce

seen reforms aimed at controlling food pathogens, such as the introduction of the HACCP procedures.[43] In a similar vein, in Europe and Japan, fast food chains and pre-cooked meals have spread rapidly.[44] The diffusion of junk food and high-calorie meals is provoking health problems, such as diabetes and other obesity-related pathologies, in populations which traditionally have not suffered these types of diseases (Aa. Vv. 2002; Kanazawa et al. 2002).[45]

With regard to Europe, the predominant food culture is connected to the preservation of local traditions. This is especially true for the Mediterranean countries, such as Italy[46] and France, while it is more nuanced in the case of the UK. The weight of local traditions finds expression in two ways. On the one hand, traditional recipes for preparing food are largely preferred to more standardized ways of cooking. On the other, great emphasis is placed on the importance of using local ingredients in food preparation. The same legal protection of the place of origin and of the geographical indications of many ingredients and food products, which plays an important role in European law (O'Connor 2004; Olszak 2001; Aa. Vv. 1990; Pacileo 2003b: 286 ff.),[47] can be seen not only as a tool to protect the economic interests of the local producers, but also as a way of strengthening the traditional food culture. This is, indeed, a justification often used to back new pieces of legislation aimed at reinforcing the protection of the geographical indications.[48]

---

trans fats in restaurants, see Severson 2006. A proposal to tax sugary soft drinks has been recently advanced by San Francisco's mayor: see McKinley 2007.

43   On the introduction of the HACCP procedures, see Chapter 2.

44   Nonetheless, the diffusion of pre-cooked (or "ready") meals is far less widespread in Europe and Japan than in the US. The difference can be explained taking into consideration both the time variable (that is, the fact that pre-cooked meals were introduced in Europe and Japan later than in the US) and the cultural variable. In this sense, the less vigorous spread of pre-cooked meals can be due to cultural resistance.

45   Obesity is becoming a worldwide emergency which has also gained the attention of the World Health Organization; see the page dedicated to this problem in the WHO website <http://www.who.int/topics/obesity/en/>.

46   In Italy, the Ministry of Agriculture and the Ministry of Culture have recently issued a Ministerial Decree providing that Italian traditional foodstuffs are considered part of the national cultural heritage: see Ministerial Decree, May 29, 2008.

47   Art. 22 of the Agreement on Trade-Related Aspects of Intellectual Property Rights (TRIPS Agreement, April 15, 1994) provides protection for geographical indications. The first paragraph states that "Geographical indications are, for the purposes of this Agreement, indications which identify a good as originating in the territory of a Member, or a region or locality in that territory, where a given quality, reputation or other characteristic of the good is essentially attributable to its geographical origin."

48   The intersection between cultural factors and economic interests in the case of the protection of geographical indications illustrates the difficulties that we can face when we try to distinguish between the two. Economic interests play an important role in shaping the relevant legislation, but the cultural predisposition favoring local food facilitates the advocates of these interests. On the other hand, the same cultural predisposition we have

Moreover, those who prepare food are considered more as craftsmen than as producers. Such an observation is important because it supports the underlying idea that ingredients play a pivotal role in the process of food preparation and that human manipulation should be reduced to a minimum.

The fact that human intervention is limited, even with regard to foodstuffs which are usually considered natural, can be easily questioned, since the level of manipulation of the primary ingredients is high in most cases. But what counts here is the perception of the production process rather than its realities. Crucial in this perception is the idea that the human interference is residual in the case of foodstuffs labeled as "natural." What must be stressed, therefore, is that – for Europeans – food must preferably be the product of a natural process (Lupton 1996: 85 ff.; Kershen 2003: 13–14).

This has important consequences with regard to food safety. If the (predominant) European cultural predisposition favors "natural" food, then there will be a higher tolerance for defects due to the characteristics of the ingredients used. Consumers will tend to downplay the risks that come from the "naturalness" of the food. This seems the case, for example, for the risks derived from the consumption of cheese made with raw milk (Echols 2001: 8). Taking into consideration that, in some areas of Europe, cheese produced with non-pasteurized milk is considered part of the local culinary tradition, sheds light on why such a product is not perceived as particularly dangerous. The same is true with regard, for example, to the consumption of raw pork sausages or of raw shellfish. The fact that these dishes are part of the tradition of the local community, past patterns of consumption, and the scant alarm triggered by the risks deriving from them, are all factors which partially explain why consumers tend to have an overly optimistic view of the dangers the dishes pose. On the contrary, Europeans tend to have a negative perception of the use of technology in food production. The adoption itself of the precautionary principle in the food safety context can be seen as the cultural emblem of European sensibility regarding the protection of the food chain from the assaults of technology.[49]

Why this is so should be quite clear, in the light of the considerations developed so far. If the cultural predisposition is to favor food which is perceived, marketed or in any event labeled as "natural" (Echols 2001: 17–18), products which, on the contrary, are clearly the result of an industrial process will be seen as threatening the traditional cultural values characterizing the society. This is the case, for

---

mentioned can be strengthened by economic interests, in the sense that economic actors can magnify the importance of local food culture, for example, through marketing techniques or the heuristic of fear. On the importance of preserving local traditions in Italy and France as a way of affirming national identity, see Aime 2008: 86 ff.

49   See art. 7 of the EC Regulation 178/02. For further details on the precautionary principle in the food safety context, see Chapter 2.

example, for the rejection in some countries of genetically modified organisms.[50] The dividing line between the perception of a foodstuff as natural or industrial can be thin. For example, in the case of beef, it can be perceived as natural so long as consumers do not know that the animals have been fed with hormones. But once such information spreads, then the idea associated with this type of meat is that it is the product of an industrial process.[51]

Japan has similar features with regard to food culture. Indeed, in this country too, local traditions are emphasized and strongly protected. The importance of using local ingredients is connected not only with the need to employ them for the preparation of traditional dishes, but also to the idea of purity (Cwiertka 2007; Maclachlan 2006: 249; 2002: 179; Vogel 1992: 123–4).[52] Ingredients coming from local areas and/or produced according to traditional methods are considered pure, in opposition to ingredients coming from abroad, which are seen as impure or, at least, are regarded with suspicion. The rise of the mad cow scandal in Japan offers

---

50   A study conducted in Italy on the use of biotechnologies in food and drug production seems to confirm the comment. While most of the people interviewed expressed positive opinions (except for some ethical concerns) on the role that biotechnologies could have in the development of new drugs, the opinions are exactly opposite in the case of the production of foodstuffs. Here the same (bio)technology is perceived as posing a menace to public health. The results of the study can be explained through the different media coverage that biotechnologies enjoyed in the cases of drug production and food production. The fact that the media highlighted the positive aspects of the use of biotechnologies in the drug context, while stressing the risks of such technologies in food production, could have heavily influenced the responses to the study. But another explanation could be advanced in terms of cultural preferences. The use of biotechnologies for creating new drugs does not pose the same (cultural) resistances that emerge if these are used to produce foodstuffs (Neresini, Bucchi, Pellegrini 2002). Similar results can be found in European Commission – Special Eurobarometer 225, *Social Values, Science and Technology*, 92 ff. (June 2005). While 54% of those interviewed think that we should never, or only in exceptional circumstances, develop genetically modified crops, the percentage is reduced to 35% when the question concerns developing genetically modified bacteria to be used for cleaning up the environment. For a study underlying the importance of feelings and affect in perceiving the risks posed by GMOs, see Townsend 2006. As to the importance of culture in explaining the regulatory divide between Europe and the US with regard to agricultural biotechnology, see Kershen 2003.

51   The example we have sketched is modeled on the growth hormone scandal which occurred in Europe in the 1980s.

52   Analyzing the consumer movements opposing the deregulation of food additives, both Patricia Maclachlan and David Vogel stress the fact that consumer organizations have a long tradition of fighting against agricultural liberalization on the basis of (food) safety concerns. Such movements tend to treat the importation of foreign food as a potential source of contamination; based on these considerations they support anticompetitive agricultural policies, such as restrictions on food imports. For similar considerations, see S. Vogel (1999: 193–4). On the idea of purity with regard to the import of foreign blood and the spread of the HIV epidemic in Japan, see Feldman 1999.

good examples in this regard. In the aftermath of the discovery of the first BSE case, public institutions, consumer groups and the media tended to highlight the risks that the importation of foreign beef created, rather than the risks posed by local production. Similarly, in reporting that a Japanese citizen contracted vCJD, all the sources stressed the fact that this person had been in the UK for a few weeks and that, therefore, he probably had contracted the disease abroad. In both cases, the dichotomy impure/pure food, as well as the contraposition between foreign and local foodstuffs, implies diffidence towards products which are perceived as extraneous to tradition. Such diffidence has important consequences on the perception of the safety of the "extraneous" foodstuffs. Being deemed impure, what is foreign is easily perceived also as unsafe, especially in cases when suspicion about its integrity is raised. In line with this remark, it is no surprise that the consumption of traditional food is perceived by Japanese citizens as a way of affirming their own national identity.[53]

The Japanese experience, thus, highlights the important link between food and national identity: traditional cuisine becomes an element by which the members of a community identify themselves. The prominence that the food/identity relationship assumes in the Japanese context is brought about by the high degree of homogeneity in this country, especially in comparison to Europe and the US. A good example is the consumption of whale meat. Despite the international pressures to halt whaling, Japan is in the forefront in the defense of whale hunting, even if under the justification of research purposes.[54] The role that culture and culinary tradition play in Japan's rejection to stop whale hunting is pivotal (Hirata 2004a). The perception that international norms prohibiting whaling are unjust since they are in conflict with Japanese tradition and tend to deny the country's identity, explains the firm stance that Japan has assumed on the issue.

Similar considerations can be drawn with regard to the production and use of rice. Rice is a product deeply embedded in Japanese culture and perceived as an element defining national identity (Wojtan 1993). Given the importance it has for the traditional values of Nipponese society, along with the need to protect local farmers' economic interests, the import of foreign rice has long been limited. Such limitation, in its turn, has given rise to a long drawn-out controversy between the US and Japan concerning the liberalization of the rice market (Davis 2003).

---

53   Cwiertka (2007) points to the fact that the birth of a Japanese traditional cuisine would be the product of the Meiji Restoration, which created uniform culinary traditions in order to render them a symbol of national identity.

54   See "Japan's Whaling Fleet Sails despite International Censure," Environment News Service, November 20, 2007, at <http://www.ens-newswire.com/ens/nov2007/2007-11-20-01.asp>. The only concession Japan has made to international pressure has been to halt the hunt of one species of whale, the humpback: "Japan to Drop Humpback Whale Hunt," *USA Today*, December 21, 2007, at <http://www.usatoday.com/news/world/environment/2007-12-21-japan-whaling_N.htm>.

On the one hand, the fact that local food is perceived as being pure and, on the other, the observation that food contributes to defining the national identity, influence the perception of the risks that foodstuffs can pose. Similarly to what we have observed in relation to Europe, in Japan too there is a tendency to downplay the risks that local foodstuffs pose. For example, the risks that the consumption of raw fish can entail for human health are perceived as less severe than the risks posed by meat consumption.

Finally, the US presents a food culture which is not based on tradition in the sense we have indicated for Europe and Japan. The heterogeneous composition of American society implies also the lack of a common culinary tradition. In a country built by immigrants, each group brought its own cuisine. But this does not mean that we face a mosaic of original ethnic cuisines. The lapse of time, the lack of original ingredients, and the cultural and spatial distance from the societies where the original culinary practices developed are all factors which have weakened food traditions. What we are confronted with, rather, is an elaboration of the original practices and a cross-fertilization of different national traditions. The final result is a sort of culinary syncretism, where each cuisine no longer retains its traditional features. It is, therefore, impossible to speak of culinary traditions in the sense of either Europe or Japan. Nonetheless, we can still speak of a food culture in the case of the US. Lacking a strong traditional background, American food culture has been more shaped by economic interests than in Europe and Japan, especially after the end of World War II. The rise of the so called "hamburger culture" is a blueprint of this (Schlosser 2005; Spurlock 2004). The aggressive marketing campaigns conducted by the fast food chains have heavily influenced American tastes (Schlosser 2005: 6). In a country where, despite the mix of different cultures, the Anglo-Saxon matrix has always played a leading role, the main meal of the day has often included meat (predominantly beef) and potatoes. The "hamburger and French fries" dish promoted by the fast food chains can be seen as a development of this traditional meal. Therefore, by connecting to an already existing culinary tradition and highlighting it, companies such as McDonald's and Burger King have attracted crowds of customers.

This has not been the only means by which the fast food industry has been able to exploit the food preferences of American consumers. For example, marketing campaigns have focused on children by representing fast food restaurants as places where they can have fun, meet friends and get nice gifts (Schlosser 2005: 42 ff.).[55] The influence that children have on family decisions, such as the ones concerning food, is enormous and this can help to explain the rapid spread of the fast food chains. Another factor which has been stressed in order to gain new customers is the idea that fast food restaurants provide an affordable dinner for every family, regardless of social status or income. The possibility of dining out

---

55   It should be noted that the heavy impact that fast food ads have on the food choices of the children is often used as one of the core arguments to claim the liability of fast food chains in provoking health problems, such as obesity and diabetes.

on a regular basis, made feasible by the low-price policy implemented by the fast food companies, has represented social progress for many families.

The fast food example sheds some light on the perception of food risks in the US. A key factor in the fast food industry's success has been the widescale industrialization of the food manufacturing processes which the companies have implemented over the years. Meal preparation in fast food restaurants closely resembles an assembly line (Schlosser 2005: 68 ff.). Each employee has her own specialization and takes care only of one stage in the preparation of the dish. In the same vein, the use of high-tech machinery for food preparation is widespread. The same industrialization feature can be found in most of the foodstuffs to be found on supermarket shelves. The coupling of industrialization and food is more embedded in American culture than in European and Japanese ones. This implies that the risks which technology may pose in food production are perceived as less alarming in the US than in countries where the cultural background is hostile to the employment of food production technologies. Rather, technology is perceived as an important factor capable of controlling risks which are naturally present in the foodstuffs.

In the US, the lower degree of cultural resistance to the industrialization of the food sector is due to the lack of homogeneous culinary traditions which, on the contrary, are present in Europe and Japan. The picture is of course rapidly evolving, due to globalization which affects the production and marketing of foodstuffs. This implies an increasing convergence towards models in which food traditions are weakened and, therefore, become more and more interchangeable.

A final observation must be made. We noted before that it is easy to question the idea that "natural" food exists nowadays. The widespread use of pesticides, additives and other chemicals in the production of almost all foods seems to contradict the processed/unprocessed dichotomy on which we have relied to draw the distinction between risk perceptions in Europe and Japan, on the one hand, and the US, on the other. But again the point is that we should not refer to the realities of contemporary food production, but to the perception of such production processes.[56] While European and Japanese consumers need to be reassured that the food they consume is not the result of an industrial process, even if this is not true, American consumers seem to pay only spasmodic attention to this aspect. They are not overly concerned about the industrial *vis-à-vis* the natural character of the food they purchase.

This does not mean that they are totally unconcerned about other aspects of food production. As we will see in Chapter 2, American consumers are more concerned about the risks of food contamination as a consequence of a terrorist attack, or about the dietary aspects in the consumption of certain foods than their

---

56 Lupton (1996: 91) notes: "While the natural/artificial and unprocessed/processed oppositions are clearly central in defining 'good' or 'healthy' and 'bad' or 'unhealthy' food, they are cultural constructions that ignore the conditions of food production and distribution in modern societies."

European and Japanese counterparts. Indeed, it is by referring to these two types of threats that recent reforms concerning the food safety framework have been enacted in the US. If we take both the case of the risks flowing from the processed/ unprocessed contraposition, or the risks depending on terrorist attacks/dietary habits, what matters is the perception of such risks more than their statistical likelihood or extent. Europeans and Japanese are statistically exposed to the same risks of terrorist attacks to the food supply as Americans, and the converse is true with regard to the risks arising from the use of technology in food production. Some highlight certain types of threats because of the operation of cognitive and cultural backgrounds which address their perception.

The Role of Culture in the Mad Cow Crisis

The cultural cognition paradigm may be employed to explain the different reactions triggered by the BSE epidemics in the US, Europe and Japan. Some of the observations developed in the previous section can already shed some light on the role that culture has played in magnifying or downplaying the risks connected to mad cow disease.

We have noted that the hamburger culture is a distinctive feature of US society. But more generally meat, and in particular beef, has largely been considered the standard meal for American families, as confirmed by the statistical data on the per capita consumption of beef. The average American consumes about 43 kilograms of beef per year.[57] As shown in Tables 1.2 and 1.3, both the quantity of beef and total amount of meat consumed in the US far exceeds consumption levels in Europe and Japan.

Table 1.2   Per capita meat consumption in kilograms in three geographical areas (year 2004)

	Beef	**Pork**	**Poultry**	**Total**
US	43.2	30.1	44.6	117.9
Europe (25 Member States)	18.2	43.4	16.0	67.6
Japan	9.3	20.1	13.5	42.9

Source: The data have been extrapolated from the tables reported in the USDA website, at <http://www.fas.usda.gov/dlp/circular/2006/06-03LP/bpppcc.pdf>.

57   The data refers to the years from 2001 to 2006. See the tables reported in the USDA website, at <http://www.fas.usda.gov/dlp/circular/2006/06-03LP/bpppcc.pdf>. In 1961, beef consumption was 42.8 kilograms per person per year. The consumption level increased in the following years (53.3 kilograms in 1970), and declined starting from the end of the 1970s (49.8 kilograms in 1979) up to the 2000s, when it came back to the 1961 level. The data are reported in Simpson, Farris (1982: 284–5).

Table 1.3 **Per capita meat consumption in kilograms in five countries (year 1999)**

	Beef	**Pork**	**Poultry**	**Total**
US	45.3	31.7	49.4	126.4
Japan	11.7	17.0	13.7	42.4
France	26.8	38.4	24.1	89.3
Italy	26.3	36.3	18.4	81
UK	19.7	25.0	28.6	73.3

Source: See the statistical data available at the webpage <http://www.allcountries.org/uscensus/1370_per_capita_consumption_of_meat_and.html>.

To say that the American food culture is a meat culture is not an exaggeration. The stable and elevated patterns of consumption imply a high degree of confidence in the product "beef" which in turn supports the conclusion that American consumers (and institutions) are less sensitive to the risks that this commodity can pose than are consumers in other areas of the world. Moreover, the cultural environment previously described has played an important role in rejecting the idea that beef could be a dangerous product. Once the BSE problem emerged, therefore, it was not difficult to minimize the risks that the disease could create for public health, by referring to the everyday experience of the (safe) consumption of beef. One of the main findings of a recent study aimed at measuring the determinants in the perception of the BSE/vCJD risk has concerned the importance of the variable "preference for beef" in offsetting the extent of the so-called "worry dimension," that is, the perception of the importance of a threat (Setbon et al. 2005: 824).

Such a finding seems to provide direct support for the contention that the cultural confidence we have in a product or activity affects our perception of the risks that the activity/product can pose. Moreover, doubts about the meat supply's safety have meant questioning one of the few catalysts of American food culture, that is, the one centered on the consumption of hamburgers, veal steaks, and so on.[58] There are, of course, other reasons that may contribute to explaining the downplaying of the hazards connected to beef and BSE. For example, the protection of the economic interests connected to the beef industry has played an important role in minimizing BSE risks. It is clear that the widespread diffusion of alarmist information about mad cow disease would have been a financial disaster for the relevant industries.[59] But such an explanation is

---

58 Schlosser (2005: 6) notes: "A hamburger and french fries became the quintessential American meal in the 1950s, thanks to the promotional efforts of the fast food chains."

59 A clue to the interests of the beef industry to prevent the spread of alarmist information about BSE can be found in the vicissitudes which have involved Oprah Winfrey

not exhaustive since, as noted previously, the same interests are also present, and well represented, in Europe and Japan.

The fascination for beef in Europe is not as strong as it is in the US. Even if the consumption level cannot be considered low, pork is the most widely consumed type of meat in Europe.[60] The differences in the beef consumption levels between the US and Europe can be explained by taking into consideration two elements. First, the accessibility to beef in the two geographical areas is different. As shown in Table 1.1, the cattle population in the US is larger by far than those in the UK, France and Italy, even if we aggregate the data relating to the latter three countries. The huge amounts of grazing land available in the US have made it possible to raise more cattle than in Europe. In its turn, the large quantities of beef produced by American ranchers have made it easier to buy at a reasonable price.

Second, in Europe, the image of the safety of beef was compromised in the 1980s by the growth hormone scandal (Chichester 2005; Sien 2007; Chang 2004). The scandal was reinforced by the emphasis placed on other health risks that, in general, red meat consumption could generate (Truswell 2007; Smith 2007). The growth hormone affair contributed to the creation of an environment of suspicion towards the use of new technologies in the beef production context. The development of such an environment has found support in the cultural idea that food must be as natural as possible, while intensive processing worsens the quality of foodstuffs and creates new health risks.

Another factor to take into account is how the first news of the BSE risk was presented in the old continent. The social amplification of the BSE risk in Europe is largely due to the spread of news that the BSE epidemic's origins lay in the particular technology used to produce the ruminants' feed. Public attention focused more on the fact that humans, and human technology in particular, had given rise to the terrible disease, than on the real extent of the BSE risk. A survey of journal articles concerning the BSE epidemic shows that the link between the use of technology and the disease is highly emphasized. Environmental groups blamed producers and public institutions, stressing that the former had turned cows into cannibals, while the latter facilitated this transformation. The image of a rash use of technology in food production had the power to trigger a host of

---

and her talk show. The Texas beef producers brought a suit against the anchorwoman for having broadcasted a show in April 1996 during which one of her guests expressed alarmist opinions about the possibility of an outbreak of BSE in the US. The plaintiff asked for compensation after suffering huge economic losses in the days following the show. The request of compensation was rejected by the District Court for the Northern District of Texas: *Texas Beef Group* v. *Oprah Winfrey*, 11 F. Supp. 2d 858 (Northern Tex. D. Ct. 1998).

60　　The Mediterranean countries (Italy and France, for example) consume more meat than northern European countries, such as the UK. For example, in 1994, the per capita consumption of beef was 17.3 kilograms in the UK, 26.6 in Italy and 26.7 in France: see the data reported in the table at <http://151.121.3.140/dlp2/circular/1998/98-03LP/Tables/table13.pdf>. The data are confirmed also for the years preceding 1994, even if with regard to the total consumption of meat (beef, pork and poultry); see Hughes (1995: 6).

emotional responses, magnifying the real salience of the BSE risk and involving some values considered basic to the existence of European society.[61]

The perception that these values are endangered in fact determines a rejection of the activities/products thought responsible for the danger. In the case of BSE, preference for natural foodstuffs and distrust of artificial ones may be regarded as the basic value which was threatened by the new disease and which led to the risk amplification.

The case of Japan differs from what has been described so far. Beef cannot be considered part of the Japanese diet. The traditional image of beef is, indeed, that of a foreign and impure food. Until 1868, consumption of meat from four-legged animals was prohibited due to Buddhist precepts (Cwiertka 2007: 24 ff.). During the Tokugawa period (1603–1867), this prohibition was relaxed and the slaughtering of animals for meat began to spread. Nonetheless, slaughter was considered an impure activity, to be performed by members of disadvantaged groups, which had long been discriminated against by the rest of society (Longworth 1983: 70–71).[62] Despite the abolition, with the Meiji reforms, of the ban on consumption of meat from four-legged animals, its use in Japanese cuisine remained uncommon. This in part was due to the high prices Japanese consumers must pay for beef, prices which, in turn, depend on the scanty supply of this meat. But it has been noted that this problem could be solved by permitting larger imports of beef from abroad, a policy which Japan has gradually implemented only in recent years (and until the explosion of the mad cow crisis) (Davis 2003).

One of the most often-cited justifications for rejecting the increase in beef import quotas related to safety concerns, with the claim that foreign beef would be less safe than that from domestic production (Longworth 1983: 17–18).[63] On the other hand, it is true that if we compare the per capita consumption of beef in 1961 and nowadays, we note a marked increase.[64] Things are changing, therefore, but the preference of Japanese consumers is still clearly for fish products, as shown in Table 1.4.

---

61   Setbon et al. (2005: 823–5) note in their conclusions that the risk perception in the case of BSE/vCJD cannot be reduced to the cognitive dimension but must take into account also the cultural variable, meant as value-based considerations about the extent of a risk. In particular, their analysis "gives empirical support to the hypothesis that risk perception is more tightly centered on feelings, ethical and social values, i.e. determined by what might be called emotion, and value-based judgments." Similarly, Breakwell, Barnett (2001: 20) stress the importance to specify the cultural variables which characterize the environment where the risk amplification occurs.

62   Those working in the meat and leather industries formed the segregated class of the so-called *Burakumin*, that is, the "people of the hamlet," since they were forced to live in special villages outside the cities (Upham 1987: 78).

63   Longworth (1983: 76) notes that the liberalization of the beef sector has never ranked as a top priority for the consumers' movements, which have preferred to focus their attention on other problems.

64   In 1961, the per capita beef consumption (in kilograms) was 1.6; in 1970, 3; in 1979, 4.9; the data are reported in Simpson, Farris (1982: 284–5). In 2001, beef consumption

**Table 1.4   Fish consumption and production in five countries
          (average 2001–2003)**

	Fish consumption (per capita/kg)	Fish production (tons in live weight)
France	33.5	873.239
Italy	24.4	489.943
UK	20.7	873.238
Japan	64.7	5.836.343
US	22.6	5.447.176

Source: The data have been extrapolated from the table available at the FAO (Food and Agriculture Organization), at ftp://ftp.fao.org/fi/stat/summary/summ_04/applybc.pdf.

The cultural background concerning beef cannot be considered to favor this type of product. Rather, beef has traditionally been viewed with suspicion due to the perception that it is impure. This is an important factor in explaining the strong emotional and legal reaction that the mad cow crisis triggered in Japan. But there is also another factor which helps in understanding the dynamics behind the occurrence of risk magnification. Similar to Europe, in Japan we are also dealing with a clear preference for food which is perceived as natural. This preference is also evident in Japanese cuisine, which traditionally does not hold with excessive processing or flavoring of food. The fact that the origin of BSE was due to the modern technologies of feed production has, as in Europe, resulted in a cultural rejection of what was perceived to be the product of human manipulation. A final remark which can contribute to explaining the alarm triggered by mad cow disease relates to the foreign/local dichotomy. The feeling that what is pure is local and what is dangerous is foreign is something we can find in any society. But in Japan, such feeling is particularly strong, probably due to historical reasons.[65] The isolation

---

was 11.2, in 2004, 9.3; the data are available at the USDA website <http://www.fas.usda.gov/dlp/circular/2006/06-03LP/bpppcc.pdf>.

65   In this context, I can only sketch some notes on the historical developments which have determined the segregation of Japan from the rest of the world up to the so-called "Meiji Restoration" (1868–1912). During the Tokugawa period (1603–1867), the *shogun* initiated a policy of the progressive isolation of Japan from the rest of the world, closing the harbors, expelling foreigners and promoting an autarchic economy. Facing pressures from Western countries, which were intent on opening new markets in the East, the *shogun* leadership fell. The end of the shogunate determined the restoration of full imperial power and, more important for our discourse, the opening of Japan to the outside world and the beginning of an era of reforms in which the West assumed the role of reference point. For an introduction to Japanese history, see Sansom 1963; Henshall 2004. With specific reference to the legal history of Japan, see Henderson 1965; Haley 1991: 44 ff. On the importance

from the outside world which has long characterized Japanese society, parallel with a strong sense of nationalism, can shed some light on the reasons behind the high sensitivity to the foreign/local dichotomy. All these elements have played some role in shaping the contours of the mad cow crisis in Japan, amplifying the risks arising from this disease.

Culture and Legal Change

The analysis conducted in the second section of this chapter was aimed at showing that culture plays an important role in the way human beings perceive risks. It is now time to draw some conclusions on the importance that these findings may have in understanding the processes of legal change. The goal is to underline how knowledge of the cultural context in which legal reforms occur can help us not only to explore more fully the mechanisms by which legal change happens, but also the methodological importance that cultural studies may have for comparative law (Nelken, Feest 2001).

With regard to the process of legal change, it is evident that cultural context is able to influence the reception of foreign legal norms and institutions. It might be said that cultural context determines the acceptability of a norm. To be clear, culture is one of the variables that contribute to make a norm acceptable. The historical background of the legal system, the financial and political interests it protects, the prestige the foreign model enjoys or the imposition of such model by other subjects in a (military or economic) position of supremacy, are some of the other variables to be considered. The choice of focusing on the role of culture is motivated by the fact that it is a paradigm often neglected *vis-à-vis* the abovementioned other variables, which are more evident and/or more easily quantifiable. But the difficulties we face when we try to single out the cultural factor should not prevent us from stressing its importance.

Comparative scholars and political scientists have dedicated many works to topics such as legal transplants (Watson 1974; Ewald 1995b; Graziadei 2006), norm diffusion (Hugill, Dickson 1988; Jörgens 2005) and circulation of models (Sacco 1991a, 1991b; Somma 2005). Before dealing specifically with the relationship between culture and risk regulation, it is interesting to note that there are cases in which, despite the strong pressures to adopt a given solution, or the prestige that this solution enjoys, legal systems refuse to implement a certain legal model. In order to clarify such an outcome, it can be helpful to introduce the notion of "cultural match" (Checkel 1999; Cortell, Davis 2000). The idea of cultural match has been advanced to explain the mechanisms underpinning the reception of international norms by national states. The expression "cultural match" is intended to denote the correspondence between the content of a norm

---

that Western-style cuisine had in molding Japanese cooking during the restoration of the imperial power, see Cwiertka 2007: 18 ff.

and the values, traditions, institutions present in the society that this norm should resemble. The basic idea behind the notion of cultural match is that a norm will be adopted in a legal system in so far as it conforms to the cultural environment characterizing that legal system.[66] Therefore, a legal rule will be refused, or at least will give rise to "cultural resistance," if its adoption is perceived to threaten the traditional values of society.[67]

One of the sectors where, more often, we witness the adoption of foreign legal models by national states is precisely in cases when such states must deal with a new risk. Here, indeed, parliaments examine the solutions implemented in other countries before intervening (or declining to intervene) to control such a risk. Risk regulation can, in this sense, be regarded as a field test, to verify the theory that culture matters.

The causal chain connecting culture to risk regulation, on the other hand, is quite straightforward, at least at the level of the theoretical model.[68] The reasoning proposed here is syllogistic. If culture contributes to determine risk perception and the latter influences the way a legal system regulates given activities (in the sense that the regulation will be enacted or tightened only if the risk is perceived as real and salient), then risk regulation is (at least in part) determined by cultural preferences. The cultural match matters here.

The operational mechanism of the cultural match closely resembles that of the cultural perception of risk. In both cases, the cultural values are able to direct the salience/importance in one case of a risk, in the other of a norm. Moreover, the two mechanisms cannot be differentiated in their functioning. Beyond the fact that the two are similar, it is evident that a society's perception of an activity as a risk deeply influences the subsequent step concerning the expediency of adopting a norm to deal with such a risk. The norm will probably be rejected if the risk is considered to be non-existent or minimal, and enthusiastically adopted when the risk is deemed high.

This kind of reasoning contributes to explaining why Japan rapidly adopted an administrative food safety framework which is very close to the European model, while the US did not even feel the need to think about reforming its own food safety apparatus. The BSE risk, with its connections to the processed/unprocessed

---

66 Although they do not use the notion of cultural match, similar considerations are expressed in the writings of other legal scholars and legal anthropologists; see Rouland 1988; Feldman 2006; Sacco 2007. Some international law scholarship underlines that the reception of international norms occurs through dynamic processes of acculturation and socialization of those same norms: in other words, states would conform, through socialization/acculturation, to world-level cultural models (Goodman, Jinks 2003; Koh 2005).

67 Sacco (2007: 49) notes that resistance to imitation will be stronger when the reform is encroaching a factor perceived as defining the group's identity.

68 As noted before, it might be complicated to single out with mathematical precision the role that culture has in risk regulation *vis-à-vis* other variables, such as economics, political interests, cognitive mechanisms.

dichotomy, is at odds with the European and Japanese cultural background, which is very sensitive to food products' purity and naturalness. The threat that such a risk implied for the cultural values of the European and Japanese societies made a reform plan acceptable which involved almost all aspects of food safety. The same cannot be said with regard to the US, since here we are contending with a different cultural background and, therefore, ample reforms could not be deemed acceptable, as they were in Europe and Japan.

Introducing the variable of culture into the analysis of legal change complicates things further (Nelken 2006). If it is true that taking cultural background into consideration is an important step in increasing our understanding of what determines a legal change, on the other hand we must be aware that we are including a further variable in the equation, to the detriment of the predictability of the final result. Why does culture enrich and at the same time complicate the comparative discourse on legal change?

In my view, there are two basic reasons. First, culture is difficult to grasp. It is, indeed, difficult to define and measure the role of culture in the processes which lead to legal reforms; but it is also difficult to understand fully the cultural environment of a society which is often alien to us (Geertz 1983; Nelken 2006: 946).[69] Second, culture interacts with so many other variables (economic, cognitive, political, institutional and social) to such an extent that identifying the role of one with respect to the others becomes hard. The food context, once again, offers a good example. To what extent are our food choices the product of cultural preferences or of marketing techniques? Are they determined by the availability of certain foodstuffs and, therefore, by the channels of distribution? The answers to these questions are not straightforward. If we say that marketing techniques heavily influence our food choices, at the same time we could also maintain that cultural preferences direct the choice of the economic operators to market certain products rather than others.[70] The influence, therefore, becomes reciprocal, creating a sort of circular pattern of interactions. But my goal is not so ambitious as to define the exact boundaries of the role that culture plays in the process of legal change. The purpose is only to demonstrate that culture matters, even if it is not clear (or may be impossible) to understand to what extent. One limitation revealed by the discourse is that the possibility of predicting the process of legal reforms is seriously undermined. If the interactions between the different variables are so entangled and chaotic as to make isolating them difficult, then it

---

69   For Graziadei 1999, an historical comparative method can provide a preliminary solution to the problem of studying legal cultures alien to us.

70   Maclachlan (2006: 252) emphasizes the fact that food manufacturers did little to oppose the strict regulatory measures concerning GMOs urged by consumer movements and then adopted by the Japanese government. The author justifies the producers' choice with the fear that they might lose market share, especially those connected to the consumer cooperative movement.

will be just as problematic to discern any general pattern to explain legal change (Nelken 2006: 943).

From the methodological point of view, the functionalist method has been dominant within comparative law scholarship (Michaels 2006; Graziadei 2003; Curran 1998: 66 ff.). The essence of functionalism is to observe how a specific problem is solved by different legal systems, comparing the solutions and highlighting similarities and differences. Functionalism is, therefore, an anti-formal method of enquiry, since its focus is on how problems are actually solved. But such a method has often disregarded the context in which the solutions to the problems have been implemented. Moved more by pragmatic needs than theoretical considerations, functionalists, in other words, have neglected the socio-cultural environment in which the norms operate.[71]

Despite the traditional focus on the functions, recent times have witnessed a rising interest in studies which deal with the influences that the context has in the development and implementation of legal reforms.[72] In truth, the founding father of the functionalist method, Ernst Rabel, did not discard the study of the context in which legal reforms occur as irrelevant (Gerber 2001). On the contrary, he asserted that, in order to understand the function that a rule performs, attention also must be paid to the context in which such a rule operates.[73] The problem was that he did

---

71 An example of functionalist methodology applied to comparative law is contained in the two volumes collecting some of the writings of Basil Markesinis (1997, 2001). Critics have underlined the scant attention paid by functionalists to the context (Geertz 1983: 232; Legrand 2003).

72 Curran (1998: 51) notes: "Thus, a valid examination of another legal culture requires immersion into the political, historical, economic and linguistic contexts that molded the legal system, and in which the legal system operates." Hanson, Yosifon (2003: 179 ff., in partic. 183) propose the use of *critical realism* as a legal theory able "to begin with real humans and to build models from there, rather than to begin with models [such as law and economics or bounded rationality models] and then view and interpret humans through them." Rodolfo Sacco (1989) has borrowed from linguistics the notion of cryptotype to underline the importance that hidden factors (as such not explicit in a legal system) have in molding the operational rules to be implemented. In this sense, culture can be considered one of the cryptotypes present in a legal system. The idea that there are rules which, even if not articulated, are nonetheless able to govern a society is present in von Hayek (1973: 74 ff.). From a different point of view, a fruitful cross-pollination has been occurring in recent years between comparative law and scholarship concerning law and society. Comparative scholars apply sociological tools of analysis more and more frequently to the legal systems, while law and society scholars have borrowed some of the results developed by the comparative law movement. In his recent book, Roger Cotterrell (2006) sustains the importance that sociology of law and comparative law exchange ideas also with regard to the methodologies to be applied.

73 Gerber (2001: 200) notes: "The function/context label suggests that function and context are separate and independent analytical functions, the former to be performed before the latter. In Rabel's writings they are not so clearly distinguished. The conceptual boundary is far more fluid. The analyst has to understand the function – the concrete reality

little to clarify which method to use in studying context (Gerber 2001: 200). The consequence was (and still largely is) that, despite the formal recognition of the importance of context, Rabel and his disciples focused mostly on the functions, neglecting the analysis of the context.

A second factor which has contributed to downplaying the role of context in comparative law studies is connected to the success of Alan Watson's idea of legal transplants. Debating with the legal scholars advancing the so-called "mirror theories" of law, under which law is the by-product of external social factors such as economics, politics, and so on (Kahn-Freund 1974),[74] Watson elaborated his legal transplants theory, by which law is unrelated to external social variables: on the contrary, it would be subject to autopoiesis.[75] Even in this case, in a similar way to the functionalist method, Watson's idea has been, at least in part, misapplied by his followers. The moderate version of the Watson's legal transplants theory does not reject the influence that social variables, and culture in particular, play in molding legal rules. According to this thin version, therefore, we should also take into account the social factors forming the context in which legal change occurs.

Which conclusion should we draw with regard to the role of culture in comparative law? As we have seen, the idea that context matters, albeit sometimes in muted terms, has been present from the very beginning of comparative law studies. Nonetheless, its importance was neglected in subsequent years, due to the (misunderstanding of) two elements – functionalism and legal transplants

---

– to which legal norms relate, but she can do so only by looking at what they do in context. Cognitively, the two operations are intertwined."

74   The idea that a strong relationship exists between law and local traditions can be traced back to authors such as Montesquieu and von Savigny, who conceived of legal institutions as the product of local factors; on the importance of these authors for the comparative law movement, see Monateri 1999.

75   Ewald (1995b: 491–3) distinguishes between weak and strong versions of the mirror theories: the first responds to the principle "Law and economics, politics, religion, etc. are closely related," while the second answers to the paradigm "Law is only the product of economics, politics, religion, etc." Similarly, he also distinguishes between weak and strong versions of the legal transplants theory. According to the first, economics, politics, religion, and so on, contribute to shaping the law, although the pivotal role is played by the legal transplant mechanism; under the latter, economics, politics, religion, and so on, do not mold the law at all. It should be added that the idea that legal change can be implemented regardless of the socio-cultural context in which it should occur is a useful notion to some "global" institutions, such as the International Monetary Fund (IMF) or the World Bank (WB). It is, indeed, easier to impose legal paradigms on developing countries if we depict the process of legal change as something which can happen regardless of the context. Ugo Mattei (2003: 28–9) claims that the use of law and economics discourse by international legal actors (the IMF and the WB) has become an instrument for imposing global, decontextualized rules. Monateri (2003: 583) highlights the non-neutrality of comparative law and the use of it by elites to diffuse Western models, for example, through the notion of efficiency "a magic keyword in the rhetoric of the borrowing elites."

theory – mentioned before. Despite such marginality, some comparative scholars, as well as academics from other disciplines (in particular, political scientists, anthropologists and sociologists), have developed studies also taking into account the cultural environment where legal changes occur (Twining 2005).[76] Recent times have witnessed a new-found attention being paid to this aspect of comparative studies (Caterina 2008: 218–19; Legrand 1999; Nelken, Feest 2001; Twining 2005).[77] My work places itself in the path of this new sensitivity to the cultural context in which the law operates. We should shirk the "all or nothing" perspective with regard to the debate between the followers of the mirror theory and those of the legal transplants theory (Ewald 1995a). As noted, the moderate versions of both the functionalism and of the legal transplants theories converge in the consideration that legal change depends on factors in part external to the law (economics, politics, culture, and so on), in part within the law (imitation, inertia, and so on). The conclusion, therefore, is that we must pay attention to the legal forces, but also to the socio-cultural variables which operate in determining the adoption of a given rule.[78]

In this first chapter, I have tried to sketch the socio-cultural environment characterizing three legal systems in relation to a specific field of enquiry: the legal reforms concerning the food safety framework. In addition, I have sought to offer a theoretical account of why the socio-cultural context matters in studying the process of legal change. In the following chapters, I will describe the legal models and forces which have led to the implementation of legal reforms. As we will see, imitation has played an important role in choosing which model to adopt in governing food safety. This is the case for Japan, which has borrowed the European products liability directive with few changes. Similar considerations can be made with regard to the implementation of the administrative legal framework of controls. But imitation by itself cannot explain the process of legal change. The socio-cultural environment in which reforms occur provides the ground in which such reforms can develop.

76	For a critique of the recent theories offering mostly contextualist accounts of legal norms, see Markesinis 2003.

77	As to the role of the lawyer, Monateri (2003: 592), speaking about the borrowings of foreign legal models, meaningfully writes: "What a comparative lawyer can do, as a comparativist, is to reveal the unofficial and to critique those processes of meaning-production as social and political realities, particularly in a world of contaminations."

78	The analysis of the cultural context is strictly intertwined with the study of the historical roots which form the background of that context. Rodolfo Sacco has stressed the importance of historical studies for comparative law in many of his writings (1992a: 25 ff.). James Whitman (2004) has compared the different privacy rules adopted in Europe and the US, highlighting the different cultural context in which these rules have been created and the influence it had in molding them.

Chapter 2
The Administrative Regulation of Foodstuffs

Elles [les lois] doivent être tellement propres au peuple pour lequel elles sont faites, que c'est un très grand hasard si celles d'une nation peuvent covenir à une autre.

C.L. Montesquieu, *De l'esprit des lois* (Chronologie, introduction, bibliographie par V. Goldschmidt), Livre premier, Chapitre III, Paris, 1979, 128

Any legal system relies on a mix of *ex ante* and *ex post* controls to guarantee the safety of foodstuffs placed on the market. In the following pages, I will analyze the set of administrative regulations forming the *ex ante* approach to protecting consumers' health. Administrative rules concerning food safety are countless: to try to present an overview of them would be a vain attempt. Moreover, this being a case study of the legal changes brought about by the BSE crisis, it would be beyond this work's scope to deal with areas of food safety not directly related to the topic. Therefore, I have chosen to focus my efforts in two directions. First, I will describe the general framework governing food safety in the US, Europe and Japan, paying particular attention to the norms, procedures and institutions regulating the production and marketing of meat. In addition, I will briefly deal with the international norms (that is, international standards and agreements) concerning the regulation of the food trade. The dominant role they are assuming in the global context, and their ability to influence local laws, makes it necessary to dedicate some pages to them. Second, I will study in detail the regulations and decisions in the three legal systems under consideration, which have been adopted to curb the spread of the BSE (and related vCJD) epidemic. The chapter sections mirror this choice; the first part will be dedicated to an analysis of the general framework which has been set up to guarantee the safety of meat, the second to a description of the international norms governing food safety, and the third to scrutinizing the specific rules concerning BSE and vCJD. The last part of the chapter will evaluate the institutions and rules described. Using a precautionary paradigm of analysis, I will try to assess which legal system has been most sensitive to the risks posed by mad cow disease. Anticipating the conclusion, we will see that a clear division exists between Europe and Japan on one side, and the US on the other. The gulf can be partly explained in the light of the theory of cultural risk perception I outlined in Chapter 1.

Before analyzing the details of the legal reforms that have been enacted in the wake of the mad cow crisis, it is apt to introduce some data concerning the scientific and political features characterizing BSE and vCJD. Having a clear picture of these data is a crucial step for fully understanding the intricacies and problematic aspects which characterize the legal reforms.

The Scientific Features of Mad Cow Disease

BSE (bovine spongiform encephalopathy) is a neurodegenerative disease belonging to the group of TSEs (transmissible spongiform encephalopathies). It is caused by an abnormally configured protein, called a prion.[1] The very existence of this protein has long been questioned and it was only in 1982 that the neurologist Stanley Prusiner isolated it, proving its existence definitively.[2] To clarify, not all prions cause TSEs, but only the type of prions which are abnormally structured, that is, whose structure is altered. This variation is able to be transmitted to other (new) prions: their spread determines the occurrence of TSEs. A further distinguishing characteristic of prions is their resistance to traditional methods of inactivation. In particular, they seem to be resistant to inactivation through heat, radiation and other standard chemical treatments (Lledo 2001: 48–9). The prions' resistance to inactivation helps to explain their diffusion, but also the difficulties encountered in curbing their spread.

Prions are typically found in the brain and in the nervous tissues (spinal cord, ganglia, and so on). They aggregate within the brain, modifying its normal structure and causing the formation of plaques which destroy the nervous tissue. Due to the destruction caused by these aggregations of prions, the brain assumes a sponge-like aspect, characterized by the presence of "holes," corresponding to the plaques. It affects mainly cattle, and more rarely, other animals.

It is not clear how the disease originated. Some scientists think that it is the product of a genetic modification which occurred naturally, while others believe that it is the bovine version of scrapie, a disease found in sheep, which has many features in common with BSE (Lledo 2001: 27 ff.). The disease is transmitted from animal to animal by the ingestion of materials tainted with prions. Contamination is facilitated if the ingested materials consisted originally in nerve tissue, such as brain matter and ganglia, due to the high quantity of prions in these materials. But prions can also be found, though in low quantities, in other animal parts, such as muscle tissues; for this reason, contamination also occurring through the consumption of materials other than nerve tissue cannot be excluded. Speculation has been advanced that prions might be present also in milk but as yet no proof of this thesis exists.

The spread of BSE was caused by the use of so-called "MBM" (meat and bone meal), a feed produced by reprocessing animal carcasses into flour, subsequently mixed with "traditional" ingredients, such as soybeans. MBMs were used for two purposes. By adding proteins of animal origin to the traditional feed, its nutritive properties were enriched, permitting faster growth of the animals. The second reason is due to the need to dispose of the huge amounts of residual material left

---

1   The word "prion" stands for proteinaceous infectious particle. On prions and their role in TSEs, see Phillips of Worth Matravers 2000: vol. II: *Science*; Lledo 2001; Weissenbacher 2003.

2   Prusiner was awarded the Nobel Prize for Medicine in 1997 for this discovery.

after slaughtering. The costs associated with the disposal of the left-over carcass parts can be huge; the possibility of reprocessing them in order to obtain another product (animal feed), which could be marketed, was perceived as a further business opportunity. But the opportunity represented by such reprocessing was also at the heart of the BSE problem.

Indeed, the reprocessing of BSE-infected animals in MBMs has probably given rise to widespread contamination of the entire food chain. For example, one theory connecting the emergence of BSE to scrapie, hypothesizes that the disease was transmitted to cattle because of the reprocessing of sheep carcasses contaminated with scrapie into animal feed. Given the resistance of prions to traditional inactivation methods, they were able to survive through the reprocessing and, therefore, to be transmitted to cattle through the consumption of MBMs.

BSE symptoms typically manifest themselves as difficulties in standing and in other neurological signs, such as sudden movements; given the strange behavior which seemed to characterize the affected animals, BSE is also popularly known as "mad cow disease." It is invariably fatal and no treatment is known at this stage. The incubation period is about four years.

The variant Creutzfeldt-Jakob Disease (vCJD) is a disease belonging, as does BSE, to the TSEs, with the difference that it affects humans.[3] vCJD presents many similarities with CJD (Creutzfeldt-Jakob Disease), an extremely rare disease occurring naturally in humans (Will et al. 1996). Both diseases are caused by prions and both lead to neurodegenerative disorders. Both are fatal for their victims and no therapy has proved to be effective, not even in slowing the disease's development. Furthermore, there is no *ante mortem* test to determine the existence of abnormal prions in the person suffering the condition. The only possibility of detecting the disease's presence is a *post mortem* analysis of the victim, in particular verifying the occurrence of the characteristic holes in the brain.

Despite the similarities, there are also differences which distinguish the two types of disease. First, while in the case of the CJD, the symptoms appear on average in people aged 60–65 years, vCJD affects younger people, on average 30 years old. But there are cases of vCJD which have also affected teenagers. This seems to mean that the incubation period for vCJD is shorter than in the case of the CJD. In any case, there are many uncertainties as to the time required for vCJD to develop: estimates range from five to more than thirty years. It has been also hypothesized that genetic predisposition could influence the length of the incubation period.

---

3   The occurrence of vCJD was in some way anticipated by the existence of kuru, a widespread disease among the Fore people in Papua New Guinea. Like BSE and vCJD, Kuru belongs to the TSEs and it is invariably fatal. Its spread was caused by cannibalism, practiced by the Fore tribe. In particular, the practice by the women and children of eating the brain of the deceased, as an act of mourning, is thought to have ensured the disease's spread.

The second set of differences concerns the symptoms. Psychic symptoms are more accentuated in the case of vCJD than in CJD, while the neurological symptoms appear to occur relatively late in vCJD (Zeidler et al. 1997). Also the average length of the disease varies: five months for CJD, a little over a year with vCJD. The last main difference between the two concerns the contamination mechanisms. CJD may originate from different sources. Some of the cases are hereditary, that is, caused by a genetic alteration which can be passed on. Other cases are sporadic, occurring for the first time in an individual. Finally, some cases are due to iatrogenic transmission. Especially in the 1980s, the practice of recovering human growth hormone (HGH) from pituitary glands (including from humans) infected with CJD determined the transmission of the disease to patients receiving HGHs. Conversely, vCJD has only one origin: the consumption of meat contaminated with BSE.

The BSE Scandal

On March 20, 1996, Stephen Dorrell, the Secretary of State for Health, announced to the British Parliament the shocking news that some young people had contracted a new disease, called variant Creutzfeldt-Jakob Disease and that the origin of the disease was probably linked to the consumption of BSE-tainted meat.

The 1996 announcement may be considered the turning-point in the BSE crisis. It was particularly shocking, since in the preceding years the British government, but also the European institutions, had adamantly denied that the BSE posed any risk to the health of consumers. The announcement also triggered a host of fears among British citizens, concerned that the few cases of vCJD which had emerged in those years were only the beginning of an epidemic of unforeseeable limits. Third, the announcement moved the British and European parliaments to set up commissions of enquiry to investigate the scientific and political background which had allowed the risks connected to BSE/vCJD to be underestimated.

Before analyzing the main results of these public enquiries, it should be noted that the first signs of a possible emergency were present well before March 1996. The first cases of BSE in the British cattle occurred in 1984, but it was only in December 1986 that the State Veterinary Service announced the discovery of a new animal disease, BSE (Phillips of Worth Matravers 2000: vol. I: *Findings and conclusion*, 1). In 1989, the first cases of species jump were proved, detecting episodes in which BSE affected animals other than cattle, such as cats. Meanwhile, the British and European institutions enacted legislation prohibiting the use of animal feed. But, due to the exceptions to which these regulations were subjected and to their poor enforcement, large quantities of animal feed continued to be distributed, even after the ban.

Taking into consideration the cases of cross-contamination, some scientists began to advance the hypothesis that humans could be affected by the BSE agent as well. Despite these alarming signs, both the British government and the

European Commission stopped further scientific and regulatory initiatives in the years 1990–1994. The reasons for halting the process can be understood if two elements are taken into consideration. First, an English study into BSE, the so-called "Southwood Commission," created in 1988, had reached the conclusion that mad cow disease did not pose any risk to humans. Second, given the low number of BSE cases present in continental Europe, and under pressure from the British authorities, the European Commission concluded that BSE was a British affair, deserving marginal attention at European level. It was only in 1994 that the European Commission, facing an increasing number of BSE cases occurring outside the UK, decided to enact new regulatory measures to curb the spread of the disease. In the same year, the first cases of a new, mysterious disease, which would later be named vCJD, begin to seize the attention of scientists and health authorities.

In 1996, as mentioned, the announcement made by the Secretary of State for Health revealed itself as the factor capable of generating a series of changes. Apart from the alarm that had been generated, that the link between consumption of BSE-tainted meat and vCJD could mean a massive spread of the terrible human variant of the disease in the future, another element triggered fear and rage among consumers. This element concerned the mechanism which had permitted the epidemic's propagation. As noted, its diffusion was chiefly due to MBMs, that is, to the technology used to produce feed, by which carcasses were processed and transformed into flour mixed with "traditional" feed ingredients. The fact that cows, herbivorous animals, were transformed into cannibals provoked a feeling of revulsion in the minds of European citizens. Consumer and environmental associations used this as an example of the risks that the use of the technology can run, when applied to the field of food production.

In July 1996, the European Parliament set up a committee of inquiry to investigate the political responsibilities in the management of the BSE epidemic. A year later, in December 1997, the British Parliament adopted a similar solution, creating a commission, chaired by Lord Phillips of Worth Matravers, to review the actions taken in dealing with BSE. Both the reports[4] point to the many deficiencies that characterized the actions taken by the European and British authorities. In particular, they denounced the behaviour of the competent institutions, which underestimated the magnitude of the risks. Market interests were preferred over questions of public health, by selectively emphasizing the risks revealed by science and by impeding sources of independent investigation or minority scientific opinions. In addition, enforcement of the regulations enacted to curb the spread of BSE was judged to be weak.

---

4   The Report, commissioned by the European Parliament, was released February 7, 1997: see Medina Ortega 1997. The BSE Inquiry Report, made by a Commission chaired by Lord Phillips of Worth Matravers, was published in October 2000; see Phillips of Worth Matravers 2000.

With specific reference to the European experience, the institutional reasons which permitted the poor handling of the BSE crisis are linked to so-called "comitology" (Joerges, Vos 1999; Bergström 2005). Under this institutional arrangement, each directorate (sub-divisions within the European Commission) had their own committees to manage their various tasks. The Directorate of Agriculture, which had primary responsibility for the management of the BSE crisis, had several scientific committees, providing risk assessments in different fields relating to agricultural matters. In theory, these committees had some degree of autonomy, but *de facto* they were all under the political guidance of the directorate. This made the committees very susceptible to political and economic influences, especially in the case of the Directorate of Agriculture, which is economic by nature. Moreover, the fact that risk assessment and risk management were carried out within the same body facilitated the downplaying of the problem, through an opaque and unidirectional application of scientific knowledge. The European report suggests two lines of reform. The first concerns the distinction between the phases of risk assessment and risk management, with the creation of an independent authority charged with the risk assessment tasks. The aim was to guarantee a more independent and transparent use of science than in the past. The second line of reform regards the 1985 directive on product liability. The extension of strict liability to primary agricultural products was conceived as an appropriate tool to provide more efficient protection of consumers' health.

Both lines of reform can be found in the proposals contained in the 1997 Green Paper on the General Principles of Food Law.[5] The first reform implemented concerned product liability. On May 10, 1999, Directive No. 34 reformed the 1985 directive, extending the strict liability regime to include primary agricultural products. With regard to the reform of the administrative framework governing food safety, this was preceded by the White Paper on Food Safety, published on January 12, 2000 (Chalmers 2003: 534–8; Alemanno 2008: 4–5).[6] The document lays out the main points of the reform, which was to be enacted two years later by Regulation 178/2002. As we will see in detail in the following pages, a tripartition between risk assessment, management and information was introduced. At the same time, the regulation created the European Food Safety Authority (EFSA), a body charged with the task of carrying out the risk assessment phase. Risk management remains under the control of the Commission, while the risk information duties are shared by the Commission and the EFSA. Other important tools introduced by

---

5   Commission Green Paper, COM (1997) 176 final, April 30, 1997. In 1997, the Commission decided to charge Directorate XXIV, renamed "Health and Consumer Protection Directorate," to deal with all the issues relating to the protection of public health. The reform was aimed at preventing the dangerous mix between economic interests and protection of consumer health, as was the case within the Directorate of Agriculture. In any event, risk assessment and risk management were still carried out within the same framework.

6   Commission White Paper, COM (1999) 719 final, January 12, 2000.

the 2002 reform concern traceability, the use of a precautionary approach in risk management, the consumers' right to be informed and the rapid alert network.

The reforms involved in the Japanese reorganization of its food safety framework seem to have been conducted at a more marked pace than that witnessed in Europe. The first case of mad cow disease was discovered in September 2001 and immediately triggered a high state of alarm among consumers, which determined a sharp decline in beef sales. In order to support the domestic beef industry, the government set up a compensation plan a month later, paying subsidies to the farmers.[7] But towards the end of 2001 and the beginning of 2002, foreign beef was mislabeled as domestic, in order to gain access to the compensation plan.[8] The occurrence of the first BSE cases, the perception that the government was only weakly counteracting this new emergency, and other food scares (such as the mislabeling affair), provoked widespread mistrust in the safety of the Japanese food chain. The government decided to answer citizens' widespread fears by reforming the food safety framework (Yasui 2004).[9] The bulk of the reforms have concerned the creation of the Food Safety Commission, an authority modeled on the EFSA and charged with the assessment of food risks.[10]

In the US, as mentioned in Chapter 1, mad cow disease has not triggered the same level of concern as was present in Europe and Japan.[11] The first case of BSE occurred in the US in December 2003 and was followed by two other cases, one in 2005 and the other in 2006. Some voices have sought to advocate that the mad cow disease might have been the factor capable of initiating comprehensive reform of the American food safety framework. But these voices remained isolated: only *ad hoc* measures have been adopted, so far, to curb the spread of BSE. To be precise, the absence of general reform initiatives was not explicable on the basis that American institutions managed the BSE risk in a perfectly efficient way. For example, in 2002 the US General Accounting Office published a report concerning the federal measures taken to prevent an outbreak of BSE in the US (US General Accounting Office 2002). The document expressed several concerns with regard to the soundness and sufficiency of the regulatory initiatives adopted so far. But since it did not make reference to the need to reform the overall food safety framework, it triggered only new *ad hoc*, anti-BSE measures.

---

7   "Mad cow subsidies recovered," *The Japan Times Online*, November 30, 2003; "Meat boss gets seven years for bilking state amid BSE scare," *The Japan Times Online*, May 28, 2005.

8   "Snow brand searched in mislabeled beef probe," *The Japan Times Online*, February 3, 2002.

9   "Food safety bills aimed at restoring public trust," *The Japan Times Online*, February 8, 2003.

10   The Commission was created under Act no. 48, May 23, 2003.

11   For a detailed description of the mad cow affair in the US, see Rampton, Stauber 2004.

The Local Administrative Frameworks for Ensuring Food Safety

The American Model

Describing the US administrative framework governing food safety is a complicated task. Its fragmentary nature, the myriad of public bodies involved to a greater or lesser extent in the structure, the procedural and substantive rules regarding each single institution make it difficult, in the limited space available, to provide a complete picture. Therefore, I will only sketch in the main institutions involved and their roles. What I will scrutinize to a greater extent is the role played by the US Department of Agriculture (USDA), the body in charge of guaranteeing the safety of meat put into (interstate) commercial circulation, a topic more directly related to the development of my work.

In order to clarify the different tasks characterizing the institutions which exist in the American system, the best solution is to set out a historical overview of the development of the food safety framework. The USDA's foundation dates back to 1862: its goal was, and in large part still is, the protection and promotion of American agriculture. Pursuant to this pro-business matrix, food safety was not included among the tasks of the Department of Agriculture (Merrill, Francer 2000: 78; Hutt, Merrill, Grossman 2007; Roots 2001; Babuscio 2005: 152 ff.). But when, a few years later, the need for food safety regulation emerged, it appeared natural to attribute the new, but related, responsibilities to the USDA. In 1889, the Bureau of Chemistry was created within the USDA: its mission was to investigate the adulteration of foodstuffs, drugs and beverages. At almost the same time, the first laws concerning food purity were enacted, in particular at state level. Their goal was limited to preventing adulteration and, in addition, they concerned only specific products, such as tea, milk and butter (Regier 1933; Merrill, Francer 2000: 78–9).

Towards the end of the nineteenth and into the beginning of the twentieth century, many initiatives relating to food safety were undertaken. The head of the Bureau of Chemistry, Mr. Wiley, followed a very aggressive approach in pursuing his bureau's mission and was soon in conflict with the powerful agricultural lobbies and his superiors at the USDA. Not only did he incessantly investigate those who committed food frauds, but he also called for new regulations introducing stricter food standards. He received support from the press in his battle. A handful of so-called "muckrakers" began to write articles on the many frauds taking place in the marketing of foodstuffs, as well as on the unsanitary conditions typical of these products' manufacturing process. The muckrakers mounted a public campaign, invoking the adoption of a more severe regulatory approach to food safety (Regier 1933). The publication of Upton Sinclair's book *The Jungle* in 1906 may be considered as a milestone in the campaign (Sinclair 1906). The novel describes working conditions in the Chicago meatpacking industry in the early years of the twentieth century. Although Sinclair's main purpose was to reveal the terrible conditions under which immigrants were forced to work, the book became famous for its denunciation of the unsanitary practices used in meat production and packing.[12] The joint efforts of the head of the Bureau of Chemistry and the press led to the enactment of two statutes, which laid the foundations of the existing American food safety administrative framework, in 1906 and 1907 respectively.[13] The first was the Pure Food and Drug Act (PFDA), charging the USDA with the task of promoting food and drug safety through appropriate monitoring systems: furthermore, it prohibited the distribution of adulterated food in interstate commerce. The second was the Federal Meat Inspection Act (FMIA), which created the system of meat inspection which in large part still exists. The Bureau of Chemistry was given responsibility for the implementation of the PFDA, while the enforcement of the FMIA was entrusted to the Bureau of Animal Industry (Merrill, Francer 2000: 79).

The friction between the Bureau of Chemistry and the USDA's top management continued, despite the enactment of the PFDA and FMIA. The bone of contention related to the research and enforcement duties, both assigned to the Bureau of Chemistry. The opponents of the Bureau of Chemistry argued that a conflict existed between these two types of duties and that they had to be assigned to two distinct bodies. This line of reform was followed in 1927, when Congress entrusted the enforcement duties to a new office within the USDA: the Food, Drug, and Insecticide Administration (FDIA). In 1930, the tasks relating to insecticide control were removed from the new office and its name became simply the Food and Drug Administration (FDA) (Merrill, Francer 2000: 81). It should be noted that in these early phases, the FDA was not an independent agency, but was under USDA control. The overlap between food safety concerns and the promotion of the agricultural market was, thus, still present.

Meanwhile, President Franklin D. Roosevelt began to promote a raft of reforms inspired by a more interventionist approach by the government, in both the social security and economic arenas (Jackson 1970). One of these major reforms was the enactment of the Food and Drug Cosmetic Act (FDCA), which replaced the PFDA in 1938 and is still today at the core of food safety regulation in the US.[14] The new law reinforced the existing rules, instituting new procedures and providing for stricter standards.[15] With specific reference to foodstuffs, it empowered the FDA:

---

12   *The Jungle* describes the life of a Lithuanian immigrant working in a meatpacking plant in Chicago. Although fictitious, Sinclair based the novel on the findings of a seven-week investigation he undertook in the Chicago meatpacking district.

13   The enactment of the two statutes occurred after 190 proposals were advanced to reform the food safety framework in the years between 1879 and 1906. The powerful lobbies existing in the Congress (and especially in the Senate) were able to reject all attempts to reform the system, until the 1906 events occurred (Regier 1933: 3–5).

14   21 USCA 301–97.

15   Although unrelated to food safety, one of the milestones of the 1938 reform was the introduction of the pre-marketing approval for new drugs. It should be noted that the FDCA was enacted in the aftermath of a scandal involving an untested drug, whose ingestion caused 107 casualties; see Merrill, Francer 2000: 81.

1. to inspect factories and facilities where food is produced and stored,
2. to set tolerance limits for substances that are unavoidably unsafe,
3. to establish identity and quality standards, and
4. to impose the labeling of ingredients.

In the same year, Congress empowered the Federal Trade Commission (FTC) to regulate the advertising of food (Merrill, Francer 2000: 82).

In 1940, President Roosevelt removed the FDA from the USDA control, setting it up as an agency under the supervision initially of the Federal Security Agency and later of the Department of Health and Human Service. Perpetuating the division introduced in 1906 through the enactment of two laws, one dedicated to food in general and one specifically to meat, Roosevelt's reorganization plan maintained the attribution of the meat inspection functions to the USDA and, in particular, to one of its offices, the Food Safety Inspection Service (FSIS; Merrill, Francer 2000: 84).[16]

The last important reform involving the food safety framework occurred in 1970. Up to then, first the USDA, and subsequently the FDA, had regulated the use of pesticides on crops and set quantity limits on food residuals. But President Nixon, in creating the Environmental Protection Agency (EPA), deemed it appropriate to entrust the new agency with the task of setting the tolerance levels for pesticides in foodstuffs. The EPA can only fix these levels, while the USDA and the FDA have the duty of enforcing the limits (Merrill, Francer 2000: 87–8).

Because of its historical development, the American food safety system appears to be extremely fragmented. The USDA, through the FSIS, overviews the safety of meat and poultry,[17] including their labeling; the FDA controls the quality and labeling of the other foodstuffs and feed products; the EPA sets the tolerance levels for pesticide residuals; the FTC promotes and enforces regulations on misleading food advertising; the Center for Disease Control (CDC), together with the National Institute of Health (NIH), the USDA and the FDA, is concerned with epidemiological investigations and control of food borne diseases; the Commerce Department is responsible for inspection and surveillance in relation to seafood (Merrill, Francer 2000: 90).

To further complicate the picture, state agencies and departments may be involved in the administration of food safety. Although the management of the meat safety system is mainly operated at federal level, local institutions, ranging from Agricultural to Health Departments, still play some role and mainly operate in two directions. First, they are entrusted with the task of overseeing the retailing of foodstuffs, both at grocery stores and restaurants. Indeed, the federal agencies

---

16   Originally, the FMIA entrusted the Bureau of Animal Industry to enforce its provisions: this bureau was later renamed the Bureau of Animal Husbandry and, eventually, the Food Safety Inspection Service (FSIS).

17   The surveillance of poultry products was added to the tasks of the USDA in 1957, with the Poultry Products Inspection Act.

and departments described so far only monitor the processing level and do so exclusively in relation to interstate commerce. The second field of intervention concerns the inspection of small processing plants or slaughterhouses. This inspection service is performed in cooperation with the USDA or the FDA, since the federal bodies usually focus their controls only on large producers (Merrill, Francer 2000: 110–11). It is important to note that the same fragmentation existing in the federal framework is experienced also at state level, with different departments, offices and agencies playing a role in guaranteeing the safety of foodstuffs (Merrill, Francer 2000: 112). Beyond the specific regulatory problems concerning the meatpacking sector that we will shortly consider, the large degree of fragmentation, which is a hallmark of the American framework, has motivated some authors to call for comprehensive reform in order to surmount the persisting divisions. In particular, concentrating the dispersed functions within an existing governmental body or a newly created authority has been deemed desirable (Merrill, Francer 2000; O'Reilly 2004).

The large number of institutions involved in the American food safety system implies a significant variance in the procedures implemented to guarantee the purity of specific foodstuffs. Each agency or department tends to lay down its own procedures which, of course, concern only the products regulated by that body. This constitutes one of the main differences between the US system and the European and Japanese ones which, as we will see, have recently created a comprehensive scheme providing for procedures to be applied to nearly all foodstuffs. Moreover, this feature impels me to focus solely on an analysis of the procedures implemented by the USDA, and in particular by the FSIS. The consequence is that, at least with regard to the US, the analysis will be limited to the meat and poultry sector.

Before going into details of the regulation of the meat sector, a brief clarification is required. Indeed, despite the variety of institutions and procedures, there is a common analytical process concerning the adoption of regulatory choices which deserves to be mentioned. This process is called the "Cost Benefit Analysis" (CBA) (Adler, Posner 2006; Adler 2003; Antle 1995). Under Executive Order 12866 of September 30, 1993, the US President has imposed the use of CBA upon all the agencies which are part of the federal government, when adopting their regulatory decisions.[18] Section 1(a) states that "In deciding whether and how to regulate, agencies should assess all costs and benefits of available regulatory alternatives, including the alternative of not regulating." Part (b) of the same section, at point 7, provides that "Each agency shall base its decisions on the best reasonably obtainable scientific, technical, economic, and other information concerning the need for, and consequences of, the intended regulation." The way in which CBA is implemented in practice leaves room for some differences. In its strictest form, the costs (implementation of damage-mitigating technologies,

---

18   58 FR 51735 (1993). Executive Order 12866 revoked Executive Order no. 12291 of 1981, which first introduced the CBA (although under the name of Regulatory Impact Analysis) for all the federal agencies.

decrease in productivity, and so on) and the benefits (saving of lives, reduction of injuries, minimization of environmental damages, and so on) of a given regulatory action are ascertained and, then, priced. The comparison between the costs and benefits in monetary terms allows a decision to be taken as to whether to adopt that course of action (Brent 2006; Zerbe, Dively 1993). Other forms of CBA also seek to take into account social or political concerns.[19] In both cases, the CBA is used to cope with situations of uncertainty. It helps to establish some points for dealing rationally with the problematic aspects flowing from uncertain situations (Pennisi, Scandizzo 2003).

The mention of the CBA in the food safety context is justified by the fact that it is also used by the USDA.[20] This can be considered one of the main reasons why, in the specific context of food safety, a divide exists between the US, on one side, and Europe and Japan, on the other. Since Europe and Japan use a precautionary approach in dealing with food safety, it appears natural that their regulatory choices would be more sensitive to food risks than the choices implemented in the US. But, as we will note in greater detail in the last section of the chapter, Europe and Japan do not always apply a precautionary approach in the field of food production, while the use of CBA by the US sometimes acquires a precautionary flavor. In other words, the divide between the US and Europe and Japan goes beyond the mere contraposition between precautionary principle and CBA.

As to the regulation of the meat sector, the FSIS is the branch within the USDA entrusted to monitor the meatpacking plants. With regard to the slaughterhouses, the control duties are performed jointly by the FSIS and the Animal and Plant Health Inspection Service (APHIS), another branch of the USDA charged with the task of protecting plant and animal health. Actually, two different systems of control coexist. The first was introduced in 1907 with the FMIA and consists in organoleptic analysis of the meat. The law requires that each carcass entering a plant for processing is subjected to inspection by sight, touch and smell in order to single out any which appear to be unfit for human consumption. The carcasses deemed fit are stamped by the inspectors and can then enter the processing phase (Manoukian 1994: 564; Lassiter 1997: 447 ff.). It must be added that meatpacking plants can operate only if federal inspectors are present: in cases in which the FSIS detects repeated failures to conform to the prescribed regulations and standards, it can decide to withdraw its inspectors, so halting, in fact, the operation of the facilities.

The organoleptic system of inspection does not require any microbiological testing of the meat. This is due to the fact that the system was created in the 1907, when microbiological analysis was largely unavailable, and to date has hardly been

---

19   For example, Sunstein (2005) proposes a soft version of the CBA that he calls "libertarian paternalism." The proposal is criticized by Mandel, Gathii 2006. Another example of a revised interpretation of the CBA is in Adler 2004.

20   See the Office of Risk Assessment and Cost Benefit Analysis (ORACBA) at the USDA website <http://www.usda.gov/agency/oce/risk_assessment/>.

reformed at all. But the incredible advances in microbiology make organoleptic inspection both obsolete and ineffective in guaranteeing the safety of the meat put onto the market. It is thus no surprise, that, alongside the 1907 system, other control mechanisms have been created. One of them concerned the introduction of the Hazard Analysis and Critical Control Point (HACCP) procedures in meatpacking plants in 1998 by the USDA (Johnson 2004: 160).

The HACCP is a system which aims at preventing the contamination of food during the production phases, through a series of preventive measures. It is typically an *ex ante* procedural framework of control which, by identifying the processing stages which appear to be most risky with regard to food safety, sets up the devices likely to minimize such risks. Any HACCP system requires the implementation of seven steps (Schuller 1998: 88–9). First, the hazards that can compromise the purity of the foodstuff must be recognized. The second step consists in identifying the points in the chain of production at which such hazards can materialize. These are the so-called "critical control points" (CCPs). For example, with regard to the BSE risk, a normal CCP is when the backbone of the cow is separated from the carcass, since it might happen that, by cutting it, leftovers of spinal cord could contaminate the meat. Third, tolerance limits must be established. These are the maximum levels under which the food safety hazard is deemed acceptable. The tolerance values set for salmonella in the meat are a typical example: if, through microbiological testing for this agent, it is found that the level of salmonella is under what is considered the maximum limit, then the meat can be put into commercial circulation. The fourth step requires that monitoring procedures are created to verify compliance with the tolerance limits set out in the preceding steps. Microbiological tests, chemical analysis and visual inspection are all examples of monitoring procedures. If a deviance from the standards is ascertained, then corrective action must be taken: this is the fifth step of any HACCP procedure. In the salmonella example, recall of the meat not within the fixed limits is an example of a corrective measure. The last two steps require, respectively: the maintenance of a record-keeping system concerning the analysis and actions adopted, and verification procedures concerning the effective operation of the HACCP scheme.

Any producer must adapt these seven steps to the specific characteristics of their firm, identifying the specific risks inherent in the production process which, in turn, depends on the manufacturing methodologies used. It should be noted that HACCP procedures are not approved by the FSIS before their implementation, but are self-validated by the producer. What the FSIS can do is to verify both the effective compliance with the procedures and their ability to guarantee the manufacture of safe foodstuffs (Schuller 1998: 89). In its supervisory role, there are some limits that the FSIS must observe. For example, with regard to microbiological testing, the initial rule laid down by the USDA provided that the FSIS could only carry out sample tests on raw meat for salmonella, while tests for E. coli had to be conducted by the producers, without any monitoring by the FSIS (Schuller 1998: 87). But this framework has been dismantled. In the months following the new USDA rule, the FSIS attempted to implement testing guidelines for salmonella. Under these guidelines, if the FSIS, through sample testing, ascertained three failures in meeting the tolerance levels set for salmonella, it could withdraw its inspectors, thus halting the producer's activity. A meat processor whose plant was closed because of its repeated failures challenged the USDA authority to establish (through the FSIS) the testing guidelines.[21] Basing their decision on the notion of adulteration indicated by the FMIA, the judges stated that the USDA had exceeded its regulatory authority and could not withdraw its inspectors from the plant.[22] The decision had the effect to rule out the salmonella tests previously performed by the FSIS.

It is clear that the HACCP system places much more reliance on the producers than the 1907 FMIA did; while in the latter federal inspectors play a crucial role, in the HACCP, the major role is performed by the producers. The reform has, therefore, accomplished not only the goal of modernizing the controls which are performed, but also of slimming down the system, by reducing the involvement of the federal government. Along with the lack of a control framework allowing the detection of microbiological contamination, one problem in fact was that the large amounts of meat which are processed nowadays in the meatpacking plants make it almost impossible for the inspectors to certify each carcass. With regard to the coexistence of the organoleptic controls and the HACCP, there has been discussion whether the latter replaces the former, or not.[23] On the one hand, the previous system has never yet been formally abrogated; but, on the other, it seems a waste of resources to implement both controls. What *de facto* is happening nowadays in the meatpacking plants is that the FSIS inspectors spend most of their time checking the records kept by the producers, with the consequence that the visual inspections of the carcasses are much less frequent than in the past (Hinderliter 2006: 746; Machado 2003: 821).

The European Food Safety Framework

The current European food safety framework differs from the American system in many respects, as a consequence of the far-reaching changes that followed in

---

21   *Supreme Beef Processors, Inc.* v. *United States Department of Agriculture*, 275 F.3d 432 (Ct App. 5th Circ. 2001).

22   In particular, the FMIA allows the FSIS to withdraw its inspectors only when they find that the meat is adulterated, that is, under the definition of the FMIA, rendered unfit for human consumption. Since salmonella is largely a natural contaminant of meat and might be present regardless of the processing operations carried out in the plant, testing for salmonella cannot be considered a good indicator for adulteration, at least within the technical meaning indicated by the FMIA (Johnson 2004: 168–9).

23   Merrill, Francer (2000: 104) think that, although not in the organoleptic form, the FMIA in any event mandates the inspection of each carcass; Schuller (1998: 90–91) believes that the role of the federal inspectors is limited only to ensuring that the requirements imposed by the new HACCP system are respected.

the wake of the mad cow crisis (Chambers 1999).[24] Indeed, before the reforms were enacted in 2002, the resemblance between the US and Europe was much more noticeable. First, it should be noted that food regulation was one of the first areas into which the European Community intruded. The numerous national laws dealing with the production and marketing of foodstuffs constituted a major barrier preventing the development of a common market in one of the key sectors for the development of the European Economic Community (EEC). It is no surprise that the European institutions decided to promote an array of directives, regulations and decisions with the aim of harmonizing the norms on specific foodstuffs (Vos 2000; Sgarbanti 2003).[25] This strategy parallels the initial competence of the USDA, that is, the promotion of interstate commerce in food and agricultural goods. Thus, in both legal systems, the early food regulations had a very similar slant: they showed a pro-business attitude, paying scarce attention to the safety profile. Moreover, initially a general framework of intervention was lacking: most of the initiatives were *ad hoc*, concerning only particular, limited classes of foodstuffs.

Second, the pivotal role in regulating food at the European level has traditionally been played by the committees.[26] Following their creation, food regulation shifted from targeted sets of initiatives to a more organic and comprehensive approach. The food safety framework was composed of three committees: the Scientific Committee on Foodstuffs (SCF), the Standing Committee on Foodstuffs (StCF), and the Advisory Committee on Foodstuffs (ACF) (Vos 2000: 229–30). The SCF was entrusted with the task of offering scientific opinions on the safety of food products, in order to provide a technical basis upon which to program future actions. The StCF could be regarded as the political arm of the system, in the sense that it guaranteed the political support of the member states for the decisions taken by the European Commission (EC). Finally, the ACF was the body representing the interests of the different stakeholders involved in the food sector (farmers, processors, retailers, consumers, and so on). The final decisions on how to regulate particular aspects of food production and marketing were taken by the EC, after having consulted the three committees and discussed the proposed regulations. Although not yet in its full-fledged state, the division between the phases of risk assessment, carried out by the scientists sitting in the SCF, and risk management, performed by the Commission in cooperation with the StCF and the ACF, was already present.

---

24   For a comparison between the American and European regulations with specific regard to the beef industry, see Houston 2006.

25   The case law of the European Court of Justice (ECJ) has been fundamental in ensuring the implementation of the principle of free circulation of agricultural products: see, for example, ECJ July 11, 1974 (C-8/74, the so-called "Dassonville case"), *European Court Reports* 1974, 837, and ECJ February 20, 1979 (C-120/78, the so-called "Cassis de Dijon case"), *European Court Reports* 1979, 649.

26   The expression used to refer to the role of committees in the European law-making process is comitology. On the role of committees in the European context, see Vos 1999: 110 ff.; Joerges, Vos 1999; Bergström 2005.

This system collapsed in the years of the BSE scandal. The inquiry ordered by the European Parliament revealed major mistakes in the management of the crisis. In particular, the committees appeared subject to political pressure and manipulation, severely impairing their ability to provide reliable and/or independent advice. The BSE experience had, moreover, pointed to the lack of a conceptually and scientifically sound system of risk analysis for food safety. The past initiatives of the European Community in this field were still inspired by an *ad hoc* approach, without a general framework able to address the complex problems deriving from the intersection between law, science and politics (Vos 2000: 232–3). The inquiry, thus, advocated a comprehensive reform capable not only of solving the manipulation problems, but also of creating a conceptual framework for dealing with risk analysis in the specific field of food safety. The Green Paper in 1997, followed by the White Paper in 2000, drew the outlines of the future regulation of the sector. This regime was to be enacted two years later, with Regulation no. 178 of 28 January 2002. Although the title of the Regulation makes reference only to foodstuffs,[27] the law embraces, significantly, both food and feed products, a regulatory choice suggested by the lesson learnt from the BSE epidemics.

Regulation 178/2002 introduced many innovations in comparison with the system used in the past (Capelli, Silano, Klaus 2006; Aa. Vv. 2003: 114 ff.). First of all, the philosophy embraced by the new law is radically different from the traditional approach. As mentioned, due to its historical origins, the major goal of the European Community in the food field has been pro-business. This approach has played an important role in underestimating the risks connected to the spread of BSE. The primary aim was more by way of defending the economic interests behind the meat industry than of protecting consumers' health. Therefore, the first step in the reform process was to implement a pro-consumer attitude to food regulation, in which the promotion of public health was the most important goal (Vos 2000: 234).[28] Articles 5 and 8 of Regulation 178/2002 embody this attitude, stating that the primary goal of food law is to protect consumers' interests and health: the promotion of the free movement of foodstuffs in the Community is subordinated to the respect of the other norms laid down in the Regulation.

The second point of reform has introduced a conceptual framework within which the investigation of the risks posed by food products can operate. Art. 6 provides that "food law shall be based on risk analysis" (Gradoni 2003a). In its turn, art. 3.10 defines risk analysis as a process composed of three elements: risk assessment, risk management and risk communication. The first is a procedure by which a hazard is identified and its magnitude evaluated according to scientific parameters (art. 3.11). The scientific analysis must be conducted in an independent

---

27   Regulation no. 178/2002 of the European Parliament and of the Council of 28 January 2002 laying down the general principles and requirements of food law, establishing the European Food Safety Authority and laying down procedures in matters of food safety.

28   Germanò, Rook Basile (2005: 245) note that with Regulation 178/2002 there has been a shift from food security to food safety.

and transparent manner (art. 6.2). Taking into account the results of the risk assessment, along with other political, social and economic factors, the policy of selecting the most appropriate action is implemented: this second phase is called risk management (art. 3.12).

Finally, risk communication consists in the exchange of information between the interested parties with regard to the nature and extent of the hazards and the initiatives taken to deal with them (art. 3.13; Losavio 2007: 209 ff.).[29] Any potential threat to consumers' health should go through this tripartite framework of analysis. While risk assessment and risk management are consequential one with the other and pertain to two distinct authorities (respectively, scientific and political), risk communication can be implemented simultaneously with the first two and is carried out both by scientists and politicians. Articles 9 and 10 reinforce the risk communication stage of the analysis. Art. 9 provides that the enactment of food law must be preceded by an open and transparent public consultation process. Art. 10 states that whenever a particular food is suspected of posing a risk to human health, public authorities must inform the public "identifying to the fullest extent possible the food or feed, or type of food or feed, the risk that it may present, and the measures which are taken or about to be taken to prevent, reduce or eliminate that risk."

Under art. 7, if, after the phase of risk assessment, uncertainties remain as to the existence or extent of particular hazards, precautionary measures may be applied. In other words, during the phase of risk management, the precautionary principle may be used in order to shape policy decisions when a situation of scientific uncertainty persists.[30] But its adoption is limited by some constraints specified in the same article. The precautionary measures must be temporary, in the sense that they can be maintained as long as more advanced scientific results are

---

29   Recently the European Commission has published a proposal for a Regulation on the provision of food information to consumers; the proposal can be downloaded at the URL <http://ec.europa.eu/food/food/labellingnutrition/foodlabelling/proposed_legislation_en.htm>.

30   The conceptual roots of the precautionary principle can be traced back to the writings of the German philosopher Hans Jonas and the German sociologist Ulrich Beck: see, respectively, Jonas 1984 and Beck 1992. The second author argues that, in order to avoid apocalyptic disasters in the future, humankind must adopt a precautionary approach towards the risks that modern societies and technologies create. The first implementations of the precautionary principle were adopted in the 1970s in Germany, in particular, through a series of environmental laws. Soon after, the precautionary principle was also included in some international agreements concerning the protection of the environment. For a survey of the historic passages which led to the legalization of the precautionary principle, see Izzo 2004: 28 ff. See also European Court of First Instance September 11, 2002 (T-13/99), *European Court Reports* 2002, II-3305, and id. September 11, 2002 (T-70/99), *European Court Reports* 2002, II-3495. For a justification of precautionary measures taken during the BSE crisis to curb the spread of the disease, see European Court of Justice, May 5, 1998 (C-180/96), *European Court Reports* 1998, I-2265 (in particular, points 98 ff.).

achieved. Moreover, the measures must be proportionate to the goal of protecting consumers' health, not restricting the trade more than necessary for the fulfillment of such objective. In this sense, economic and technical feasibility should be taken into account, in order to avoid measures disproportionately affecting production interests (Basili, Franzini 2004; Wiener 2003; Gradoni 2003b; Izzo 2004; Marini 2004; Santonastaso 2005; Sollini 2006; Galasso 2006; Germanò 2007: 49 ff.).[31]

Section 4 of the Regulation puts in place some general requirements. The distribution of food which is injurious to health or unfit for human consumption is prohibited (art. 14). In particular, the assessment of the unhealthiness of the food must be carried out taking into account its normal conditions of use, the information provided to the consumers, its cumulative toxic effects and, more in general, its long-term effects on subsequent generations as well.[32] The conformity of the food to the provisions laid down by European law creates a presumption of safety, but such presumption can be reversed if, despite the conformity, there are reasons to suspect a safety deficit.[33] The responsibilities in fulfilling such requirements are shared between food operators and public authorities (art. 17). The former have a duty to put products on the market which are safe and that respect the applicable norms,[34] while the latter must ensure the enforcement of the food law provisions, monitoring the activities carried out by the food operators, as well as informing the public of potential health threats.

The final measure under section 4 introduces a requirement intended to play a pivotal role in the future food safety framework. Art. 18 imposes the traceability of "food, feed, food-producing animals, and any other substance intended to be, or expected to be, incorporated into a food or feed." Traceability means an identification system which permits operators, public authorities and consumers to retrace the components (and the corresponding suppliers) which have been put into the food during the production and marketing phases. The goal is twofold. First, it makes it easier to single out the ingredient which rendered a particular batch of food unsafe. Once the contaminant has been identified, corrective action

---

31   See the Communication of the Commission on the Precautionary Principle, COM(2000)1, February 2, 2000. For a cautionary tale on the use of the precautionary principle by the European Union, see Cazala 2004; Löfstedt 2003.

32   Germanò, Rook Basile (2005: 256–7) note that the prohibition on putting foodstuffs onto the market which may have deleterious long-term effects might be in conflict with the development risk defense included in European product liability law.

33   In the case of feed, art. 15 provides for requirements similar to those set out in art. 14. In particular, it is forbidden to market feed which is unsafe, that is, which can "have an adverse effect on human or animal health; make the food derived from food-producing animals unsafe for human consumption."

34   Art. 19 of the Regulation reinforces the responsibilities of the food operators, providing that they must withdraw the products they have reason to believe pose risks to public health. Along with this duty, they also must inform public authorities and consumers of the potential risks. These duties extend not only to food producers, but also to distributors and retailers.

can be taken. For example, the contaminated batches can be withdrawn;[35] fines for having violated food law provisions can be imposed; the operators responsible for having put the contaminant into circulation can be sued for the damages suffered. Second, it reassures the consumers about the origin and quality of the foodstuff. The fact that references to facilitate traceability must be included in the labeling not only allows consumers to avoid products over which there is public alarm, but also permits them to purchase foodstuffs produced or processed by operators they trust.

The last important innovation introduced by Regulation 178/2002 was the creation of the European Food Safety Authority (EFSA), an independent body whose mission and tasks are stated in articles 22 and 23.[36] Under these measures, the EFSA provides the EC and the Member States with scientific opinions concerning the safety of specific foodstuffs, promotes the development of scientific studies (as well as the collection and analysis of data) in the field of food safety, and informs the public of the possible risks depending on the consumption of particular foodstuffs. In other words, the EFSA is charged with both the assessment and communication of the risks, but it does not play any role with regard to their management. Indeed, risk management is carried out by the European Commission together with the Member States, albeit sometimes in an adversarial position in their regard.[37]

The clear separation between risk assessment and risk management is a consequence of the BSE scandal and was one of the most important reforms suggested in the 1997 Report commissioned by the European Parliament. The goal is to keep political and economic considerations away from scientific opinions, avoiding the overlap between them which characterized the committees' experience and which led to the underestimation of the risks during the BSE epidemic. This idea is reinforced by some provisions contained in the Regulation, stressing

---

35   Art. 19 places on food operators the responsibility of recalling products which have already reached the market, when such a measure is necessary to protect consumers' health.

36   The first activities of the EFSA started in 2003, but it was in 2005 that the Authority moved to Parma (Italy) as its official and definitive headquarters, and has begun to work steadily. For a survey of the origins of the EFSA, see Chalmers 2003; Alemanno 2008.

37   Art. 36 of the EEC Treaty provides that the Member States can derogate to the principle of free circulation of goods when there is a documented suspicion of danger to public health. There are several examples where a Member State has prohibited the importation of foodstuffs whose safety was questioned. The European Court of Justice has tried to strike a balance between the opposing needs to ensure the smooth development of the common market and the right of the states to protect their citizens' health. See, for example, ECJ September 9, 2003 (C-236/01), in *Foro italiano* 2004, IV, 245 with commentary by Barone, supporting the legitimacy of a decision of the Italian government to halt the import of genetically modified products which were marketed in other Member States, and ECJ December 13, 2001 (C-1/00), in *Foro italiano* 2002, IV, 269, with commentary by Bellantuono, finding against the French government for having prohibited the import of British beef after the ban on this meat was lifted.

the importance of independence (art. 37), transparency (art. 38), confidentiality (art. 39) in the performance of the tasks attributed to the Authority. The main goal is to avoid secretive practices when conducting the risk assessment, as occurred in the past.[38]

It should also be noted that the EFSA does not have a monopoly of risk assessment and communication. As to the latter, many bodies share the duty to publicize information on the possible risks associated with the consumption of food, such as, in addition to the EFSA, the European Commission, the Member States, independent scientific organizations, and so on. With regard to risk assessment, there are agencies or offices at the level of the Member States which provide scientific opinions as well. Most of the Member States have set up independent agencies to carry out risk assessment: this is the case in the UK, with the Food Standard Agency, and in France, with the *Agence Française de Sécurité Sanitaire des Aliments*.[39] Other Member States rely on the analysis performed by offices within their ministries, as in Italy.[40] Leaving aside the issue of whether or not to create an independent agency, the ensemble of the EFSA, national authorities, ministries and independent organizations forms a collaborative network for the performance of risk assessment functions (art. 36). The intention is to attribute a position of prominence to the EFSA, in the sense that it should be considered the hub to which all information and scientific studies (gathered or developed at local level) are sent and from which such information is communicated to the periphery.

Articles 24 to 28 are dedicated to the organizational structure of the EFSA (Chalmers 2003: 538–42; Alemanno 2008: 7–12). The bureaucratic direction of the Authority is conferred on the Management Board and the Executive Director, while the scientific tasks are performed by the Scientific Committee and the Scientific Panels. The former is "responsible for the general coordination necessary to ensure the consistency of the scientific opinion procedure, in particular with regard to the adoption of working procedures and harmonisation of working methods" (art. 28.2). It also deals with scientific issues which do not fall within the expertise of any panel or which are multisectoral.[41] However, most of the scientific opinions are given by the Scientific Panels. Such groups, which are permanent,

---

38   Articles 40, 41 and 42 stress the importance of a greater involvement of the interested parties in the process of risk assessment, providing for a right to access to the documents and imposing on the EFSA a duty to disseminate information.

39   For a description of the agencies of food safety created at the level of Member States, see Babuscio 2005: 83 ff. Usually the national Agencies carry out only risk assessment tasks, thus paralleling the separation between risk assessment and management present at European level.

40   See the joint Decree of the Ministry of Health and the Ministry of Agriculture of July 26, 2007 providing for the institution, within the Ministry of Health, of the *Comitato nazionale per la sicurezza alimentare* (National Committee for Food Safety), whose tasks pertain mainly to scientific risk assessment.

41   In such cases, the Scientific Committee can also set up *ad hoc* working groups.

are composed of scientists with special expertise concerning particular categories of products or hazards.[42] The intention behind the decision to adopt a framework providing for subdivision into panels was to facilitate the organization of the work and aims at providing reliable, independent scientific opinions.[43]

The final articles of Regulation 178/2002 concern the rapid alert system and the management of crisis situations. The rapid alert system is a network through which information concerning health risks deriving from the consumption of food or feed is spread to all the actors concerned (art. 50). The major role in the management of the system is performed by the Commission, which operates along with the EFSA and the Member States. However, other bodies can be included in the network, such as international organizations or third countries which may be affected by the risks. Once a possible hazard is identified, information about it is transmitted to the Commission, which is in charge of spreading the news. The EFSA can be called upon to provide scientific and technical support in order to assess the real extent of the hazard; in addition, the Member States can share the scientific opinions that their own agencies or ministries have developed. The states have also the duty to announce the precautionary measures they have adopted at national level to deal with the potential emergency.

The rapid alert system can be considered another by-product of the BSE crisis. Indeed, the divisions in committees and offices within the Commission, the poor coordination between the Member States and the European institutions and the fragmented nature of the scientific opinions all constituted major hurdles in managing that crisis. The goal is to create a dedicated circuit from which information can be spread efficiently and quickly, two fundamental features for dealing with any emergency.[44]

An overview of the European system is not complete without a description of the methods of hygiene and monitoring created to ensure food safety. Some of these measures are common to all foodstuffs, while others are specific to products of animal origin, included meat (Germanò, Rook Basile 2005: 273–4; Losavio 2004).

---

42 Art. 28.4 provides the setting-up of eight panels: 1) Panel on food additives, flavorings, processing aids and materials in contact with food; 2) Panel on additives, products and substances used in animal feed; 3) Panel on plant health, plant protection products and their residues; 4) Panel on genetically modified organisms; 5) Panel on dietetic products, nutrition and allergies; 6) Panel on biological hazards; 7) Panel on contaminants in the food chain; 8) Panel on animal health and welfare. In the case of technical or scientific developments, the number and/or names of the panels can be changed.

43 The Scientific Committee and the Scientific Panels can provide their opinions if requested by the Commission, the European Parliament, or a Member State, if Community law requires the EFSA to be consulted, or on their own initiative (art. 29). They can also promote scientific studies, as well as collect and analyze data concerning their fields of investigation, irrespective of whether a specific opinion is sought.

44 Articles 55, 56 and 57 provide for a general plan for crisis management, as well as the institution of a crisis unit: their functions relate to the creation of a common framework of reference within which to administrate efficiently food safety emergencies.

The measures in common are set out in Regulation 852 of 2004.[45] Art. 1 draws up a list of the principles which should shape the rules and procedures to be followed by operators. Responsibility for the safety of foodstuffs put onto the market rests on the food operators, who must guarantee this aspect throughout the whole chain, from primary production to the final retailing stage. The implementation of the HACCP principles, along with adherence to microbiological and temperature requisites laid down in accordance with risk assessment methodologies, is aimed at ensuring the safety of foodstuffs at the operational level.[46]

Art. 4 distinguishes between primary production and post-primary production: while the former is subject to the requirements provided in part A of Annex I of the Regulation, so far as regards the latter, the norms contained in Annex II must be fulfilled. The most notable consequence of this subdivision is the exemption from the application of the HACCP procedures in respect of primary production (art. 5, sect. 3). Furthermore, operators must also comply with microbiological criteria and temperature control requirements and carry out sample analyses on their products. Establishing the different criteria and requirements, as well as the procedures for the sample analysis, is the responsibility of the Standing Committee on the Food Chain and Animal Health, under the provisions set out in art. 14. Art. 5 regulates the adoption of procedures based on the HACCP principles and imposes a duty on operators to provide the relevant documentation proving compliance. The adoption of the HACCP system in Europe parallels the solution implemented in the US, with the difference that, while in the latter the system is limited only to the meat sector, in the European Union it is of general applicability. Art. 6 regulates food establishments. Every food operator has a duty to register any "establishment under its control that carries out any of the stages of production, processing and distribution of food." When a provision of Regulation 852/2004 itself, a Member State's law, or a decision taken by the Standing Committee on the Food Chain and Animal Health so requires, the establishment is subject not only to registration, but also to approval.

As mentioned, there are also norms specifically applicable to products of animal origin. In particular, there are two regulations to mention: Regulation 853/2004[47] and Regulation 854/2004.[48] The first important provision is contained in art. 4 of Regulation 853/2004: food operators can only put products on the market

---

45   Regulation no. 852 of 29 April, 2004, on the hygiene of foodstuffs. For a comment on this Regulation, see Germanò, Rook Basile 2005: 273–4.

46   Art. 1 also makes reference to good practice guidelines which should help food operators to fulfill the hygiene requirements and implement the HACCP principles. These indications are not mandatory and are to be adopted on a voluntary basis. The HACCP system was first introduced in Europe in 1993, by Directive no. 43 of 14 June 1993.

47   Regulation no. 853 of 29 April, 2004, laying down specific hygiene rules for food of animal origin.

48   Regulation no. 854 of 29 April, 2004, laying down specific rules for the organization of official controls on products of animal origin intended for human consumption.

which are manufactured in registered (or approved) establishments and only if the norms under Regulation 852/2004 are fulfilled. If approval of the establishment is required, the applicable procedures, as well as the necessary requirements, are set out in Regulation 854/2004. The fact that, so far as establishments are concerned, mere registration or (more burdensome) approval is required, carries another consequence with it (art. 5, Regulation 853/2004). If the establishment is approved, then the product must normally carry a health mark or, in more limited cases, an identification mark. If the establishment is registered, the operators may apply an identification mark on their products.[49] Since slaughterhouses are subject to approval, health marks are usually required, in the case of meat. The requisites necessary to obtain the health mark are set out in Regulation 854/2004. Under art. 4, the system of controls includes the verification of the HACCP procedures and direct inspections of specific products of animal origin, such as fresh meat, live bivalves, raw milk, and so on. With regard to meat, art. 5 provides that the official veterinarian can stamp a health mark on the carcass only if it does not present any deficiency, on performance of *ante mortem* and *post mortem* inspections and laboratory testing.[50]

Comparing the US and European Models

If we compare the solutions adopted in the US in the field of meat controls to the ones applied in Europe, we note a blend of similarities and differences. The similarities consist in the adoption of the HACCP procedures in both cases, as well as in the application of a health stamp (or mark) which should ensure the safety of the meat product put onto the market. The differences subsist in the controls underlying such marking. While in the US, the inspection method is mainly visual and has been *de facto* replaced by the HACCP in very recent years, in Europe, we confront a more thorough system of controls, which combine inspections of the animal before and after slaughter, as well as microbiological testing of the meat.[51] Moreover, in Europe, the HACCP procedures accompany this system of controls and do not replace them.

There are also more general features distinguishing the American and European experiences in the field of food safety. The first, and more obvious, concerns the fragmentation which marks the US framework *vis-à-vis* the more systematic and comprehensive scheme in the European Union. The difference should not be overemphasized, in the sense that up to only a few years ago, the European situation

---

49   Annex II, section I of Regulation 853/2004 governs the regime for the appropriate application of identification marks.

50   The procedure to be followed to apply health marks is set out in Annex I, section I of Regulation 854/2004.

51   As we have seen, microbiological testing in the US has been limited only to salmonella in raw meat and, moreover, is severely constrained by the courts, which have stated that the USDA has exceeded its powers in imposing such tests.

was very similar to that on the other side of the Atlantic. But it bears witness to a major change in the philosophy behind food safety, a change which has occurred in Europe but not as yet in the US. The shift consists in the conversion from an attitude which is sensitive to food security and the facilitation of (interstate) trade to one in which consumer protection plays a pivotal role (Sgarbanti 2003; Albisinni 2003a). While the BSE crisis was the catalyst capable of triggering such a conceptual shift in Europe, the US seems to pay the consequences of a sort of lock-in effect, still stuck in the old ways of working and conceptual frameworks which shaped the reforms in the first decades of the twentieth century.[52] As noted in Chapter 1, in my view the roots of the difference lie in the cultural values that the BSE crisis has endangered: values closer to the European rather than to the American mentality and, therefore, able to generate a wave of reforms in the old continent. To be true, signals that such a change could also occur in the US have been emerging over recent years. But the change appears to be following a different path, focusing more on dietary problems.[53]

The differing philosophies embraced by the two systems bring with them a train of more specific differences. Thus, a second major distinction pertains to the division between risk assessment and risk management. In order to guarantee better protection of consumers' interests through the provision of independent and reliable scientific information, one benchmark of the European reform has been the attribution of the risk assessment and management to two distinct bodies (the EFSA and the Commission, respectively). On the contrary, in the US, both functions are carried out within the same institution, the USDA in the case of meat. Furthermore, risk communication in Europe is clearly part of the risk analysis process and great emphasis is placed on this factor: we can say that consumers have a right to be informed about food risks (Losavio 2007). Nothing similar exists in the American system. While it is true that, in recent years, some states, with the aim of curbing the spread of obesity, have passed legislation making it obligatory to inform consumers about the dietary features of food put onto the market, such initiatives are far away from constituting a generalized right to be informed regarding food risks (Thompson 2004; Neal 2006; Fisher 2006).

Another difference concerns traceability (Petersen 2004). Again, Europe has put great emphasis on the possibility of retracing the (many) passages that a particular foodstuff undergoes before being put into commercial circulation, considering it an essential means both of informing consumers and facilitating the

---

52   The lock-in effect is tightly intertwined with path dependency. For an overview on these phenomena, see Gerhardt 2005; Licht 2001; Hathaway 2001; Liebowitz, Margolis 1995.

53   In his first months in office, President Obama has underlined the need to bolster the food safety system by reforming and reorganizing it (Harris 2009), but there are also doubtful voices as to his real intent to reform the sector (Severson 2008). Recent initiatives by the FDA seem to follow the new policy recommended by President Obama (Harris, Martin 2009).

recall of dangerous products. In the US, a kind of traceability has only emerged since 2002 and for purposes other than those which inspired the European reform. In the aftermath of the terrorist attack of September 11, the US Congress passed the Public Health Security and Bioterrorism Preparedness and Response Act (hereinafter the Bioterrorism Act) on June 12, 2002. Although there is no reference to the term "traceability," the Act seems to create a system which can follow the transformations and additions which the end-product has undergone. Sections 305 and 306 require, respectively, the registration of facilities which manufacture, process, pack, or hold food and the maintenance of records permitting the inspectors to trace where specific ingredients arrived or whence they came.

There are quantitative and qualitative differences between this form of traceability and that introduced in Europe. First, whereas in Europe traceability concerns all food products, sections 305 and 306 of the Bioterrorism Act apply only to the FDA. This means that the registration/tracking system does not apply to meat products, which are under the supervision of the USDA. The difference is partly overcome by the fact that the slaughterhouses, in order to be able to operate, need USDA inspectors to be present and, thus, to be registered. Moreover, the implementation of the HACCP procedures requires the conservation of records concerning the different stages of production. But the major difference concerns the qualitative aspects of traceability. The purpose of the Bioterrorism Act is to prevent terrorist attacks on the food supply, by maintaining a strict control both over domestic production and the import of foodstuffs. There is no reference to the interests of consumers in knowing the ingredients present in the food they purchase, just as there is no clear indication that the monitoring system is connected to a recall mechanism. We can summarize the differences between the two systems by saying that, whereas in Europe traceability is aimed at safeguarding consumers' health, in the US, its goal is the protection of national security.

Last but not least, an important element of differentiation concerns the precautionary principle. In the food trade in particular, the precautionary principle has been often a bone of contention between Europe and the US. It is no surprise, therefore, that this principle has been inserted into Regulation 178/2002, nor that the US seems to disregard it. The rejection of the precautionary approach by the US is well represented by the consistent resort to the CBA as the only tool able to provide viable solutions. The divide between the two systems can be seen both as the final result, but also the origin of the differences described so far. It is the final result, because the differing philosophy (pro-consumer or pro-business) entails a more accentuated or more muted precautionary approach to food risks. But it is also the origin, in the sense that adopting the precautionary principle shapes, or at least reinforces, the pro-consumer philosophy embraced by the competent institutions and the technical options necessary to implement it.

Japan's Food Safety Reforms

Japan finds itself in a position closer to the European Union than to the US. Until 2003, its food safety framework was similar to that of Europe before the mad cow crisis. There was no distinction between risk assessment and management: both phases were carried out by the Ministry of Health, Labour and Welfare and by the Ministry of Agriculture, Forestry and Fisheries. Each ministry had one or more offices charged with tasks related to food safety, which ranged from the assessment of the threats posed by foodstuffs, to the inspection of food facilities, through the establishment of quality and safety standards. But in Japan, too, the BSE crisis triggered an array of reforms which have profoundly altered the existing framework (Nottage 2000b).

The enactment of the Food Safety Basic Law[54] in 2003 introduced many of the reforms present in European Regulation 178/2002 (Yasui 2004). The first of them was the establishment of the tripartite arrangement for risk assessment, management and communication. The BSE emergency, along with other contemporaneous food scandals, has likewise highlighted, in the Japanese context, the dangerous effects that the coexistence of risk assessment and management within the same institution can produce. The solution has been not only to distinguish the three functions referred to above, but also to confer responsibility for them to two distinct bodies. Risk assessment is carried out by the newly created Food Safety Commission, an independent agency whose members are appointed by the prime minister.[55] The risk management phase is run mainly by the Ministry of Health, Labour and Welfare through the Department of Food Safety, with a more restrained role played by the Ministry for Agriculture, Forestry and Fisheries.

The two functions are connected, in that the ministries can request evaluations from the Food Safety Commission which, in turn, can recommend policy action, along with the results of the scientific investigations. Moreover, the commission can promote scientific studies related to food safety and monitor the implementation of policies adopted on the basis of the risk assessments carried out, evaluating their efficacy in achieving the desired results. In performing such duties, the commission must ensure that its actions conform to the principles of independency and transparency.

However, the tasks of the commission are not limited to risk assessment, but also extend to risk communication. This function is shared with the ministries charged with risk management. Similarly to the European approach, the goal of risk communication is, to the maximum extent possible, to disseminate information about the risks posed by foodstuffs. Coherent with this approach, risk communication is conceived of as a networking function in which different bodies

---

54 Law n. 48, May 23, 2003. An English translation of some of the Japanese laws, included the Food Safety Basic Law, is available at <http://www.cas.go.jp/jp/seisaku/hourei/data2.html>.

55 The Food Safety Commission began to operate in 2005.

participate, exchanging information, data and opinions. Indeed, the spreading of information involves not only consumers, but also food business operators, international organizations, ministries, local governments, private research institutes, and so on. Finally, the organization of the Food Safety Commission mirrors the subdivision in committees implemented by the EFSA. Today, there are three general committees (the Planning Expert Committee, the Risk Communication Expert Committee and the Emergency Response Expert Committee) and thirteen specific expert committees, including groups on genetically modified organisms, novel foods, additives, pesticides, and so on.

Another fundamental piece of legislation concerning food safety is the Food Sanitation Law,[56] enacted in 1947 and amended several times since then. The purpose of the law is specified in art. 1: "to prevent the occurrence of health hazards arising from human consumption of food, by making necessary regulations and taking any measure so as to work for the protection of the health of the people." The law regulates the phase of risk management and can be divided in three parts. The first states the prohibition on the distribution of any food, additive or raw material which is rotten, contaminated or otherwise injurious to human health. Art. 9 prohibits the sale of meat which is derived from diseased animals.

The second part is dedicated to the establishment of standards relating to food, additives, containers and labels. Mention must be made to articles 13 and 14 which, under the title "Comprehensive Sanitation-Controlled Manufacturing Process," refer to the HACCP procedures. The HACCP was adopted for the first time in 1995 in Japan, through the amendment of the Food Sanitation Law. Under art. 13, the Ministry of Health, Labour and Welfare can approve manufacturing methods implemented in specific facilities for those in respect of which an application has been filed. These methods are nothing other than procedures based on HACCP principles. The approval of the procedures is preventive and on an *ad hoc* basis, in the sense that it may concern only individual facilities. HACCP procedures are implemented in Japan in a way that is different from what we have seen with regard to the US and Europe. While in the latter cases, no *ex ante* approval is required, in Japan such endorsement constitutes a necessary condition in order to make the HACCP system operative. The authorization requires three conditions: the existence of standards for the type of food which is manufactured or processed in the facility for which the application is filed, the examination of documents, and on-site inspections. Art. 14 provides that HACCP approval must be sought every three years.

The third part of the Food Sanitation Law concerns the system of inspections and controls aimed at ensuring that the norms applicable in the field of food safety are respected. The controls are carried out by the Ministry of Health, Labour and Welfare and, in particular, by the Inspection and Safety Division. In performing the inspections, an important role is also played by the local prefectures. The Ministry

---

56   Law no. 233, December 24, 1947. The Act has been recently amended by law no. 87 of July 26, 2005.

establishes a central plan of inspection, while every year each prefecture prepares a plan of control confined to their area of competence. Art. 25 provides that a food product cannot be put on the market if it does not bear a label "stating that it has passed the examinations," that is, it has passed through the system of controls set out under the inspection plan.

The Food Sanitation Law contains two meager articles dedicated to labeling. Art. 19 states that the Ministry of Health, Labour and Welfare can adopt standards to regulate the labels to be applied to food products: no product can be marketed without satisfying the standards, once they have been established. Under art. 20, false or exaggerated claims in labeling (and advertising) of foodstuffs is prohibited. A more comprehensive and organic discipline is contained in the Law Concerning Standardization and Proper Labeling of Agricultural and Forestry Products.[57] The purpose is to improve the quality of the food products put into circulation and to help consumers to make careful choices by providing proper labels (art. 1).

In order to accomplish these goals, the law has created the so-called JAS (Japanese Agricultural Standard) System. This is a certification system under which the JAS mark can be attached to a food product if it satisfies the requirements laid down by the system itself. The Ministry for Agriculture, Forestry and Fisheries manages the system, providing for a five-yearly review. It is important to note that the manufacturers do not have any obligation to submit their products to the JAS system. It works, in fact, on a voluntary basis and products lacking the JAS mark can be marketed.[58] The procedure is quite simple. Before the amendment of the law, producers wishing to obtain the JAS mark had to submit their products to a competent body in order to have the product graded, that is, assessed in its degree of conformity with the standards applicable.[59] The reform provided that the producers can have their facilities and manufacturing procedures certified as being in conformity with the JAS standards. In this way, all the goods produced in that facility or according to that procedure can obtain the JAS mark.

In 1999, important amendments were introduced with regard to the labeling of foodstuffs. The basic distinction concerns fresh food and processed food: regarding

---

57   Law n. 175 of 1950: the last amendment entered into force on March 1, 2006. The law must be read along with Enforcement Ordinance no. 291 of 1951 and the Enforcement Regulations contained in Ministerial Ordinance no. 62 of 1950, both amended simultaneously by law 175/1950.

58   The JAS system mirrors other voluntary certification systems, administered by public institutions, implemented in Japan, such as the SG (Safety Goods) system. On the SG system, see Ramseyer 1996.

59   The products which can obtain the JAS mark are: 1) beverages, foods, fats and oils; 2) agricultural, forest, livestock and fishery products; 3) any other good manufactured using the abovementioned products. The bodies which can perform the grading are the prefectures, the Center for Food Quality, Labeling and Consumer Services, and registered grading organizations. Section 3 of the law regulates the registration of the grading organizations which are different from the prefectures and the Center for Food Quality, Labeling and Consumer Services.

the former, only the name and place of origin must be indicated, while for the latter, the ingredients, the net contents, the name of the producer, the expiration date and the preservation method are also required. Special rules apply to food containing allergens or genetically modified components.[60] In both cases, the label must indicate the presence of these elements, in order to inform the consumers of the possible risks the product may pose.

The labeling regime is strictly connected to the issue of traceability (Clemens 2003a). There is no rule in Japan imposing a duty to trace the ingredients for all foods:[61] on the contrary, traceability has been introduced on *ad hoc* basis and progressively extended to an increasing number of products. In the case of traceability, too, the BSE crisis can be considered as the triggering factor. In July 2002, the Japanese government adopted special measures to deal with BSE, which included the duty to trace all the cattle raised in the country. With regard to imported beef, the JAS system should certify the traceability of the meat put onto the market. Additionally, the government expressed the intention to make traceability mandatory for seventy products by the end of 2007.[62] It is worth noting that Japanese producers and retailers are increasingly using traceability as a tool to provide consumers with assurances about the safety and quality of the products (Clemens 2003a: 4–5). Japan is one of the more advanced countries in experimenting with new technologies to implement traceability mechanisms (Rich 2006).[63]

The final aspect of the Japanese food safety legislation to be analyzed concerns the standards and controls provided specifically for the meat sector. The Abattoir Law contains the rules created to regulate slaughterhouse management and meat processing.[64] All slaughterhouses, or other facilities in which the meat is processed,

---

60 For genetically modified foods, see Notification no. 517 of the Ministry of Agriculture, Forestry and Fisheries of March 31, 2000. Genetically modified foods are also subject to pre-market approval, as in Europe.

61 The government planned to enact a law during 2009 extending traceability to all food products; see "Government mulls food traceability law," *The Japan Times Online*, July 6, 2008.

62 See "Food Safety and Traceability: Knowing What Is on Your Plate" <http://www2.jma.or.jp/foodex/en/other/vol04.html>.

63 Many producers, especially in the meat sector, attach labels to the products including their photos, too, in order to provide the consumers with tangible proof of the genuine origin of what they are purchasing. A chain of supermarkets installs computers in their aisles through which the consumers can check the origin, ingredients and other features of the meat they are buying. The technologies most often used to implement traceability systems are RFID and QR codes. RFID (Radio Frequency Identification) is composed of a tag attached to the product which transmits a radio signal containing information (about the origin of the product or the ingredients, for example). The signal can be read through appropriate readers, such as also mobile phones. QR codes are the modern version of the bar codes.

64 Law no. 114 of 1953. See also the Abattoir Law Enforcement Ordinance no. 216 of 1953 and Abattoir Law Enforcement Regulation no. 44 of 1953.

must obtain permission from the prefectures or the mayor of the cities within which they operate (art. 4). In order to reinforce this provision, only the meat slaughtered in facilities for which permission has been obtained can be marketed (articles 13 and 15). Inspections are carried out both *ante* and *post mortem*, in order to identify animals or carcasses which are diseased or otherwise unfit for human consumption (art. 14): the controls are performed by inspectors of the local prefectures or cities (art. 19). Microbiological testing is not imposed as a general means of control, but can be used in cases in which the inspectors suspect that the carcass is infected, along with histopathogenical analysis. Furthermore, microbiological tests can be part of the HACCP procedures applicable to meat-processing plants.

Some comparative remarks can also be made in the case of Japan. First, the style of the Japanese legislation seems to be more meager than the American or European examples. Norms are not very detailed and ordinances, along with second-level regulations enacted by the competent ministries, play an important role. This is not peculiar to the food safety field, but is a more general characteristic of Japanese legislation. The so-called administrative guidance is one of the ways by which ministries have traditionally directed the behavior of market operators (Young 1984).[65] The informal, non-mandatory directives expressed by functionaries of the competent ministries, together with the threat of ostracism in the case of non-compliance, proved to play an important role in shaping Japanese economic life. Following this line of interpretation, it is no surprise that some of the instruments that have been imposed by law in Europe, such as traceability and conformity to minimal quality and safety standards are left, in Japan, to voluntary implementation by food operators. The JAS system, but increasingly the application of traceability, testifies to the ability of the Japanese producers to make their actions conform to the policies of intervention indicated by the bureaucratic elites, regardless of the imposition of a specific, normative duty.[66]

The second comparative observation goes back to the remarks with which I opened the description of the Japanese food safety framework. The reforms that took place after 2003 made it clear that Japan has followed the European model. The emphasis placed on the division between risk assessment and management, the creation of the Food Safety Commission, the importance attributed to risk communication and labeling are all elements leading to consider the Japanese approach to food safety as precautionary. Despite the lack of any reference to the precautionary principle in the relevant legislation, Japan has implemented a series of measures to protect consumers in a preventive way. Furthermore, the philosophy behind such measures seems to be in line with the one inspiring the European reforms: the protection of consumer interests. Art. 1 of the Food Sanitation Law was amended in 2003 in order to insert, among the other purposes of the law, the

---

65   For criticism with regard to the notion of administrative guidance, see Miwa, Ramseyer 2004.

66   A seminal analysis on the bureaucracy role in addressing social change in Japan is in Upham 1987.

defense of public health. The JAS system restates the same goal, as well as the Food Safety Basic Law. Along with Europe, Japan has thus begun the shift from a food security to a food safety paradigm.

The last remark concerns the event that triggered the reforms. Even with regard to this element, there is a strong parallel between the European and Japanese experiences. In both legal systems, the BSE crisis has been the crucial factor for promoting an organic and comprehensive reformulation of the existing food safety schemes. This is due, in my view, to the ability of this epidemic to threaten some cultural values considered as fundamental in both societies. The menace of the destruction of these values, implicit in the spread of the disease, has been an extraordinary engine of reform, while consumers' fears and their amplification by the media is the fuel which has made the engine run.

The International Dimension of Food Safety

Food safety is a field which is not dominated exclusively by national legislation (Echols 2001). It also offers an international dimension which is represented by quality/safety standards on the one hand, and international agreements on the other. The importance of international standards and agreements depends on the global dimension with which the trade in foodstuffs has increasingly become acquainted. The local provisions regulating food safety reflect the cultural preferences predominant in the area, but also hamper the development of international trade. In the food arena in particular, a clash between local and global dimensions is taking place. It is no surprise that many campaigns of the so-called "anti-globalization" movements focus their attention on the food trade, invoking economic and public health concerns to fight the spread of globalization.[67] But it is no surprise, at the same time, that food business operators support the establishment of international standards and agreements in order to enlarge the market in which to sell their products. Governments sometimes seek to reconcile the local and global perspectives, developing tools which try to strike a balance between the two. This is the case for the efforts to introduce a sort of precautionary principle and references to economic sustainability in international agreements (Poli 2004). But the final results are often weak compromises, generating disputes at the operational level.[68]

---

67 Joseph Bové is the paradigmatic figure of a French activist who has gained worldwide attention by conducting campaigns against globalization in the food context. For further information see <http://en.wikipedia.org/wiki/Jos%C3%A9_Bov%C3%A9>.

68 The application of art. 5.7 of the Sanitary and Phytosanitary Agreement, as we will see, has given rise to many disputes in the international arena, with conflicting positions between the European Union and the US.

Food Safety and Private Standards

As mentioned, there are two mechanisms through which food safety operates at international level. The first is the establishment of uniform safety and quality standards, meaning technical norms aimed at regulating market-based activities (Charnovitz 2005). The standards may derive from various sources. Sometimes they are created at intergovernmental level; sometimes by international organizations; sometimes by associations representing food operators.[69] In addition, they may be incorporated in international agreements.

In all cases, the goal is to create a uniform frame of reference in which all the operators can play by the same rules. This should not only facilitate the development of a global common market, but also raise the level of quality and safety of the foodstuffs traded on this market. Indeed, all operators must abide by the minimum requirements established by the applicable standards. Furthermore, the resulting system integrates safety and quality aspects. This is a consequence of the increasing importance placed on consumer choice: for consumers, quality means also safety. Ensuring food quality thus implies ensuring food safety.

This reference to an integrated quality/safety framework also explains, to some extent, the widespread recourse to voluntary international certifications. Certification is a procedure by which (usually[70]) private bodies inspect and certify that a given food operator follows production methods which are in conformity with the standards for which certification is sought.[71] The final product leaving the food operator's plant should guarantee a high level of quality and safety, since it has been manufactured according to certified methods of production. The voluntary nature of the certifications simply means that there is no legal obligation to implement them: but competition and market forces can create a *de facto* duty to certify the products.[72] There are many types of certifications, each one with its own

---

69   For example, in the field of wine production, the *Organisation Internationale de la Vigne et du Vin* has developed standards related both to the manufacturing of wines and to their labeling.

70   The bodies that award certifications are usually private, but sometimes there are exceptions. This is the case of Japan, where the JAS mark is essentially the product of a certification procedure administered by a public body.

71   Examples of specific certifications for the food sector are: the British Retail Consortium (BRC), the International Food Standard (IFS) and the Global Good Agricultural Standards (GLOBALG.A.P.). On the increasing delegation of regulatory and standardization powers by States and European institutions to private subjects, see van Waarden 2006: 53 ff.; Cafaggi 2005.

72   Global retailing companies are increasingly requiring that the products they purchase are certified according to BRC, IFS or GLOBALG.A.P. standards. Since most of the production is nowadays distributed through these retailers, selling non-certified products means not having access to a fundamental channel of distribution.

standards.[73] The safety and quality characteristics of the final product, therefore, depend on the certification sought by the operator.

With regard to the setting of food standards, the Codex Alimentarius Commission deserves a special mention.[74] This body was established in 1962 under the Food and Agriculture Organization (FAO) and the World Health Organization (WHO) of the United Nations. Its task is to develop standards concerning both the characteristics of specific foodstuffs[75] and the methodologies used to manufacture them. The commission operates through committees, which possess expertise in particular scientific fields and in preparing the technical norms to be adopted as standards. The application of the standards is voluntary: but with the creation of the World Trade Organization (WTO) and, in particular, with the Sanitary and Phytosanitary (SPS) and the Technical Barriers to Trade (TBT) Agreements of 1994, the Codex Alimentarius standards have gained greater momentum. Although their application remains formally voluntary, articles 3.2 of the SPS Agreement and 2.4 of the TBT Agreement state that the measures conforming to the Codex Alimentarius standards are presumed to respect the obligations imposed by the two international acts. In this way, there is a strong incentive for states to adopt the standards established by the commission and to impose them on the national producers, since, should they wish to depart from these technical norms, they might have to justify this decision to the WTO panels (Stewart, Johanson 1998; Casella 2001; Cassese 2004; Poli 2004: 615; Arcuri 2005; Livermore 2006: 775).

Food Safety and International Agreements

A second instrument through which food safety operates at a global level is by means of international agreements. From a global perspective, the food trade is one of the most important economic sectors. At the same time, it is also a field in which protectionist measures have often been adopted, in order to preserve local markets from international competition. Food safety concerns have been the most

---

73 For example, the adoption of HACCP procedures is one of the standards most often required. In the case of HACCP procedures, moreover, the standard imposed by the certification scheme coincides with a requirement imposed by law.

74 The website of the Commission is <www.codexalimentarius.net>. Its name is derived from the *Codex Alimentarius Austriacus*, which was a set of food standards and requirements created in the final years of the Hapsburg Empire. Although not mandatory, it was used as a reference point by the Austrian courts to decide cases relating to foodstuffs. On the role of the Commission, see Poli 2004; Livermore 2006. It should be noted that, unlike the certifications mentioned before, which concern directly private producers, the Codex Alimentarius standards apply first and foremost to national states and only indirectly to the producers.

75 For example, there are standards allowing the denomination "sardine" to be applied to about twenty sardine-type species: the breach of this standard by a European Community regulation gave rise to the so-called "sardine case," adjudicated by the Dispute Settlement Body of the WTO. On the sardine case, see Poli 2004: 615–16.

commonly invoked reasons for defending such protectionist measures. Behind the shield of public health protection, states have sought to restrain or forbid the import of foodstuffs, such as meat produced with growth hormones, food products containing genetically modified organisms, beef for which BSE tests were not performed and apples affected by fire blight disease.

The reform of the General Agreement on Tariffs and Trade (GATT) in 1994 laid down the conditions for resolving problems raised by the adoption of protectionist norms masquerading as public health measures (Borghi 2004). The SPS and TBT Agreements are specifically dedicated to providing practical measures to deal with these problems.

In particular, the SPS Agreement addresses many questions concerning the potential conflict between international trade and protection of public health (Echols 2001; Claus 2003; Guzman 2004; Chang 2004; Arcuri 2005; Winickoff et al. 2005; Chichester 2005; Germanò, Rook Basile 2005: 312). As regards sanitary and phytosanitary measures, the agreement sets out provisions aimed at protecting the life or health of animals and plants *vis-á-vis* the risks posed by the occurrence and spread of diseases and the introduction of contaminants and additives.[76] The adoption of these measures is justified if specific conditions are met.

Art. 2 provides that the measures can be "applied only to the extent necessary to protect human, animal or plant life or health"; they must conform to scientific principles, to be non-discriminatory with respect to other Member States in which similar conditions occur, and must not constitute an anticompetitive device, albeit in a disguised manner (Echols 2001: 78 ff.). If the measures conform to international standards, they cannot be reviewed by the WTO litigation panels. Should they differ from the international standards (for example, from those set out in the Codex Alimentarius Commission), the state which has adopted them might have to justify such choice before a WTO panel. The justification must be based on the scientific assessment of the risks posed by the foodstuff (art. 3.3; Echols 2001: 81 ff.).

According to the WTO panels' decisions, a quantifiable risk must exist, that is, a risk whose likelihood of occurrence can be established through scientific principles. In other words, a mere theoretical risk cannot be used as a legitimate ground for

---

76   The definition of sanitary and phytosanitary measures is contained in the Annex A, point 1, of the SPS Agreement: "1. *Sanitary or phytosanitary measure* – Any measure applied: (a) to protect animal or plant life or health within the territory of the Member from risks arising from the entry, establishment or spread of pests, diseases, disease-carrying organisms or disease-causing organisms; (b) to protect human or animal life or health within the territory of the Member from risks arising from additives, contaminants, toxins or disease-causing organisms in foods, beverages or feedstuffs; (c) to protect human life or health within the territory of the Member from risks arising from diseases carried by animals, plants or products thereof, or form the entry, establishment or spread of pests; or (d) to prevent or limit other damage within the territory of the Member from the entry, establishment or spread of pests."

the adoption of SPS measures. Moreover, it has been established that there must be a rational relationship between the results of the risk assessment and the type of SPS measure adopted. This means that the measure must be proportionate to the risk identified and aimed at reducing it (Echols 2001: 83 ff.; Guzman 2004: 7–9). The relevance of risk assessment as the main basis upon which to establish SPS measures also emerges under art. 5.1 of the agreement, which states:

> Members shall ensure that their sanitary or phytosanitary measures are based on an assessment, as appropriate to the circumstances, of the risks to human, animal or plant life or health, taking into account risk assessment techniques developed by the relevant international organizations.

Despite the pervasive reference to risk assessment, the SPS Agreement provides for an exception to it. Art. 5.7 states that "in cases where relevant scientific evidence is insufficient, a Member may provisionally adopt sanitary or phytosanitary measures on the basis of available pertinent information" (Echols 2001: 106 ff.; Germanò, Rook Basile 2005: 316; Chichester 2005: 233–5). The norm covers a series of cases which closely resembles those contemplated in art. 7 of European Regulation 178/2002, under which a precautionary approach could be applied. Nevertheless, while from a European (and probably even a Japanese) viewpoint, art. 5.7 could appear as the reception of the precautionary principle, this interpretation has been sharply rejected by the US and other states. The decisions given by the WTO litigation panels are in line with the US interpretation. According to the panels, art. 5.7 does not allow SPS measures to be taken which are based on a purely theoretical scientific hypothesis.[77] Some verifiable data must exist but, since they are insufficient, they cannot form the basis for a careful and complete risk assessment. In such a case, according to the WTO arbitrators, a state can adopt an SPS measure, but the measure must be provisional in nature. More specifically, states must continue gathering data in order to fill the existing scientific gap and review the provisional measures, in the light of these new data, within a reasonable period of time.

Although the SPS Agreement has only been in existence for a short time, the litigation generated by it has proved to be important, both in quantitative and qualitative terms. Among others, cases have concerned the Australian restrictions on the import of salmon,[78] a Japanese law prohibiting the import of apples,[79] and the recent, still ongoing, dispute over the European ban on the marketing of food containing genetically modified organisms (Echols 2001: 67 ff.; Claus

---

77 For a similar interpretation of the precautionary principle, see European Court of First Instance September 11, 2002 (T-13/99), cit., and Id., September 11, 2002 (T-70/99), cit.

78 Panel Report, "Australia – Measures Affecting Importation of Salmon," June 12, 1998, WT/DS18/R.

79 Appellate Body Report, "Japan – Measures Affecting Agricultural Products II," February 22, 1999, WT/DS76/AB/R.

2003; Wong 2003; McDonald 2004).[80] The most important example for the present analysis concerns the growth hormones case (Echols 2001: 65–7; Chang 2004; Chichester 2005). Two decisions, in cases respectively adjudicated by the Dispute Settlement Body[81] and the Appellate Body[82] of the WTO, have stated that the ban implemented by the European Union on the import of beef raised with growth hormones is contrary to the provisions of the SPS Agreement, since it is neither based on a risk assessment (art. 5.1) nor constituting a temporary measure (art. 5.7). As a sanction, arbitrators have allowed the US to retaliate against Europe by suspending importation of some European goods and imposing 100 per cent tariffs up to a certain value (Chichester 2005: 246). The rationale underlying the decisions points to the rejection of factors other than science in adopting a SPS measure. For the panels, allowing elements such as consumer fears or precautionary approaches to be taken into account could pave the way for negating the very essence of the WTO, that is, the abolishment of anticompetitive policies at global level.

The growth hormones case is also instructive as regards the management of the post-decision stage. Although the arbitrators clearly found in favor of the US in this case, it has proved to be a Pyrrhic victory. The European Union, indeed, did not comply with the adjudication reached by the WTO panels. Directive 2003/74, which was designed to bring Europe into line with the WTO decisions, has maintained the ban on beef raised with growth hormones.[83] The US decided to retaliate against Europe by implementing the sanctions provided in the decisions. The European Union has counter-retaliated, claiming that the 2003 Directive complies with the requirements indicated in the rulings. The actual situation is a stalemate damaging the economic interests of operators on both sides of the Atlantic. One of the most probable outcomes will be a renegotiation of the entire growth hormones problem (Sien 2007).

These events testify to the strong economic and cultural flavor that food safety also (or, perhaps, *particularly*) acquires in the global arena. Technical norms, as well as international standards, appear unable to survive the cultural, economic and political consequences they trigger. The risk is that such norms remain as law in the books, without any operational role. The events also show the weakness of the SPS Agreement, and in particular art. 5, regulating risk assessment. The ambiguous words of the exception provided in art. 5.7 encourage counterpositions between different ways of perceiving risks, a phenomenon which has its roots in the different cultural values that characterize the US, Europe and Japan (Sien

---

80   Panel Report, February 7, 2006, WT/DS/291.

81   Panel Report, "E.C. Measures Concerning Meat and Meat Products (Hormones)," August 18, 1997, WT/DS26/R/USA.

82   Appellate Body Report, "E.C. Measures Concerning Meat and Meat Products (Hormones)," January 16, 1998, WT/DS26/AB/R.

83   See Directive n. 74 of October 14, 2003. The European Union has maintained the ban on beef raised with growth hormones claiming that new scientific evidence has showed that such hormones have negative effects on human health (Sien 2007; Chichester 2005).

2007: 576). Technical and political choices which neglect to take these factors into account are not only doomed to failure, but risk exacerbating the conflict, because states and consumers will tend to perceive them as constituting a threat to their basic cultural values.

The Specific Measures to Minimize the BSE/vCJD Risk

The European Case

As anticipated in the Introduction, this section analyzes the regulations and decisions that Europe, Japan and the US have adopted to limit the threat posed by the BSE/vCJD epidemic. Since Europe was the geographical area where the disease originated, I will begin by describing the measures taken in this legal system. Such measures are now included in Regulation 999/2001,[84] but they are the result of the progressive adoption of different actions over the span of more than a decade. The first decisions to restrict the import of certain live cattle, including calves, from the UK had already been enacted in 1989 (in 1992, the ban was extended to British cattle embryos). In 1994, a series of decisions regulated the production of feed for ruminants, providing for the ban on the use of proteins derived from mammalian tissues and for the implementation of rendering procedures able to inactivate prions.[85] Decision 96/239 of 27 March 1996 prohibited the import of any live cattle and cattle products originating from the UK.[86] In 1997, the marketing of specified risk materials (SRMs) was forbidden.[87] After having restricted the trade in meat and bone meals (MBMs), this type of feed was prohibited from 2000.

In May 2001, the European Parliament and the Council enacted Regulation no. 999, laying down what was effectively a restatement of all the measures taken in the preceding years to deal with transmissible spongiform encephalopathies (TSEs).[88] Art. 6 establishes the monitoring system for the TSEs, although the details are contained in Annex III. According to this, all healthy cattle of 30 months or more must be tested for TSEs through the rapid test called "ELISA." In the case of cows at risk, which are considered as animals showing symptoms of any disease, all must be tested at 24 months or older. With regard to animal feed, art. 7 restates the

---

84   Regulation n. 999 of 22 May 2001, laying down rules for the prevention, control and eradication of certain transmissible spongiform encephalopathies (TSEs).

85   Decisions 94/381 and 94/382, both 27 June 1994.

86   The request by the UK to annul the decision 96/239 was rejected by the European Court of Justice, May 5, 1998 (C-180/96), cit.

87   The Decision 97/534 considered brain matter, eyes and spinal cord as SRMs. The definition was expanded in 2001 to include bovine intestines and the vertebral column.

88   Regulation 999/01 has been repeatedly amended, relaxing some of the provisions originally enacted, as the BSE risk progressively diminished. I will mainly make reference to the original version of the regulation.

ban on the use of proteins derived from mammals and of rendered ruminant fat for feeding any kind of animal. Annex IV adds that, while milk and gelatin can be used for producing feed only if it comes from healthy animals, blood cannot be utilized for ruminant feed.

Art. 8, together with Annex V, regulates the marketing of SRMs. In the original version of the Regulation, the ban on specific SRMs depended on which risk category the single Member States are in. These categories, defined in art. 5 and Annex II, measured the TSE risk level to which each state is exposed. Of course, in countries where TSEs are endemic, the level of risk will be higher than in countries where they are sporadic. Consequently, the possibility that SRMs may carry the infective agents will be greater in high-risk states. This is the reason why Annex V permitted certain SRMs to be marketed in some countries, but not in others. For example, in states included in categories 3 and 4, the skull, tonsils and spinal cord were considered SRMs, while in states in categories 5, the entire head and the vertebral column were considered at risk. The current version of the Regulation provides for three categories, instead of the original five: negligible BSE risk, controlled BSE risk, and undetermined BSE risk. The treatment of SRMs consists in their removal at slaughterhouses and disposal by incineration or burial in approved landfill sites.

Finally, articles 12 and 13 provide for procedures concerning cattle suspected of having TSEs. Such animals must be confined until the results of the BSE test are known: the same restrictive measure is applied with regard to all animals in the same holding as the suspect animal. If the test confirms the presence of the BSE agents, all the body parts of the infected animal must be destroyed. Moreover, all the animals and products of animal origin which are at risk, as being or having been in contact, in some way, with the infected animal, must be destroyed. According to Annex VII, the animals in the same holding as the infected animal, its embryos and progeny and the feed which might have transmitted the TSE must be considered at risk.

The American Case

In the US, the first preventive measure aimed at coping with the BSE risk was adopted in 1989 (Odeshoo 2005; McGarity 2005; Berlowitz 2006). The APHIS decided to ban the import of live ruminants and some ruminant products, such as feed, from countries known to have BSE. In the following years, the ban was extended to all ruminant products (McGarity 2005: 322). In the 1990s, FSIS inspectors started carrying out BSE tests. The tests focused on the so-called "downer cattle," that is, on cows which are not able to stand, or show other neurological symptoms which could indicate the presence of a TSE. Not all downer cattle are tested, but only a sample; the total amount of animals checked appears to be low, especially in comparison with the total number of cows slaughtered per year.[89]

---

89   McGarity (2005: 324) reports that between 1990 and 2002 the APHIS has tested about 30,000 downer cattle out of 300 million slaughtered. The CRS Report on Food Safety

With regard to the procedures used to recover the meat, in 1994 and subsequently in 2004, the FSIS regulated the so-called "advanced meat recovery" (AMR) systems, providing that meat produced through AMR systems containing spinal cord is to be considered misbranded if marketed as "meat."[90] In other words, the label "meat" cannot be attached to products which contain spinal cord. The 1994–2004 regulations clearly aim at reducing the contamination of meat by SRMs, but their enforcement has been limited, if it is true that 76 per cent of the facilities where AMR systems were operating tested positive to spinal cord contamination (McGarity 2005: 325).

In 1997, the FDA intervened to regulate the feed sector, enacting the so-called "Ruminant Feed Regulations." In producing feed, the use of proteins derived from mammalian tissues is prohibited. But some exceptions to the general rule exist (McGarity 2005: 328; Vera 2005). First, blood, blood products, milk, gelatin and proteins derived from pigs and horses can be processed to manufacture the feed. Second, the regulations do not apply to materials which are not proteins, such as fats, oils, grease and amino acids. Third, ruminant proteins can be used in feed for chickens, pigs and pets. On the other hand, feed producers are required to maintain documentation on the products they receive containing animal proteins.

The exceptions have been criticized insofar as they leave space for cross-contamination between different species; furthermore, the regulations have been poorly enforced by the FDA inspectors, due to budgetary problems (McGarity 2005).

As to the problem of traceability, in 2002, the first attempts to create a voluntary National Animal Identification System (NAIS) began.[91] This program was the first necessary step to setting up a comprehensive system for workable tracking and recall procedures. To date, several proposals have been advanced and discussed to render the system mandatory, but none of them have been approved, due mainly to the opposition from the cattle industry which considers the NAIS as a financial burden and a source of potential future liability.

In 2004, the discovery of the first case of mad cow disease in the US led to a tightening up of the anti-BSE measures. The first measure enacted by the FSIS was the prohibition on marketing meat produced from animals selected for the BSE test until the results of the test were known.[92] As the Washington BSE case shows, until 2004, meat could be marketed even if the results of BSE testing were pending. The impossibility of recalling the potentially lethal meat distributed, caused by the lack of an identification and traceability system, posed serious safety

---

Issues in the 109th Congress (2005) notes that each year 20,000 cows are tested for BSE out of a total 36 million animals killed.

90   See 69 FR 1874 (2004), "Meat Produced by Advanced Meat/Bone Separation Machinery and Meat Recovery (AMR) Systems."

91   See <http://animalid.aphis.usda.gov/nais/>.

92   69 FR 1892 (2004),"Bovine Spongiform Encephalopathy Surveillance Program."

problems.[93] A second measure concerned the SRMs:[94] their use in producing food for humans was banned. Moreover, the rule specified that, within the HACCP system, procedures must be created to remove, segregate and dispose of SRMs (McGarity 2005: 332). The fact that most of the SRMs concern only materials coming from cattle 30 months or older has been viewed as leaving a significant gap in the protection created to deal with the BSE risk (McGarity 2005: 358–60).

With regard to the surveillance program, the rule stated that all non-ambulatory cattle must be condemned as suspect. This does not mean, however, that such animals cannot be processed for human consumption: the ban in this regard only applies if the cattle are not only suspect, but also adulterated.[95] Hence, the identification of an animal as suspect only means that special attention must be dedicated to it, but does not automatically rule out the possibility of using it for human consumption. A further rule has been enacted banning stunning devices.[96] These are machines which air-inject bolts into the animal's brain to kill it. The impact of the bolt in the brain could cause the contamination of the meat, since parts of cerebral material could end up in the surrounding tissues.

Still in 2004, the USDA expanded its testing program. The number of cows tested per year doubled from 20,000 to 40,000. For the first time since testing began, around 20,000 non-downer animals aged 30 months or older had been tested (McGarity 2005: 337).[97] While it was expanding its testing program, the USDA prohibited private meat processors from carrying out their own BSE tests. The prohibition originated in an application by a private firm, Creekstone, which exported meat products to countries in the Far East, to permit the use of a rapid BSE test on all the animals it processed for human consumption. Indeed, in the wake of the mad cow crisis, Far Eastern countries began to accept only meat which was tested for BSE. In order to maintain their market, therefore, Creekstone was forced to perform voluntary tests for the BSE. But the USDA, using its authority under the Virum-Serum-Toxin Act, refused to allow Creekstone to use the rapid

---

93   The meat recovered from the Washington cow that had tested positive for BSE was distributed in the country before the test results were known. Despite attempts to recall all the meat recovered from the infected animal, large quantities of it were consumed. The lack of an identification/traceability system proved to be a major hurdle, preventing an effective recalling process.

94   69 FR 1862 (2004), "Prohibition of the Use of Specified Risk Materials for Human Food and Requirements for the Disposition of Non-Ambulatory Disabled Cattle." SRMs include the brain, skull, eyes, trigeminal ganglia, spinal cord, vertebral column and dorsal root ganglia of cattle 30 months or older and tonsils and ileum of the small intestine of all cattle.

95   69 FR 1870 (2004).

96   69 FR 1885 (2004), "Prohibition of the Use of Certain Stunning Devices Used to Immobilize Cattle During Slaughter."

97   McGarity (2005: 348 ff.) notes that the expanded testing program is not immune from criticism: the number of animals tested is still low, the tests are not carried out in a systematic way, and monitoring is focused only on the major slaughterhouses.

test (McGarity 2005: 338 ff.). In 2007, the Columbia District Court ruled that the USDA did not have the authority to ban private testing for BSE, thus allowing producers to carry out tests on a voluntary basis.[98]

Finally, in 2004, the FDA announced a tightening-up of the regulation concerning animal feed, extending the pre-existing ban to include the use of blood, plate waste and poultry litter. Moreover, facilities using proteins prohibited for ruminants would have to be limited to producing feed for non-ruminants only. Despite the announcement, so far no decision or regulation has been enacted in this regard.

The Japanese Case

Japan was relatively late in taking its first anti-BSE measures, compared to what occurred in Europe and the US (Nottage 2003).[99] Indeed, only in 1996, was the import of beef from the UK banned: in 2000, the ban was extended to all EU countries. Still in 1996, the Ministry of Agriculture, Forestry and Fisheries issued administrative guidance asking the producers not to use MBM in feed.[100] With regard to the surveillance system, since 1996, all the TSEs have been introduced into the Abattoir Law list of diseases to be checked by meat inspectors. In May 2001 the first BSE tests were carried out, initially on cows either showing neurological problems or 30 months or older.

On September 10, 2001, the first case of mad cow disease was discovered. The finding resulted in a major tightening-up of the anti-BSE measures. First, with effect from October 2001, all cows intended for food, regardless their age, must be tested for BSE by the rapid test ELISA. If this proves positive, more accurate analyses are carried out. To date, the BSE surveillance system implemented in Japan appears to be the strictest in the world. Second, the use of MBM for ruminant feed has been officially prohibited. In addition, facilities producing MBMs for animals other than ruminants must have a separate production line, specifically dedicated to this kind of product, in order to prevent cross-contamination. Third, an embryonic system of traceability for cattle meat was established. Fourth, the use of SRMs was banned: it is mandatory for such materials to be disposed of by

98 See *Creekstone Farms Premium Beef, L.L.C.* v. *U.S. Department of Agriculture*, 2007 U.S. Dist. LEXIS 22851 (D. Ct. Columbia March 29, 2007).

99 See Food Safety Commission, "Measures against Bovine Spongiform Encephalopathy (BSE) in Japan (Interim Report)," September 2004; Food Safety Commission (Prion Expert Committee), "Food Safety Risk Assessment Related to Measures Against Bovine Spongiform Encephalopathy (BSE) in Japan," May 6, 2005.

100 The expression "administrative guidance" refers to the practice followed by the Japanese ministries and public bodies to issue 'advice notices' to the business operators on the conduct to be pursued in specific contexts. In the BSE case, one of the notices was, for example, not to use MBM in feed. Although such guidance does not have legal force, *de facto* the operators conform to it: the consequence in case of failure is boycott and ostracism. On administrative guidance, see Young 1984.

incineration. The head (excluding the tongue and cheek flesh), spinal cord, ileum and vertebral column of all cattle, regardless of age, are included in the SRMs.[101] The treatment of SRMs is much more in line with the European regulations than with the American ones, where there is an important limitation relating to the age of the slaughtered animal.

The 2002 episode involving the mislabeling of beef led, in the following year, to the enhancement and full implementation of an identification/traceability system concerning both live animals and meat products (Nottage 2003). The current system provides that each cow must have an ID number: this forms the starting-point of the traceability system, since the label of the product marketed must indicate the animal(s) from which the meat has been recovered. Some chain retailers have equipped their shops with computers by which the customers can obtain information on the meat product they are purchasing, such as the animal from which the meat was produced, its age, the farmers who raised it, and so on.[102] The final step in the battle against BSE was the ban on the import of beef from Canada first and then, in 2003, from the US. The ban was justified by the discovery of BSE cases, along with the relaxed testing policy adopted, in these two countries. Eventually, after long negotiations, a temporary lifting of the ban and its reinstatement following the discovery of meat contaminated with spinal cord, the ban was abolished in July 2006 (Takahara 2006). At any event, the import of beef is strictly regulated and slaughterhouses wishing to sell beef in Japan are inspected by Japanese representatives for compliance with the new import rules.[103]

Precautionary Approach, Food Safety, and Cultural Values

The last part of this chapter is dedicated to providing a qualitative assessment of the institutions and rules described so far, using a precautionary paradigm of analysis. The goal is not, of course, to award a prize to the system which has applied the precautionary principle most effectively. Rather, the aim is to show how the precautionary approach is a function of the sensitivity of a system to a particular risk (in our case, the BSE risk), and to demonstrate how this sensitivity in itself correlates to the cultural values embedded in that system. The institutions created to govern food safety, as well as the specific rules implemented to that

---

101   Food Safety Commission, "Measures against Bovine Spongiform Encephalopathy (BSE) in Japan (Interim Report)," cited.

102   The Jusco Supermarkets (Aeon Company, Ltd.), for example, indicate a ten-digit code on the label of the meat they sell. The customer, by inserting it into the computers provided in the supermarket aisles, can obtain the history of that product and a government certificate of BSE testing (Clemens 2003b).

103   In particular, the meat must come from cows twenty months or younger; no contamination with spinal cord or other risky material must occur. See "First U.S. beef since ban goes on sale at Costco," *The Japan Times Online*, August 10, 2006.

end, are the by-products of hidden dynamics in which culture, along with risk perception, mass media and economic interests, plays a major role. This is the reason why speaking of a system as precautionary *per se* does not mean that much, if no reference is made to the specific cultural context in which such precautions have been implemented. Any legal system, therefore, can be precautionary with respect to the others, depending on the prominence of the cultural values threatened by the risk of the month.[104]

In this sense, Europe and Japan can be considered more precautionary than the US with regard to BSE.[105] But, as noted when describing the use of cost benefit analysis (CBA) in the US, the reason underlying this difference cannot be explained merely by reference to the fact that Europe and Japan have embraced the precautionary principle, while the US has not. In the first place, Japan has not embraced the precautionary principle: it appears to use a precautionary approach with regard to *some* food risks, such as, for example, BSE and genetically modified organisms. But there are other food risks for which it does not adopt particularly strict precautions: a good example is the consumption of blowfish liver.

Europe has expressly embraced the precautionary principle in the realm of food safety, but it does not apply it in a coherent way. Indeed, there are cases in which very strict precautions are taken, in situations where no risk is known, as in the case of genetically modified organisms (Nicolini 2005; Germanò 2007: 85 ff.), and cases in which few precautions are taken, notwithstanding the fact we know that there are risks for human health, such in the case of raw cheese and homemade sausages or wine. In other words, almost any food entails some risks that are in part known and in part unknown; only some of them trigger a precautionary reaction.

With regard to the US, if they seem to downplay some of the risks that have determined the adoption of a precautionary approach in Japan and Europe, on the other hand, there are recent signals that attention to food risks linked to dietary habits is gaining momentum,[106] triggering reactions more precautionary in this regard than those occurring in Europe and Japan.

If this is the case, why has BSE brought about a crisis in the European and Japanese food safety framework, but not the American one? Why has the mad cow affair led to far-reaching reforms in the first two legal systems and few reactions

---

104 Although they do not make reference to the cultural aspect of the precautionary principle, a similar conclusion on the relativity of the precautionary approach is underlined by Wiener, Rogers 2002: 334; Vogel 2003: 579; Sunstein 2005.

105 We cannot agree with the analysis by Wiener, Rogers (2002: 331–2); as far as the authors are concerned, the US has been more precautionary than Europe with regard to the BSE risk. While it is true that the early US actions were timely and proactive in preventing the spread of mad cow disease, the partial bans concerning SRMs and feeds, as well as the meager testing policy implemented by the USDA, do not allow us to define the US approach to the BSE as precautionary.

106 This is true at least with regard to the states on both the coasts of the US. The central states seem to be more reluctant to take initiatives to deal with the risks deriving from dietary habits.

in the latter? In my view, the answer lies in the cultural values that the crisis has threatened. European and Japanese societies are, for the reasons mentioned in the first chapter, more skeptical about the use of technology in producing food. When it emerged that BSE was due to the technology used in producing feed, European and Japanese consumers were eager to catalog the disease as the nth example of science menacing the traditional way food is produced. In societies where tradition plays a pivotal role in the food culture and is synonymous of quality and safety, any technology invading the field is perceived as a threat to the values embedded in that tradition.

Mad cow disease is an example in line with past and present experiences, such as growth hormone beef and genetically modified organisms. Thus BSE has been considered not just as a disease for which there is a scientifically measurable probability of being infected, but as proof that departing from tradition entails risks. This has led to a magnification of the BSE risk which in its turn has determined, with regard to Europe and Japan, the profound legal changes described.

The case of the US is different. Here tradition, at least with regard to the food sector, has not gained center stage. In other words, food safety does not follow the "threat to the traditional way of producing food – magnification of the risks" dynamic. The magnification of the risks takes other forms. Traces of these can also be identified in the description of the American food safety framework sketched so far. For example, traceability was partially introduced in the wake of September 11, as a measure to counteract the terrorist menace. Similarly, reforms in food labeling, as well as in the composition of certain foodstuffs, have been enacted at state level as a way to fight the spread of obesity.[107] Both these examples show that, even in the American case, threats to cultural values can lead to legal changes. Threats to the security of the homeland, as well as to the idea of a healthy body, are the cultural factors which may explain the timing and type of legal changes that have occurred in the US. We are dealing here with cultural values which differ from those that triggered the reforms in Europe and Japan, but they are cultural values, nonetheless.

The differing regulatory responses to the specific BSE risk, but also the more far-reaching legal reforms which have concerned food safety, must also be read in this light. This is not, of course, the only key to interpreting the legal changes which have surrounded the mad cow crisis. Institutional, political and economic factors can help to shed some light as well. The desire to protect national industries, the pressure from interest groups, the need for more transparency and accountability in the governments' actions help to explain the reasons behind the reforms. But, as underlined in Chapter 1, they do not give the full picture. For these purposes, a culturally oriented explanation can play an important role, providing a major contribution to understanding how legal changes occur.

---

107   A recent initiative in the US has concerned the diffusion of fast-food chains. The city of Los Angeles has proposed suspending licenses to open new fast-food restaurants in its southern district for the next two years as a way of combating obesity.

Chapter 3
Tort Liability and Food Safety

One major bastion, that of negligence liability, has been carried long since, and its guns turned inward upon the defenders. Another, that of the strict liability of the seller of food and drink, is hard pressed and sore beset, and may even now be tottering to its fall.

W. Prosser, "The Assault upon the Citadel (Strict Liability to the Consumer)," 69 *Yale Law Journal* 1099 (1960)

The first goal of any liability system, included that concerning foodstuffs, is to transfer the damage suffered by an individual to the person or body (the producer, the retailer, and so on) who, by their negligent act, caused or contributed to the damage; in other words, to compensate the victim. Nonetheless, this transference functions in such a way that liability also becomes one of the means of controlling the risks posed by the production and marketing of foodstuffs. The producer has an incentive to act with care, in order to minimize the chances of causing damage and to escape liability. In view of this underlying twin meaning, food liability is a tried and tested instrument in all the countries. But its degree of success and its historical importance vary widely, depending on the legal system to which we are referring. As will be seen in more detail later, food liability in common law countries has historically played an important role, contributing largely to dealing with the hazards posed by the food industry. The same cannot be said with regard to countries belonging to the civil law tradition, where the role of food liability has been rather more marginal. Here, a complex web of administrative regulations and criminal sanctions, along with few product liability cases, seem to have been the main means of addressing the issue of food safety. The case of Japan appears to resemble the experience in civil law jurisdictions. In this country there is also a complex system, in which different branches of the law contribute to guarantee food safety. But it should be noted that, although in total there have only been a small number of food liability cases, those few instances, nonetheless, concerned highly prominent mass injury cases, which have attracted a lot of public attention and have sensitized the public institutions. The Japanese case law concerning food thus seems to have had more influence on shaping the legal landscape than in continental Europe.

The emergence of the BSE crisis has prompted the European Union to extend the strict liability rule existing for movable defective goods to include primary agricultural products, in order to provide a more effective way for consumers to obtain compensation and to force producers to manage the risks inherent in their activity more efficiently. A similar, formal extension has not been adopted by other legal systems, although the operational rules which have been implemented have in some cases mirrored this form of liability. On the other hand, the "defects" that can plague an unprocessed agricultural product are of a kind that distinguishes them from those affecting ordinary industrial products. Their uniqueness poses not only legal challenges, but also economic and conceptual problems, once legislators, courts and legal scholars advocate the use of a strict liability rule. Looking to the experience of other areas of tort liability, which share some features with the one covered here, will provide material for potential, alternative solutions.

This chapter is divided in two main parts. The first describes the solutions that the different legal systems have implemented to deal with food liability, both in general and with specific reference to primary agricultural products. The approach is historical and tries to retrace the evolution that has led to the operational rules as they are implemented by the national courts nowadays. The second part will analyze which liability rule may be considered preferable for managing the risks posed by foodstuffs more efficiently, with a particular focus on the BSE context. After having described the legal, conceptual and economic hurdles that the adoption of a strict liability rule could create, attention will be drawn to alternative solutions that could obviate these problems.

A final *caveat* should be spelled out. The focus here will be on compensation for the personal injuries suffered by consumers resulting from the consumption of contaminated food. A different set of liability problems arises with regard to farmers concerning the losses they have suffered because of the diminution in value of their cattle. Therefore, the cases in which cattle breeders have sued both the government and the producers of contaminated animal feed for the economic losses experienced in the wake of the mad cow crisis will be left out of the picture.[1]

Liability for Foodstuffs

Food Liability in Common Law

Since the thirteenth century, English statutes have provided for criminal sanctions in cases in which corrupted victuals were sold to the public. Almost two centuries later, courts began to find the seller of defective food liable for the damages

---

1   See, for example, Court of First Instance, September 30, 1998 (T-149/96), in [1998] ECR II-3841, in which the Italian confederation of farmers sued the European Union claiming the damages suffered in the wake of the mad cow crisis. A few years later, the Spanish confederation of farmers re-proposed the same claim: Court of First Instance, December 13, 2006 (T-304/01), in [2006] ECR II-4857. In both cases, the judges rejected the plaintiffs' requests.

caused to the buyer (Ames 1888: 9; Dickerson 1951: 20; Prosser 1960: 1103).[2] The remedy created by the judges was aimed at holding the tavern keeper (or the vintner) strictly liable for the damages deriving from the unwholesomeness of the food supplied. The operational rule envisaged in these rulings was plainly one of strict liability, but the legal basis upon which it was operating is not clear.

The uncertainty derives from the fact that the rule was framed as an implied warranty of wholesomeness, while the liability attached to it was modeled on the tort of deceit. This latter action was based on an act of willful or reckless misrepresentation, which induced the plaintiff to rely upon it. Liability was attached to the simple fact that a fraudulent statement was made and that the victim, relying on it, suffered damages, regardless of the existence of a contractual relation between the two (Garner 2004: 435).[3] Thus, on the one hand, the reference to the term "implied warranty" recalls the law of contracts, but, on the other hand, the historical roots of the rule envisaged by the same term are firmly entrenched in the law of torts. It should be noted that the existence of an *implied* warranty must be considered quite exceptional for that time since, for most goods, only an express warranty was available to protect the buyer. The existence of such an exception was probably due to public policy considerations and, in particular, to the need to protect public health (Ames 1888: 9).[4] Moreover, the presence of such rulings back in the fifteenth century cannot be taken as indicating a vast amount of case law relating to defective foodstuffs (or even more generally to defective goods). Indeed, the opposite is true and the number of decisions remained low until the explosion of the Industrial Revolution. As has been noted, the low incidence of cases probably depended on the high costs of litigation, especially compared to the value of the defective goods; in addition, the existing system of inspection and controls was perceived as adequate in protecting public health (Atiyah 1979: 179).

A real body of case law concerning defective foodstuffs would not develop until the nineteenth century. The economic revolution entailed a rapid growth in the number of transactions and, above all, a progressive extension of the commercial chain. Buyers were less able to inspect goods for defects and it was difficult to interact directly with the producer, since in most cases the latter no longer corresponded to the final seller (Lyon 1998: 741 ff.). As a consequence, a growing number of cases began to emerge and the courts were confronted with the need to solve the new legal problems raised by these economic developments. Two competing views could be discerned in the courts (Stapleton 1994: 10–11). The

---

2   The criminal statutes were enacted in 1266. The first case imposing strict liability on food sellers dates back to 1431: Y.B. 9 Hen. VI 53, pl. 37.

3   Scholars discuss whether the tort of deceit implied the element of *scienter* (willful intent to defraud through the false representation) or not. In the early stages of evolution, it was probably required, but then it was dropped.

4   The explanation finds further support in the fact that the early criminal laws created in the field of food safety had the clear purpose of protecting public health.

first was inspired by the economic doctrine of *laissez-faire*, which was translated in legal terms into the *caveat emptor* principle. According to this view, the risk of defects in a product had to be borne by the buyer, unless the seller had given an express warranty of fitness and merchantability of the goods. The seller could be held liable only in cases in which such a warranty existed and was breached. The competing view was more paternalistic and applied the notion of implied warranty, to provide a more effective means of protection for the buyers. The justification for such warranties was found, as in the fifteenth-century cases, in the idea that, by supplying defective goods, the seller was impugning the reliance the buyer had in the fitness of the product. This idea was conceptually close to that encapsulated in the tort of deceit. Moreover, the infringement of the buyer's legitimate expectation of reliance was in sharp contrast with the equitable precept that the contractual exchange had to be fair (Atiyah 1979: 479).

Two important features characterized the notion of implied warranty. First, the seller was strictly liable to the buyer if the implied warranty of fitness was breached. The association between breach of implied warranty and strict liability was, thus, restated and reinforced in this period. The second feature concerned the nature of the implied warranty. Whereas case law in the fifteenth century was not overly concerned with the distinction between torts and contracts (since then this distinction was far from being stated in clear terms[5]), centuries later the idea of warranties in general, and of implied warranties in particular, was aptly accommodated into the notion of contract. In other words, while in its early developments the warranty was a hybrid product, closer to tort than to contract, in the nineteenth century it came to be perceived as contractually based (Stapleton 1994: 12). In the UK, the contractual basis of the implied warranties was reinforced and legislatively restated in 1893, when the British Parliament passed the Sale of Goods Act, under which all commercial sellers owed an implied warranty of merchantability to the contractual counterpart.[6] It is important to note that the liability attached to the breach of the implied warranty concerned neither the intermediaries nor the producers, but exclusively the final sellers. This restriction was a consequence of the so-called "privity requirement": the strictness of the privity constraint prevented the buyer from suing the producer, since in most of the cases there was no direct contractual relationship between the two.

---

5   On the role played by tort law in the formation of contract law, especially in the fifteenth and sixteenth centuries; see Teeven 1990; Gambaro, Sacco 2002: 89 ff. The passage of tort law notions into contract law is witnessed by use of the "assumpsit of nonfeasance" in the fifteenth century (Baker, Milsom 1986: 378 ff.).

6   Sale of Goods Act [1893]. The original version of the Act provided that the implied warranty of merchantability could operate "*unless* inspection by the buyer had actually taken place *and* such inspection should reasonably have revealed the defect" (Stapleton 1994: 14). With regard to the sale of food and drink and the implied warranty of merchantability in the US, see Melick 1936.

Privity also proved capable of influencing tort law, thwarting the buyer, at least in the early phases, from asking the producer for damages. Indeed, once the distinction between tort remedies and contractual remedies emerged with more clarity, the buyer of defective goods theoretically had two options for obtaining relief for the damage sustained. The first was to sue for breach of (express or implied) warranties, a contractual remedy, as we have seen, that was actionable only by the buyer against the immediate seller because of the privity requirement.[7] But in all the cases in which the victim was not a person in a relationship of privity with the seller, the contractual remedy was not feasible. For these individuals, the only option available was suing in tort. But this proved to be more a theoretical option than a viable one. Judges refused to hold sellers liable to third parties when a contract was present. Imposing liability on the seller under such conditions, according to the courts, would have meant overriding the allocation of risks that seller and buyer had agreed in the contract.[8] In other terms, the risk that the product could damage a third party (either a third user or a bystander) was something not contemplated in the contract of sale and, as such, could not receive any consideration as a matter of law. The contract was deemed to regulate not only the relationship between the immediate parties, but also all the other possible consequences that could originate from it, including damage to third parties. The mechanism by which privity was able to prevent the use of tort law was known as the "privity fallacy."[9]

Exceptions to the privity bar existed. The most important, so far as the future development of the product liability regime was concerned, was the liability for inherently dangerous products. If goods *per se* entailed dangers to the public, then whoever was damaged by such products could sue the person who produced the goods, in negligence. Examples range from fireworks to poisons, through guns and explosives. The first case in which the privity wall collapsed was *MacPherson* v. *Buick Motor Co.*, decided in 1916 by the New York Court of Appeals.[10] Judge

---

7   It should be noted that a non-contractual party could sue the seller if the latter made a fraudulent misrepresentation directly and expressly to the non contractual party. We are referring, in other words, to the original form of the action of deceit, upon which, during the fifteenth century, liability for breach of an implied warranty was modeled (Deakin, Johnston, Markesinis 2003: 605).

8   The leading case is *Winterbottom* v. *Wright* [1842], 152 ER 402.

9   As Jane Stapleton (1994: 17) notes, the privity fallacy made sense in the early stages of contract and tort law, when the *caveat emptor* doctrine was predominant and all the risks deriving from the defectiveness of a product were borne by the buyer. In this context, the seller had no liability for the defects in her product and it could be deemed unfair to circumvent such a position by imposing liability through the use of tort law. Once the notion of implied warranty prevailed, the old rationale supporting the privacy fallacy lost its grip, since now the seller was the subject bearing the risks for the defectiveness of her product. The judges did not notice the change in the underlying conditions and continued to apply the privacy fallacy by a sort of inertia effect.

10   *MacPherson* v. *Buick Motor Co.*, 217 NY 382 (NY Ct. App., 1916).

Cardozo expanded the notion of inherent danger to encompass all negligently made goods, provided that such negligence could endanger the health of whomsoever used or came into contact with the goods. Cardozo also made reference to the fact that, if the producer has knowledge that her product can be used by persons other than the buyer, then she has a duty towards all the foreseeable users, to manufacture it with care.[11] An equivalent development occurred in England in 1932, with the decision in *Donoghue* v. *Stevenson*.[12] Instead of focusing on the notion of inherent dangers, the majority of the court centered its opinion on the knowledge the manufacturer had that her product could be used by individuals who were not the direct buyer. The duty to manufacture the products with care is owed not only to the final purchaser, but to all the people that the manufacturer can expect will use such product: the so-called "neighbour principle," according to the words of Lord Atkin.

The consequences of the two rulings were disruptive for the privity bar. Any plaintiff, regardless of her status as buyer, user, or bystander, could sue the manufacturer of a defective product and, having proved the producer's negligence, recover the damages suffered. The two decisions coincide, with regard to the operational rule envisaged by the judges: in both cases, the plaintiff must prove the negligence of the defendant. No reference is made to the concept of warranty and the action clearly pertains to the realm of tort law. In light of these two cases, the situation can be summed up as following. If privity of contract existed between the victim and the producer, then the first could sue the second claiming the breach of (in most of the cases, implied) warranty of merchantability and fitness: as a consequence, a strict liability rule was applied. If there were no privity, then the victim of a defective product could sue the manufacturer in negligence: in such a case, the plaintiff had the burden of proving a breach of the duty of care by the defendant.

Simultaneously to these developments occurring in the English and American legal systems, the US courts began to experiment with a different solution to deal with the problems posed by the privity fallacy. Instead of using the tort of negligence to pierce the privity barrier, in the same period that *MacPherson* v. *Buick Motor Co.* was decided, some courts focused on the notion of warranty (Perkins 1919: 91 ff.; Guiher, Morris 1946: 118 ff.; Mintener 1950). The basic tenet of these rulings was that an implied warranty of merchantability was running with the product, regardless the element of privity. In other words, the fact that the warranty was in some sense incorporated in the product allowed these courts to overcome the privity bar.[13] It is interesting to note that the cases we are referring to concern contaminated or spoiled foodstuffs: food liability appears to have been the engine promoting the development of the modern law of product liability. Indeed,

---

11   Ibid., 389.

12   *Donoghue* v. *Stevenson* [1932] AC 562.

13   The leading case is *Mazetti* v. *Armour & Co.*, 135 P. 633 (Wash. S. Ct. 1913). For references to the following case law, see Prosser 1960: 1106; Stapleton 1994: 21.

as we will see, it is primarily to this line of cases that William Prosser was to look, when drafting § 402A of the Second Restatement on Tort Law.

The fact that the courts made reference to the idea of warranties does not imply that the liability envisaged in these cases relied on a contractual basis. Rather, the opposite was true. The historical origin of the notion of warranty is hybrid and owes more to tort concepts than to contract law. The association with contract law occurred when the element of privity was required in order to claim damages in the case of breach of warranty. Privity was the element that transformed the warranty into a contractual remedy. But once the idea emerged that the warranty ran with the product, it became unnecessary to investigate whether privity between the parties existed: privity was no longer a pivotal element. The departure from the privity requirement permitted the rediscovery of the "old" nature of the warranty, that is, its tortious flavor based on the action of deceit.

The concurring opinion of Justice Traynor in *Escola* v. *Coca Cola Bottling Co. of Fresno* provides the blueprint for these developments.[14] Although the rationale of the decision was based on negligence, Justice Traynor believed that the manufacturer was to be held strictly liable to the consumer in the case of a defective product, according to an action in tort for breach of warranty: "Warranties are not necessarily rights arising under a contract. An action on a warranty 'was, in its origin, a pure action of tort' and only late in the historical development of warranties was an action in assumpsit allowed."[15]

Almost simultaneously with these judicial developments, some law scholars began promoting a more comprehensive and coherent framework to deal with the liability for defective products. The first attempts were aimed at creating a strict liability rule in tort for specific categories of products, namely food and drink (Dickerson 1951). In 1960, William Prosser wrote his seminal article, supporting the extension of tortious strict liability to all products (Prosser 1960). The drafts preceding the final version of § 402A follow this evolution.[16] The first draft provided that the new, "special" strict liability rule was to be applied only to food and beverages, in line with the already existing case law. But in the subsequent versions, the rule was progressively extended to include all goods (Stapleton 1994: 24). The extension was in part supported by a case decided by the Supreme Court of California in 1963, *Greenman* v. *Yuba Power Products, Inc.*[17] In this decision, Justice Traynor led the court to recognize clearly a new form of liability for defective products, strict and tortious in its nature, and to abandon what he called "the intricacies of the law of sales." The interventionist approach of the

---

14   *Escola* v. *Coca Cola Bottling Co. of Fresno*, 24 Cal.2d 453 (Cal. S. Ct. 1944).

15   Ibid., 466.

16   Prosser can be considered the father of § 402A of the Second Restatement on Tort Law. He was one of the reporters in the American Law Institute and was extremely influential in the various drafts which preceded the 1964 final version. On the history of § 402A, see Priest 1985; Owen 1985; Priest 1989; Schwartz 1992.

17   *Greenman* v. *Yuba Power Products, Inc.*, 59 Cal.2d 57 (Cal. S. Ct. 1963).

court was based on public policy considerations, namely to provide the plaintiff with a simpler and more effective tool to sue the manufacturer of a defective product (Stapleton 1994: 24). The same public policy considerations were claimed to support the innovative rule envisaged in § 402A, a rule which was largely in contrast with the majority of the US cases. In this sense, § 402A can be considered more the product of a concerted effort by a few academics and judges, than as the consolidation and rationalization of a trend existing in the US case law (Priest 1985).

On the other hand, it should be noted that, although the case law preceding the adoption of § 402A did not embrace strict liability, more and more courts were making use of *res ipsa loquitur*, whose operational rule resembles the strict liability rationale.[18] The employment of *res ipsa loquitur* prepared the ground both for the creation of a strict product liability rule and for its acceptance by the US courts in the following years.[19]

Food liability, therefore, played a pivotal role in the process of creating a strict product liability regime in the US. It has been a reference point to which scholars and judges have looked, inspiring their attempts to shape a rule which could provide a better remedy for individuals suffering damage because of a defective product.[20] It also presents a large body of cases, especially in comparison to the case law of civil law countries, dealing with the numerous specific features that these kinds of disputes offer.

---

18   The Latin expression *res ipsa loquitur* refers to an inference mechanism by which the judge is able to derive an unknown fact from a known fact. It is a form of reasoning by presumptions, through which courts facilitate the plaintiff's position with regard to the proof of either the causal chain or the negligence element (in some cases of both). The expression was first used in an English case, *Byrne* v. *Boadle* [1863], [1861-73] All ER Rep. Ext. 1528, in which a barrel of flour, falling out of a window in a warehouse, hit the plaintiff, who was walking in the street. Having been impossible, during the trial, to determine specifically how the behavior of the defendant had been negligent, Justice Pollock used the expression "the thing speaks for itself" to mean the superfluity of proving the element of negligence in such a case. On *res ipsa loquitur*, see Malone 1941; Prosser 1948.

19   All the Restatements, and with specific reference to our analysis, the Second Restatement on Torts (in which § 402A was inserted), are not legally binding and have only a (high degree of) persuasive force for the courts. Moreover, the Restatements, which are compiled by a private body (the American Law Institute: ALI), should only restate the cases decided in the previous years by the courts, providing a organized overview of the existing case law. This has not been the case for § 402A, which stretched the previous cases in order to create an innovative rule.

20   It is worth mentioning that the first works describing product liability law mostly dealt with food liability cases. Years before Prosser's 1960 article, in which an entire section is devoted to food cases, Dickerson's 1951 book on product liability is significantly entitled *Products Liability and the Food Consumer* (emphasis added). A few years later, a product liability casebook by Dierson, Dunn (1955) made its appearance, which reported almost exclusively decisions on defective foodstuffs (it is worth noting that the book was in fact published in the Food Law Institute Series).

The history of food liability in the US does not stop with the publication of §
402A, nor does it match this provision perfectly. In the same time-frame, when
a few judges and scholars were expanding the idea of an implied warranty of
merchantability running along with (food) products, other courts were focusing
their attention on the notion of defectiveness in foodstuffs. While in the cases
decided in the late nineteenth and early twentieth centuries, the victims sued the
manufacturers for defects which were obvious, such as the case of a piece of steel
in a cherry pie, in a growing number of cases plaintiffs were claiming damages
arising out of hazardous items in the food which could not be straightforwardly
classified as defects. The most famous examples concerned cherry stones in a
cherry pie or chicken bones in chicken enchiladas. It is clear that such objects
cannot be considered extraneous with respect to the final product, since they are
natural components of the raw material by which the final product is made. These
cases are conceptually and logically different from those concerning the extraneous
objects. Whereas with regard to the latter, a lack of care could be easily inferred (a
piece of steel does not have any relation with a cherry pie), the former were more
challenging, since the consumer could reasonably anticipate that cherries have
stones and chickens, bones.

This line of reasoning has given rise to the so-called "foreign/natural doctrine."
In the leading case *Mix* v. *Ingersoll Candy Co.*,[21] the Californian Supreme Court
stated that food manufacturers have a duty to produce food which is reasonably
fit for its purpose, that is, for human consumption. The case did not present any
privity fallacy, since the plaintiff was the direct buyer and the defendant was the
producer and final seller of the defective food. The judges, thus, were in a position
to focus exclusively on the problem of defining the term "defect." The decision is
more centered on the consumer's conduct than on the manufacturer's. To cite the
words of the court:

> It may well happen in many cases that the slightest deviation from perfection
> may result in the failure of the food to be reasonably fit for human consumption.
> On the other hand, we are of the opinion that in certain instances a deviation
> from perfection, particularly if it is of such a nature as in common knowledge
> could be reasonably anticipated and guarded against by the consumer, may not
> be such a defect as to result in the food being not reasonably fit for human
> consumption.[22]

In other words, the decision states the principle under which the consumer can
recover only the damages determined by the presence of an extraneous object
in the food. The plaintiff's claim is made easier when the foreign body itself
is actually present: in such cases, the judges tend to apply the doctrine of *res*

---

21   *Mix* v. *Ingersoll Candy Co.*, 59 P.2d 144 (Cal. S. Ct. 1936). The case concerned a
plaintiff who swallowed a chicken bone contained in a chicken pie.
22   Ibid., 147–8.

ipsa loquitur (Guiher, Morris 1946: 123–4).[23] If the object can be considered as occurring naturally, then a species of the *caveat emptor* principle should apply, with the consequence that the risk of suffering damage is borne by the buyer. In the years immediately subsequent to the *Mix* decision, many state courts adopted the foreign/natural doctrine.[24]

But the test proved to have a short and troublesome life. Early commentators strongly criticized the approach epitomized in the *Mix* decision, pointing to the fact that the doctrine deprived consumers of any protection in cases in which the manufacturer could have nevertheless prevented the damage (Dickerson 1951). The core of the criticism lies in the consideration that manufacturers had no incentive to minimize the risks that natural objects could pose. Modern production techniques could prevent a natural object from being in the food, but the producer was not urged to adopt them, since she could easily escape liability by proving that the object was to be expected in the food. From the early 1950s on, courts began to develop a different doctrine to determine the defectiveness of the food product: the so-called "consumer expectation test."[25] Instead of relying on the application of the foreign/natural test, with its mechanical and rigid consequences, judges focused on whether the consumer could reasonably expect a particular object to be present in the food, regardless of its natural or foreign nature.[26]

The process of shifting from the foreign/natural doctrine to the consumer expectation test accelerated with the progressive emergence of a strict product liability paradigm in the 1960s. The test envisaged in *Mix* v. *Ingersoll* implied a high degree of deference to the *caveat emptor* principle since, as noted, the consumer was the party bearing the natural risks of the product. In some respect, the court's decision on this specific point can be considered as a sort of relic of the old *laissez-faire* ideas, by which, as a default rule, the seller had no warranty obligation to the buyer. But this was indeed to be considered a relic at a time in

---

23   *Try-Me Beverage Co.* v. *Harris*, 116 So. 147 (Ala. S. Ct. 1928); *Nehi Bottling Co.* v. *Thomas*, 33 S.W.2d 701 (Ky. Ct. App. 1930); *Norfolk Coca-Cola Bottling Works, Inc.* v. *Krausse*, 173 S.E. 497 (Va. S. Ct. 1934).

24   See *Silva* v. *F.W. Woolworth Co.*, 83 P.2d 76 (Cal. Ct. App. 1938); *Brown* v. *Nebiker*, 296 N.W. 366 (Iowa S. Ct. 1941); *Goodwin* v. *Country Club of Peoria*, 54 N.E.2d 612 (Ill. Ct. App. 1944); *Courter* v. *Dilbert Bros.*, 186 N.Y.S.2d 334 (N.Y. S. Ct. 1959); *Adams* v. *The Great Atlantic and Pacific Co.*, 112 S.E.2d 92 (N.C. S. Ct. 1960).

25   The consumer expectation doctrine was the predominant test used by the courts under § 402A. The adoption of such a test in the context of food liability could have facilitated its spread in other areas of product liability too, in the following years, ensuring its success as *the* test in cases of defective products.

26   The consumer expectation test applied to the sector of food liability was first formulated by Dickerson (1951: 185). The first court decisions to apply such doctrine are: *Bonenberger* v. *Pittsburgh Mercantile Co.*, 28 A.2d 913 (Pa. S. Ct. 1942); *Wood* v. *Walford System, Inc.*, 83 A.2d 90 (R.I. S. Ct. 1951); *Lore* v. *De Simone Bros.*, 172 N.Y.S.2d 829 (N.Y. S. Ct. 1958); *Bryer* v. *Rath Packing Co.*, 156 A.2d 442 (Md. Ct. App. 1959); *Betehia* v. *Cape Cod Co.*, 103 N.W.2d 64 (Wis. S. Ct. 1960).

which the competing, and more paternalistic, view of an implied warranty running with the product seemed (or was claimed) to be the predominant one. *Caveat emptor* and strict liability are two principles at odds one with the other. Once § 402A was approved, it seemed natural to switch to the consumer expectation test, perceived as more in line with the strict liability phraseology adopted in that section. An increasing number of jurisdictions began to reject the foreign/natural doctrine and to adopt the new rule.[27] In recent years, almost all jurisdictions have embraced the consumer expectation test (Oter 1993; Aughenbaugh 1994; Getz 1994; Griffith 1999; Veilleux 2002; Draper 2005).[28]

The final endorsement of the consumer expectation test arrived in 1998, when the Third Restatement on Product Liability was published, replacing the old § 402A (Henderson, Twerski 2004: 568–70). Section 7 provides that

> One engaged in the business of selling or otherwise distributing food products who sells or distributes a food product that is defective under § 2, § 3, or § 4 is subject to liability for harm to persons or property caused by the defect. Under § 2(a), a harm-causing ingredient of the food product constitutes a defect if a reasonable consumer would not expect the food product to contain that ingredient.

Some remarks are needed here. The first concerns the area of applicability of the consumer expectation test. Section 7 entails a special liability regime for foodstuffs only with regard to the manufacturing defects, that is, the defects described in § 2(a). Indeed, § 2 of the Third Restatement, which is applicable to all the kinds of products, except otherwise provided, makes reference to three categories: manufacturing (§ 2(a)), design (§ 2(b)) and warning (§ 2(c)) defects. A true strict liability regime is contemplated only for manufacturing defects, while, with regard to design and warning defects, the operational rule is closer to the negligence paradigm. Section 2 reflects the evolution that product liability law has mainly undergone, since § 402A was published. Despite the fact that the strict liability epitomized in § 402A was conceived to be applied only to manufacturing defects (at that time the three defect categories did not exist and the notion of defect matched perfectly with that of manufacturing defect), courts began to expand the original

---

27 *Hochberg* v. *O'Donnell's Restaurant, Inc.*, 272 A.2d 846 (D.C. Ct. App. 1971); *Stark* v. *Chock Full O'Nuts*, 356 N.Y.S.2d 403 (N.Y. S. Ct. 1974); *Jim Dandy Fast Foods, Inc.* v. *Carpenter*, 535 S.W.2d 786 (Tex. Ct. App. 1976); *O'Dell* v. *DeJean's Packing Co., Inc.*, 585 P.2d 399 (Okla. Ct. App. 1978).

28 *Gates* v. *Standard Brands, Inc.*, 719 P.2d 130 (Wash. Ct. App. 1986); *Yong Cha Hong* v. *Marriott Corp.*, 656 F. Supp. 445 (Maryland U.S. District 1987); *Phillips* v. *Town of West Springfield*, 540 N.E.2d 1331 (Mass. S. Ct. 1989); *Goodman* v. *Wenco Foods, Inc.*, 423 S.E.2d 444 (N.C. S. Ct. 1992); *Jackson* v. *Nestle-Beich, Inc.*, 589 N.E.2d 547 (Ill. S. Ct. 1992); *Mexicali Rose* v. *The Superior Court of Alameda County*, 822 P.2d 1292 (Cal. S. Ct. 1992); *Porteous* v. *St. Ann's Café & Deli*, 713 So.2d 454 (La. S. Ct. 1998).

product liability law, through the "creation" of two new categories of defect: the design and the warning defects. On the other hand, the courts themselves refused to apply a strict liability regime to these new defects, preferring to adopt rules that, on the crucial issue of the burden of the proof, resembled the operational standard of a pure negligence rule.

The use of rules centered on the notion of reasonableness testifies to this effort to mitigate the severity of strict liability, at least with regard to the design and warning defects. These developments have influenced the drafting of § 2, which reflects the different standards to be used for the different types of defect by making reference, in particular, to the reasonableness standard in the subsections (b) and (c).[29] To sum up, in the case of defective foodstuffs, a special test of liability (that is, the consumer expectation test) is applied only for the specific category of the manufacturing defects, while for the other two categories, the general tests will be applicable.

The second observation is connected to the first and concerns the applicability of the design and warning defects. Liability for these kinds of defects seems to be limited in our context. With regard to the warning defects, there are some decided cases: it is not difficult to imagine cases in which the manufacturer is liable for having failed to inform the consumers of particular allergenic substances contained in the product, or of other inherent risks in the food.[30] Here, the discussion seems to focus on the nature of risks present in the product: if they are open and obvious, no liability can be imposed on the manufacturer. As to the design defects, it is

---

29   The new § 2 of the Third Restatement has, of course, triggered different reactions in the academic environment. The exchange between George Conk (2000, 2002), on one side, and James Henderson and Aaron Twerski on the other side (2001) is paradigmatic. The latter two authors are the reporters of the Third Restatement.

30   *McCroy* v. *Coastal Mart, Inc.*, 207 F.Supp.2d 1265 (Kan. D. Ct. 2002) and *Olliver* v. *Heavenly Bagels, Inc.*, 729 N.Y.S.2d 611 (N.Y. S. Ct. 2001), two cases in which the plaintiff alleged to have suffered damages caused by the spilling of hot beverages: both the decisions rejected the plaintiff's claim, since the risk of burns by ingesting hot beverages is clear and obvious. A similar case has occurred also in the UK: *Bogle* v *McDonald's Restaurants Ltd* [2002] EWHC 490 (QB). Cases have been more successful in which the plaintiff has claimed a duty owed by the defendant to warn either of the presence of an allergic ingredient: *Livingston* v. *Marie Callender's, Inc.*, 85 Cal. Rptr.2d 528 (Cal. Ct. App. 1999), or of the risk of bacteria contamination in raw clams: *Simeon* v. *Doe*, 618 So.2d 848 (La. S. Ct. 1993) and *Kein* v. *Sheraton Perimeter Park South Hotel*, 592 So.2d 218 (Ala. S. Ct. 1991). This latter case law will be more thoroughly analyzed in the subsection dealing with the liability for primary agricultural products. A potential wave of novel litigation has emerged over recent years, with specific reference to the risks that consuming fast food can pose to health (Benforado, Hanson, Yosifon 2004; Owen 2005: 674; McMenamin, Tiglio 2006; Walker 2006; Courtney 2006): *Pelman* v. *McDonald's Co.*, 237 F.Supp.2d 512 (S.D.N.Y. 2003), partially vacated by *Pelman* v. *McDonald's Co.*, 396 F.3d 508 (App. 2nd Circ. 2005). The claims have so far been rejected and have provoked a legislative reaction at state level, prompting the enactment of the so-called "cheeseburger bills," banning this type of lawsuit.

difficult to imagine the very idea of a design for most foodstuffs. Comment (b) of § 7 recognizes the fact that most food does not have a specific design: for further support, no case law seems to exist on the point. In this sense, the consumer expectation test is by far the most widespread test governing liability for foodstuffs in the US, not because it is the only one, but because most of the case law concerns manufacturing defects.

Finally, there is potential for development in American food liability law deriving from the adoption of the HACCP system, as seen in Chapter 2. The fact that, under this system, the producer must set standards and tolerance levels which have to be met, could determine liability. The failure to observe the procedures provided within the HACCP framework could constitute a type of negligence *per se* (Schuller 1998: 97–8). It should be noted, at any rate, that the liability arising from the failure to meet HACCP procedures pertains to the realm of manufacturing defects, with regard to which the consumer expectation test seems already to provide fair protection for the victims of food poisoning.

While the US system was developing in the direction I have described, England did not experience the same pattern of evolution (Lawson 1991). The idea of an implied warranty running with the product did not come up in English case law, which remained lodged at the alternative options of contract liability for breach of warranty and liability in the tort of negligence, depending on whether privity between the victim and the producer existed or not.[31] With regard to product liability in tort, then, the English courts continued to use the language of negligence, placing on the plaintiff the burden of proving the fault of the producer. But although the judges did not elaborate a strict liability rule as their American colleagues did, the increasing recourse to inferences of negligence has shortened the distance between the two paradigms.[32] Despite the fact that the courts did not formally resort to the *res ipsa loquitur* doctrine, the operational rationale underlying the inference seems to be fairly similar (Heuston 1977: 312–13; Brazier 1988:

---

31   A good example of the alternative between contractual and tort remedies in the field of food liability is offered by *Daniels and Daniels* v. *R White & Sons Ltd.*, [1938] 4 All ER 258. In this case, the plaintiff and his wife bought some lemonade, which turned out to contain carbolic acid, causing burns to both. While Mr. Daniels sued the defendant in contract for breach of merchantability, succeeding, his wife acted in the tort of negligence. Having failed to show the negligence of the manufacturer (who had demonstrated to have a faultless system of bottling), she was not able to recover the damages suffered. The different status of the two plaintiffs (buyer and third user, respectively) constituted a barrier preventing users and bystanders from enjoying the more effective instrument of (contractual) strict liability. It should be further noted that the liability arising out of breach of merchantable quality is an absolute one since, as the Daniels case witnesses, there is no way for the defendant to escape liability; see also *Frost* v. *The Aylesbury Dairy Co., Ltd.*, [1905] 1 KB 608.

32   See *Mason* v. *Williams and Williams Ltd.*, [1955] 1 WLR 549; *Davie* v. *New Merton Board Mills Ltd.*, [1957] 2 All ER 38. The use of inferences of proof, which has partially filled the gap between negligence and strict liability in English product liability law, is noted by Fleming 1985: 84–5 and Rogers 1989: 245.

299–301; Deakin, Johnston, Markesinis 2003: 607).[33] Besides these attempts to facilitate the position of the plaintiff, it was only in 1987 that the English legal system encountered a strict product liability regime, when the European Directive 85/374 was implemented through the Consumer Protection Act.

Food Liability in Civil Law

Until the enactment of Directive 85/374, product liability law in continental Europe was a fragmented picture, lacking conceptual clarity. Each country had its own product liability regime, the outcome, in most cases, more that of academic and jurisprudential evolution than of efforts by the national parliaments. As it is not feasible to describe the solutions adopted in each country, the analysis will be mainly confined to two legal systems, France and Italy, and moreover will be limited in its scope, focusing only on the features that can facilitate the analysis of food liability. It should also be noted that product liability, and food liability in particular, has not witnessed the same development described with regard to the US legal system. The number of cases, but also the theoretical evolution (at least up until quite recently), of this field of law has remained relatively underdeveloped in comparison to the results achieved by American judges and scholars. In this sense, European product liability can be considered to be a relatively new field.

The French legal system has followed a twofold approach (Le Tourneau 2001; Borghetti 2004; Calais-Auloy, Steinmetz 2006). Consumers who are part of the contractual chain, and who suffered damages because of a defective product, can resort to the contractual remedy provided by art. 1645 of the *code civil* (hereinafter *cod. civ.*; Gruber-Magitot 1978). This remedy allows for the recovery of the damages suffered by the buyer which have been caused by a hidden defect in the goods purchased: it is the functional equivalent of the warranty of fitness and merchantability in common law. Although originally the article was intended to protect the purchaser only with regard to the decrease in value resulting from the impaired use of the product, the French judges broadened the operational range of the norm to include all the damages that the victim had suffered. In this way, the injuries to the body or health that the buyer experienced because of the hidden defect could be compensated under art. 1645 *cod. civ.*[34]

---

33   The use of the inference of negligence by the English judges has been more cautious than the use made by the American courts of *res ipsa loquitur*. This could have influenced the development of a strict liability rule, creating a more conducive environment in the US for accepting this rule than that existing on the other side of the Atlantic. The cautious attitude of the English courts toward the use of inferences for proving negligence is witnessed by *Daniels and Daniels* v. *R White & Sons Ltd.*, cit. and *Moorhead* v. *Thomas Smith & Sons, of Saltley, Ltd.*, [1963] 1 Lloyd's Rep 164.

34   Art. 1645 of the Code Civil provides: "Si le vendeur conaissait les vices de la chose, il est tenu, outre la restitution du prix qu'il en a reçu, de tous le dommages et intérêts envers l'acheteur."

Courts have not only expanded the applicability of art. 1645 with regard to the kinds of damages to be compensated: they have also lengthened the list of claimants who can use the contractual remedy established in the norm. Through the notion of *action contractuelle directe*, the manufacturer of a defective product can be sued not only by her immediate contractual counterpart, but also by all the other parties of the contractual chain (Cozian 1969; Gruber-Magitot 1978: 14; Taylor 1999: 11).[35] In other words, sub-purchasers, who do not have a direct relationship with the producers, can nonetheless act against them on the basis of the remedy provided by art. 1645.

It is clear that the *action contractuelle directe* breaks the dogma of the relativity of the contractual relation, analogous to what happened in the US with the piercing of the privity barrier. The analogies with the US experience are further stressed by the idea, present in both legal systems, according to which the warranty of merchantability (or, in French terms, of absence of defects) runs with the product. Even though the buyer has a very convenient (contractual) remedy against the manufacturer, regardless of her position in the contractual chain, the other side of the coin is the fact that the manufacturers can raise, as against the buyer, all the exceptions they negotiated with their original, contractual counterparts.[36] This implies that if the warranty runs with the product, then the content of the warranty can be limited through the use of the same contract. As to the notion of defect, this is interpreted by the courts to mean what impairs the intended and/or normal use of the goods. In contradistinction to the US experience, a clear differentiation between manufacturing and design defects seems to be lacking.

On the other hand, if the victim of a defective product is completely foreign to the contractual chain, then she will have to resort to tort remedies (Gruber-Magitot 1978). This is in particular the case of third users and bystanders. French tort liability is based on two norms. Art. 1382 *cod. civ.* provides a fault-based general clause of liability according to which a victim can seek compensation by proving to have suffered loss, the causal link between the damage and an act of the defendant and the negligent conduct of the latter. Art. 1384 *cod. civ.* concerns the liability of the so-called *gardien de la chose* (the keeper of the thing). In interpreting this article, courts have developed a rule according to which the person who has the custody of a thing will be held strictly liable for the damages caused by that thing. Producers are equated to the "keepers of the thing," with the obvious consequence that the strict liability regime is applicable to them. A further consequence is that producers will be able to escape liability only if they are able to prove that the damage depended on *force majeure*, that is, on a factual cause both unforeseeable and unavoidable.

---

35   With regard to the "action contractuelle directe," see Cass. 1re civ., October 9, 1979, no. 78-12.502. *Revue trimestrielle de droit civil* 1980, 354, with comment by Durry; Cass. 3e civ., June 27, 2001, no. 99-14.851. *Dalloz* 2002, 1005, with comment by Brun.

36   Cass. 3e civ., May 26, 1992, no. 90-17.703. *Bulletin civil* 1992, III, 175.

Most of the debate has focused on the notion of custody, which has played a pivotal role in extending the applicability of the norm, at least with regard to product liability. The judges (employing a conceptualization that appears typically French in its abstraction) have drawn a distinction between *garde de la structure* and *garde du comportement*, in order to hold the producer liable for the damages caused by a defect pertaining to the internal structure of the product.[37] The justification for the distinction is based on the fact that the manufacturers maintain a power of direction and control over the thing: if they have such power, it is considered natural they bear the risks the product can pose. This remark explains why the victim has to prove that her damage was caused by a defect inherent in the product's structure and dependent on an organizational omission on the part of the producer.

There are few cases dealing specifically with food liability. One of the most important is the decision by the *Cour de Cassation* on July 1, 1969.[38] A company in the business of selling cheese sued the manufacturer of a batch of this product after having discovered that it was contaminated with bacteria, rendering the lot unfit for human consumption. The plaintiff claimed that the producer had violated the contractual warranty of absence of hidden defects provided by art. 1645 and that she was entitled to the payment of all the damages suffered in consequence of this breach. The Court of Appeal ruled that the plaintiff could recover only damages equivalent to the price paid for the cheese and expenses associated with the purchase;[39] the warranty provided by art. 1645 was considered inapplicable to the case, since the defect (the bacteria contamination) was undetectable by the average professional producer. The Supreme Court reversed the judgment of the inferior court, stating that art. 1645 is applicable also to cases in which the hidden defect is undetectable using average control methods adopted in the relevant industry. In other words, the court ruled that the seller's liability for hidden defects is strict and absolute, and does not permit any limitation based on negligence considerations.[40]

---

37   Cass. 1re civ., June 10, 1960, no. 58-11.013. *Dalloz* 1960, jur., 609, with comment by Rodiere.

38   Cass., chambre commercial, July 1, 1969, no. 67-11.889. *Bulletin civil* 1969, IV, 199.

39   The Court of Appeal decided to apply art. 1646 in lieu of art. 1645: the first, as specified, allows only the recovery of the price paid and of the expenses associated with the purchase. But it should be noted that French judges interpret the expression "expenses associated with the purchase" in a broad sense, also including the expenses arising from the use of the (defective) goods: the case decided by the Cour d'Appel de Nimes, April 15, 1960 is a typical example. *Dalloz* 1960, 725, with commentary by Savatier. The judges applied art. 1646 and ordered the defendant, a baker, to pay damages to the relatives of a man who died after consuming bread contaminated with a toxic fungicide.

40   The Court of Appeal, by stating that the liability of the producer may be limited where the defect was not detectable using average diligence, *de facto* introduced an argument closer to negligence terminology than to the strict liability rationale.

The second group of decisions worth mentioning concerns restaurateurs who served meals which were either contaminated or otherwise unfit for consumption, causing injury to their customers (Nicholas 1982: 49–50, Le Tourneau 2004: 792).[41] In all cases considered, the defendants were found liable on the basis of breach of the contractual warranty provided by art. 1645. Once again, the courts interpreted this norm as a form of strict and absolute liability, in which the impossibility of the restaurateur preventing, or even knowing about, the existence of the defect is without any legal consequence. The judges use the expression *obligation de securité* to stress that the restaurant keeper has a duty to serve uncontaminated food, a duty existing regardless of any fault of the defendant.[42] The way in which this strict interpretation was made possible is linked to the burden of proof in contractual liability. In such a case, the liability is fault-based but, as distinct from the case of tort liability, the debtor has the onus of proving to have acted carefully. The early French cases concern the liability of all persons (restaurateurs, and so on) who were directly and personally involved in the preparation of the (contaminated) food. It was for them to demonstrate that they did not commit any negligent act during the production process. But it is clear that it can be extremely difficult to introduce exculpatory proof, in such a context. The subsequent "invention" of the *action directe* in other areas of product liability has completed and reinforced a regime of liability with a strong contractual flavor, in contrast with the predominant (tort) solutions adopted in Italy.

Historically, the story of Italian product liability law owes its conventional starting-point to a food liability case.[43] In the so-called *Saiwa* case, the Supreme Court had the chance to lay down the operational rule that governed product liability cases in Italy, up to the reception of the European Directive on product liability in 1988.[44] The case concerned a consumer who purchased a box of cookies which turned out to have gone bad, causing the poisoning of him and his wife.

---

41   See Trib. Grande Istance Saumur, March 2, 1978. *Juris classeur periodiques* G 1979, IV, 348; Trib. Poitiers December 13, 1970. *Gazette du Palais* 1971, 1, 264; Cass. 1re civ., January 17, 1965. *Revue trimestrielle de droit civil* 1965, 665; Trib. Seine June 17, 1959. *Juris classeur periodiques* G 1959, II, 11276; Trib. Metz June 7, 1957. *Revue trimestrielle de droit civil* 1958, 244, 245.

42   This obligation is included in the category of the *obligations de sécurité-résultat*, which implies a form of strict liability on the debtor.

43   The Italian legal literature on product liability is vast. Here, I can only indicate some studies which are representative of the evolution that product liability theories have undergone over the years: Carnevali 1974; Castronovo 1979; Pardolesi, Ponzanelli 1989; Alpa, Bessone 1999; D'Arrigo 2006; Stella 2006. On the specific topic of food liability in Italy, see Pacileo 2003b: 565 ff.; Nicolini 2006; Mazzo 2007; Mercurio 2007.

44   Cass. civ. May 25, 1964, no. 1270. *Foro italiano* 1965, I, 2098 with commentary by Martorano. See also Cass. civ. April 20, 1995, no. 4473 and Corte d'Appello Roma, July 30, 1992, both in *Responsabilità civile e previdenza* 1996, 672, with commentary by De Bernardis; Giudice pace Monza, March 20, 1997. *Archivio civile* 1997, 876, with commentary by Santarsiere.

The consumers sued both the seller and the producer for damages. The Court of Appeal excluded any liability with regard to the seller, while found the producer liable on the basis of proof by inference, by which the only intermediary who could have caused the defect in the product was the manufacturer. The *Corte di Cassazione* confirmed the decision of the Court of Appeal, stating that the element of the negligence can be proved through the use of presumptions. The reference point for judges is art. 2043 of the civil code, under which, among other things, the plaintiff must prove the negligent conduct of the defendant, in order to recover the damages suffered.

The innovative point is that the court made the plaintiff's position easier as regards the burden of proof. The solution of the case runs parallel to the ones we described with regard to England.[45] The operational rule adopted recalls the *res ipsa loquitur* rationale and, at the same time, refuses to introduce a clear strict liability rule.[46] It should be noted that the Italian judges refused to follow the same path as the French courts in food liability cases, in spite of the fact that the articles dealing with the (contractual) liability for hidden defects are very similar. This may be due to two factors. First, the French preference for contractual liability *vis-à-vis* tort liability is connected to the rule of *non-cumul* between *responsabilitè delictuelle* and *responsabilitè contractuelle* (Monateri 1989). Second, the French courts, as noted, dealt with cases in which the defendants were mostly restaurateurs or people who personally prepared the contaminated food. For these defendants, it was very difficult, if not impossible, to escape liability by proving the absence of any negligence in their conduct. On the contrary, the first product liability decision in Italy concerned a case in which it was quite easy for the seller, a shopkeeper, to prove an absence of negligence, since his conduct was limited to retailing a sealed

---

45   Shifting the burden of proof is a legal stratagem which the German legal system has also adopted (Markesinis, Unberath 2002: 91 ff.). The leading case is the so-called "chicken pest case," decided by the Bundesgerichtshof (Sixth Civil Senate), November 26, 1968. *Neuen juristischen wochenschrift* 1969, 269. With specific regard to liability for defective foodstuffs, the German courts have relied mainly on the second paragraph of § 823 of the BGB, establishing an obligation to compensate in cases where a person violates a law whose goal is to afford protection to another. Food production is a sector where many protective statutes exist, providing for detailed rules aimed at safeguarding consumers. The violation of these norms determines the defendant's liability according to the second paragraph of § 823 referred to above. In addition, such a violation usually implies a shift in the burden of proof, since it amounts to negligence *per se*. It should be noted, however, that the violation of a generic norm, such as one prohibiting the sale of food which is adulterated, does not constitute negligence *per se*; only the infringement of detailed laws can trigger such a consequence. For a case of food liability, distinguishing between detailed and generic protective norms, see Bundesgerichtshof (Sixth Civil Senate) November 19, 1991. *Neuen juristischen wochenschrift* 1992, 1039.

46   The Italian Supreme Court, in the 1964 *Saiwa* case, stressed the fact that its goal was not to introduce a strict liability rule, but only to legitimize the use of presumptions in proving the negligence of the producer.

box of cookies. The fact that his role in the production process was marginal, even non-existent, has led the courts to focus their attention on tort liability, signaling the future evolution of the product liability regime in Italy.[47]

The European Product Liability Directive 85/374/CEE

On July 25, 1985, the Council of the European Economic Community enacted Directive no. 374 "on the approximation of the laws, regulations and administrative provisions of the Member States concerning liability for defective products." Given the divergences between the national product liability regimes, in part mentioned in the previous section, it has been considered necessary to create a common set of rules in order to promote more uniformity and, therefore, facilitate the movement of goods within the common market (Patti 1990; Stapleton 1994; Taylor 1999; Tizzano 2001; Whittaker 2005; Fairgrieve 2005).

The original text of the directive envisaged a strict liability rule to be applied to all the movable objects which prove to be defective, with a notable exception that will soon be analyzed (art. 2). The victim is required to prove the existence of the damage, of the defect and the causal link between the two (art. 4). Art. 6 specifies the notion of defect as occurring when the product "does not provide the safety which a person is entitled to expect, taking all circumstances into account." The article goes on to list some of the circumstances that may be taken into consideration in assessing the presence of a defect: the presentation of the product, its reasonably expected use, the time when the product was put into circulation. The manufacturer can avoid liability if she proves that her case is encompassed in one of the so-called exculpatory clauses listed in art. 7. Among these, points (b) and (e) deserve particular mention, which provide that the producer will not be liable if, respectively, "having regard to the circumstances, it is probable that the defect which caused the damage did not exist at the time when the product was put into circulation by him or that this defect came into being afterwards," and "the state of scientific and technical knowledge at the time when he put the product into circulation was not such as to enable the existence of the defect to be discovered" (the so-called "development risk defense"). The provisions contained in the directive do not preclude the application of other national norms which provide better protection for consumers (art. 13). This means that the national provisions continue to persist alongside the directive, although it is not clear to what extent the old national strict or quasi-strict liability regimes created by the national courts can compete with the Community rules.[48]

---

47 The lack of something similar to the French *action directe* in the Italian legal system has reinforced the trend to look to tort law.

48 For example, European Court of Justice January 10, 2006 (C-402/03), *European Court Reports* 2006, I-199 precluded an extension of the strict liability regime to the supplier beyond the cases provided for in art. 3.3 of Directive 85/374.

The exception mentioned before concerns the applicability of Directive 374 to agricultural products. Art. 2, in its original version, provided that the notion of product did not encompass primary agricultural products and game. This category of goods was meant to include "the products of the soil, of stock-farming and of fisheries, excluding products which have undergone initial processing." The reasons for such exclusion were rooted both in political and conceptual problems. As to the first, the economic structure of the agricultural industry is different from that of other sectors. It is characterized by small and medium-sized firms with weak financial power, particularly when compared to the pharmaceutical, automobile, or other similar industries. Imposing a strict liability regime on farmers seemed too burdensome, since they would not have the financial resources to deal with the consequences that such a rule implies. In other terms, the fear was that extending product liability to include farmers, indiscriminately, would have led to unfair results. But conceptual problems also existed. The goal of product liability law was to manage the risks that the industrial process might trigger: the presumption was that the source of the risks would have to be found in the production line. Because some natural, agricultural products by their very nature pose dangers *per se*, it seemed unfair and conceptually wrong to consider them as defective. The idea of the naturalness of the agricultural products as a bar to preventing farmers being made liable has played an important role in shaping the exception contained in art. 2.

In the months following the enactment of the directive, many discussions took place with regard to the interpretation of the term "processing." The differing liability regimes between primary agricultural and other agricultural products were, indeed, based on the consideration as to whether processing occurred or not. Beyond the generic remark that the term was intended to refer to an industrial transformation of the "natural" product, divergences existed as to the degree of transformation required to be able to speak of processing (Mazzo 2007: 125 ff.). Some authors sustained that even a minimal modification, such milling corn into flour or slaughtering an animal, could determine the applicability of the 1985 norms, while others claimed that the transformation had to alter the nature of the agricultural product (Ferrero 1989: 47; Troiano 1989: 517; Cubeddu 1990: 210; Capizzano, Petrelli 1990: 171 ff., 182; Martorana 1992; Carrozza 1995). The question can be more aptly put in terms of risks that the processing generates in the product. On the one hand, it can be sustained that the directive is applicable only with regard to the risks that the industrial production process autonomously creates; on the other, the fact that the transformation in some way hides preexisting defects in the agricultural product may be considered sufficient to determine the applicability of the 1985 norms (Cubeddu 1990: 209).

It has also been noted that it is difficult to draw a clear line differentiating what is natural and what is the product of transformation in modern agriculture, since contemporary production practices intervene markedly in the natural process, blurring any preexisting distinction. Given the extensive use of pesticides, fertilizers and other artificial components, all agricultural products are, to some extent, the outcome of a technological, not completely natural, process.

Art. 2, in its original version, left all these questions unanswered and posed difficult problems of interpretation that, in part, were to lead to a reformulation of the norm in 1999. The choice to extend strict product liability to all agricultural products was reasserted few years later. Art. 21 of Regulation 178/2002, which, as we have seen, created the new European food safety framework, contains a provision aimed at connecting the new administrative framework to the liability system, by stating that the provisions of the regulation will not prejudice the application of the 1985 directive, as amended. The European lawmakers have thus intended to assign a pivotal role to the products liability system: the role of gatekeeper for European food safety, to be exercised jointly with the administrative controls set out in the 2002 regulation.

The Japanese Product Liability Law

Japan has only recently enacted a product liability law, closely resembling the European model: law no. 85 of July 1, 1994 (Aa. Vv. 1996; Young 1996; Marcuse 1996; Melchinger 1997; Cohen 1997; Nottage 2004). Despite the newness of the statute, the country had already developed a quasi-strict liability regime for defective products through a reinterpretation of art. 709 of the *Minpo* (the Japanese civil code), regulating tort liability.[49] The development of this regime is mostly due to a series of mass injury cases, which forced Japanese judges to develop new mechanisms for protecting plaintiffs more effectively. Some of the cases involve the production of defective foodstuffs which caused injury to a large number of consumers. In this sense, food liability, despite the fact that the cases are not particularly numerous, has played a decisive role both in advancing the tort system and in guaranteeing food safety.

The first, in the mid-1950s, is the so-called Morinaga case concerning the deaths of 130 babies, and neurological damage suffered by many thousands more, because of the consumption of milk contaminated with arsenic (Ottley, Ottley 1984: 51). The second case dates back to the early 1970s: cooking oil was contaminated with a highly noxious chemical agent, causing the death of 142 people and injuries to more than 10,000 consumers (Kitagawa 2006: § 4, 4–9). While the Morinaga case did not result in a judgment, because the parties reached a pre-trial settlement by which the producer compensated all the loss suffered by the babies and their families, the cooking oil case led to a series of findings against the producer, the supplier of the chemical contaminant and the government. The

---

49   The Japanese product liability system, both prior to and after the enactment of the 1994 statute, does not completely coincide with the tort provisions, but it is composed of a web of different provisions which guarantee some form of remedy for consumers. Among these, the so-called "SG" (Safety Good) label deserves a particular mention, used to guarantee the safety of certain products and allowing for the recovery of damages caused by defects through a quasi-insurance mechanism (Ramseyer 1996).

government was sued on the ground that it had violated its duty to monitor and prevent the (mis)conduct of the firms involved in the accident.[50]

In the cooking oil case, the judges were confronted with the equivalent legal problems that the European judges were dealing with at the same period, that is, the struggle to find legal tools by which the final purchasers and third users could obtain compensation for the damages suffered because of a defective product. Confronting the alternative between contractual and tort remedies, the Japanese courts rejected the former, reasoning that no contractual relationship existed between the final purchaser and the producer.[51] The pandectist matrix of the *Minpo*, along with the important influence that German legal scholarship has traditionally played in Japanese private law, has probably influenced the interpretation given in this regard. If the contractual solution could not be accepted, liability in tort seemed to be the only viable path. In line with this position, an innovative interpretation was given to art. 709 of the *Minpo*, which *per se* requires the plaintiff to prove the traditional components of the tort of negligence (that is, the damage, the defendant's negligence and a casual link between the two). The innovation consisted in the redistribution of the burden of proof, through the use of inferences and presumptions. Since the plaintiff's position was problematic, being difficult for her to prove an act of negligence by the manufacturer, the court began to require the defendant/producer to prove having acted diligently. Along with this shift in the onus of proof, the judges heighten the duty of care required of the producer, stating that, when a person engages in a dangerous activity, then she has an obligation to implement all the appropriate means to avoid, or at least reduce, the potential damage.[52] The combination of the two elements created a quasi-strict liability operational rule, even if, at least initially, it applied exclusively to cases

---

50 Government involvement in mass injuries cases due to defective products is a characteristic of Japanese product liability law prior to the enactment of the 1994 statute. This feature has been present since the early case law; in the Morinaga case, but also in other, almost contemporary cases concerning defective drugs, the plaintiffs sued not only the producer, but also the government for having failed to exercise due care in supervising the firms which caused the damage. This has happened also in the Minamata Disease Case, in which the government was held liable for having failed to enforce the provisions contained in the Food Hygiene Law: D. Ct. of Kumamoto, March 30, 1987, reported in Uga 1999: 197.

51 It should be mentioned that in an early case, relating to an episode of mass contamination from salmonella contained in *tofu* curds, the court applied a contractual remedy, thus piercing the privity barrier. The case represents an exception to a general trend favoring the application of tort law and was not followed by other decisions. See *Kanmaki* v. *Ohashi*, D. Ct. of Gifu, December 27, 1973, reported in Kitagawa 2006: § 4, 21–2.

52 Prior to their application in the field of product liability, the shift in the burden of proof and the increase in the duty of care (but also the idea of the sufficiency of a probabilistic causal link) were developed in a series of environmental liability cases, the so-called "Big Four Pollution" cases (Gresser, Fujikura, Morishima 1981).

of mass injuries. In most recent decisions, the same operational rule has also been extended to individual claims (Cohen 1997).

The passage from judicially created, quasi-strict liability to a full strict liability rule occurred in 1994 when, as mentioned, the new product liability law was enacted.[53] The articles contained in the new statute closely mirror the provisions of the European Directive 85/374, with some important exceptions (Reimann 2003a). The first is that the norms apply not only to the consumers, but to all persons who have suffered injury or loss because of a defective product (art. 2; Aa. Vv. 1996: 302). The second concerns the limitation period. While the European Directive provides for a ten-year limitation period (art. 11), running from the time the defective product is put into circulation,[54] the Japanese equivalent contemplates the same ten-year period, but running from the time when the damage is recognizable if the damage is due to a progressive accumulation of noxious substances or manifests itself after a long latency period (art. 5).

Art. 2 provides for the definition of product, that is, any movable which has been transformed or processed. According to the commentary to the statute, this definition does not include, among other things, primary agricultural products, since they are neither transformed nor processed (Aa. Vv. 1996: 305). These products, then, remain subject to the general provisions of the civil code, and in particular to art. 709 of the *Minpo*. Art. 2 also contains the definition of "defect," intended as

> ... the lack of safety that the product ordinarily should provide, taking into account the specific characteristics of the product, the ordinarily foreseeable manner of use of the product, the time when the manufacturer, etc., delivered the product, and other circumstances concerning the product.

There are two cases in which the manufacturer can escape liability (art. 4). The first exempts the supplier of raw material or components, when the defect is due to the compliance with the instructions given by the producer; the second is the development risk defense.[55] Japanese law shrinks the number of cases under which the manufacturer cannot be held liable with respect to the European Directive, even if it maintains the two most important ones.

The recent product liability case law presents two decisions concerning defective foodstuffs. The first was decided by the Osaka District Court on September 10, 1999 and concerned food poisoning from E. coli bacteria occurring in an elementary school (Rothenberg 2000: 484–5; Nottage 2004). The outbreak

---

53   The law entered into force one year later, on July 1, 1995.

54   Along with the ten-year limitation period, a shorter three-year limitation period is provided, running from time on which the consumer is aware of the damage, the defect and the identity of the producer (art. 10).

55   The commentary to the statute uses the expression "state-of-the-art defense": Aa. Vv. 1996: 319-320.

struck more than 8,000 people and a schoolchild died because of complications. The parents of the latter sued the city of Sakai, responsible for the elementary school where the poisoning occurred, both in negligence and for having violated the new product liability law. It was questionable whether the local government could be considered a "producer" according to the definition contained in art. 2.[56] The judge did not take a position on the problem, ruling that the local government had anyway acted negligently and ordering it to pay damages. In particular, the government was alleged to have omitted to inform the school of the necessity to heat the meals thoroughly in order to kill all the potential, noxious bacteria. This decision is formally in line with the provisions of the 1994 statute, since art. 6 provides that the norms of the civil code are concurrently applicable along with the special regime for product liability. But *de facto* the judge has avoided deciding an important interpretative question concerning the extension of the producers' category.

The second case coincides with the first decision in applying the new product liability statute (Rothenberg 2000: 489–90).[57] In 1998, a young woman purchased an orange juice in a McDonald's. Immediately after having drunk the beverage, she began bleeding from the mouth and needed medical attention. The analysis revealed that the bleeding was due to an injury in the throat probably caused by something present in the juice. The court found for the plaintiff ruling that, even if the latter was unable to prove the specific substance that caused her injury, nor the way it ended up in the beverage, the producer could be found liable in any event, because the damage undoubtedly arose from some defect in the product. The judge seems to make wide use of inferences in the decision. The pivotal principle, by which the plaintiff has to prove the existence of a defect, is to some extent blurred by the fact that the damage occurred in the first place, appears to be sufficient to determine the defectiveness of the product. On the other hand, a web of circumstances pointed to the fact that the injury could only have been caused by a foreign body in the beverage: the absence of possible, alternative explanations might have played a key role in the decision.

---

56   The definition of producer contained in art. 2 states: "(3) As used in this law, the term 'manufacturer' means any of the following: (i) any person who, by way of business, manufactured, processed, or imported the product (hereinafter just 'manufacturer, etc.'); (ii) any person who, by putting his name, trade name, trademark, or other feature (hereinafter 'representation of name, etc.') on the product, presents himself as its manufacturer, or any person who puts a representation of name, etc., on the product in a manner which may cause that person to be mistaken as the manufacturer of that product; (iii) in addition to the persons indicated in the preceding item, any person who puts on the product a representation of name, etc., of another person who can reasonably be determined to be the manufacturer-in-fact of the product in light of the manner of the product's manufacturing, processing, importation, or marketing of the product and other circumstances" (Aa. Vv. 1996: 303).

57   *Katsurawa* v. *McDonald's*, D. Ct. of Nagoya, June 30, 1999. For a translation of the decision, see Nottage 2004: 215 ff.

The description of Japanese product liability law should be completed by making brief reference to the role that extrajudicial mechanisms of compensation play in this legal system (Ramseyer 1996). Such mechanisms can be categorized in two groups. The first refers to the certification of specific classes of products as safe. The Product Safety Council, at the request of relevant producers, sets safety requirements for particular groups of goods: each producer can choose whether to submit its products to the Council's test or not. If the product is submitted and passes the test, then a SG (Safety Goods) label can be posted on the good. If it is not submitted or fails the test, the good can be marketed anyway, but without the SG label. What it is interesting is that, if the SG product causes injury or loss to the consumer because of the presence of a defect, then the victim will be compensated on the basis of a scheme comparable to insurance. The consumer has to prove the existence of the defect and the causal link between defect and damage, as in a product liability action. Not all products are covered by this scheme and food products do not seem to have been included.[58]

The second group concerns the activities carried out by the National Consumers Affairs Center of Japan (hereinafter NCAC), which has several local centers (the Consumer Information Centers, hereinafter CICs). Among the many initiatives promoted, the centers also offer mediation services, to facilitate the solution of disputes concerning alleged malfunctions of a product. The service is connected to another activity performed by the CICs, called "information counseling," by which the centers collect information and reports relating to problems that consumers have experienced in using specific products.[59] The data collected are used not only to solve prospective disputes, but also to suggest design improvements to the producers, as well as in the techniques used in manufacturing the goods or, finally, in the warnings given.

The so-called "*konnayaku* jelly case" provides an archetypal example (Nottage 2000a: 228 ff.; Rothenberg 2000: 486 ff.). *Konnayaku* jelly is a popular food in Japan, sold as a snack and similar to gelatin. In the mid-1990s, several choking accidents involving children were reported to the CICs, caused by the ingestion of the jelly snacks. The centers took two initiatives: first, they released public notices signaling the choking hazard; second, they urged the producers to make the snacks softer and to upgrade the warnings on the jelly packs. After other accident reports, the CICs released new statements urging the producers to make further improvements to the snacks. In addition to the exchange of information and suggestions between the centers and the producers, a few claims for compensation

---

58   As we have seen in the preceding chapter, Japan has created a certification procedure implemented on a voluntary basis (the JAS system) with regard to foodstuffs. The difference of the JAS system with respect to the SG system is given by the fact that no insurance mechanism is provided for the first.

59   The NCAC runs a database, called PIO-NET, which collects all the reports and information about malfunctions relating to goods, allowing constant monitoring of the safety and reliability of many classes of products.

were filed against some of the producers.[60] The CICs were involved from the beginning and facilitated the settlement of the claims, all of which concluded with the payment of damages to the deceased children's parents.[61]

Liability for Primary Agricultural Products

National courts and legislators have implemented specific rules in dealing with primary agricultural products contaminated by viruses or other noxious substances. First of all, it is appropriate to provide a definition of what a contaminated primary agricultural product is. By this expression I am referring to goods which have not been processed and that naturally (or originally) contain substances (viruses, bacteria, prions, and so on) rendering them dangerous for human beings. It is clear that these "defective" foodstuffs present problems which are to some extent different from those concerning food products contaminated during the production process. In the latter case, the defect is in one way or another created by the manufacturer during her activity, while in the former, the flaw existed before the manufacturing process, even if a duty to eliminate this "natural" defect may be imposed on the manufacturer under certain circumstances. This difficulty can be observed both in the decisions given by the courts and in the historical evolution of the statutory provisions dealing with this particular aspect of food liability.

In Europe, the original exemption from the norms laid down in the 85/374 Directive for primary agricultural products was due precisely to these considerations: imposing strict liability for the presence of natural defects appeared too burdensome for the manufacturers. But in 1996, the BSE scandal emerged, generating a series of consequences among which was the amendment of art. 2 of the directive, in 1999 (Ponzanelli 2001b; Nicolini 2006: 106 ff.; Mazzo 2007: 141 ff.). The European institutions have, it seems, adopted a clear position in this regard, extending the product liability regime to include primary agricultural products. The solution has the merit of overcoming the hurdles of interpretation which the distinction between processed and unprocessed goods raises. At the same time, it creates other problems that will be analyzed in the following pages. It should be noted that, although the amendment was intentionally created to deal with lawsuits concerning BSE, no case has been so far decided and the few which have been filed, have been dropped. In other words, the consumers have preferred to resort to other means for obtaining a remedy for the loss suffered.

Beyond the vCJD context, very few cases have been decided concerning primary agricultural products in Europe. A French court has ruled that the professional

---

60 The cases usually involved the death of children by choking (Nottage 2000a: 232). In October 2008, the largest jelly manufacturer, Mannan Life Co., decided to halt the production of this kind of product (Matsutani, Martin 2008).

61 Nottage (2000a: 233) notes that, even if the CICs have played a role in settling the claims related to the jelly snacks hazards, there is no product liability ADR center dealing specifically with food products, while similar centers exist for other categories of goods.

seller of unprocessed agricultural goods is strictly liable toward the consumer for the defects present in the product, applying the product liability provisions.[62] But, in another case, the *Cour de Cassation* has refused to accept that imperfections in wheat can be considered defects.[63] If the scarcity of decisions makes it difficult to predict the path that tort liability for primary agricultural products will follow in the future, it is also important to notice that criminal law has been increasingly applied to control the marketing of adulterated primary products such as meat, in particular. For example, criminal sanctions have often been invoked to deter the sale of meat contaminated with salmonella (Assumma 1987: 391 ff.; Piccinino 1988: 299 ff.; Pacileo 2003a, 2003b: 129 ff.; Lazzaro 2003; Bernardi 2003; Piergallini 2004).[64]

In the case of Japan, primary agricultural products are excluded from the scope of the law, as mentioned. The reasons for such a choice are similar to those which supported the exclusion of these goods in the original version of the European Directive. As a consequence, in the Japanese system, the distinction between processed and unprocessed products is still of fundamental importance, since liability can only be incurred in respect of the former products. The commentary prepared jointly by several government agencies assists in clarifying what is meant by the term "processing." The English term used to translate the Japanese expression is "to manufacture" and it "refers to a series of actions which includes designing, processing, inspecting and labeling the product" (Aa. Vv. 1996: 304). The term has been interpreted loosely by the courts: for example, in one case, the simple operation of salting fish has been interpreted as processing (Nottage 2004). The commentary seems to suggest a more restrictive notion of manufacture, making reference to the creation of a new product based on raw material.

The most famous case involving liability for a "defective" primary agricultural product is the so-called "blowfish case," decided well before the enactment of the product liability law.[65] A famous kabuki actor died after having consumed a large portion of blowfish liver, a traditional dish in Japanese cuisine; the organ of this fish can be very dangerous if not properly prepared, as a lethal toxin occurs naturally in it. The court found for the plaintiff, stating that the chef and the restaurant had the highest duty of care in carrying out a particularly dangerous

---

62 Cour d'Appel Toulouse, February 22, 2000. *Juris classeur periodiques* G 2000, 10429, with commentary by Le Tourneau: the case concerned horse meat contaminated with trichinae (Le Tourneau 2004: 1293).

63 Cass. 1re civ. July 15, 1999. *Bulletin civil* 1999, I, 252, 1999. As to Italy, there is no decision dealing with liability for primary agricultural products.

64 See Italian Cass., sez. pen., December 20, 2004. *Foro italiano* 2005 II, 308; Cass., sez. pen., July 13, 2004. *Foro italiano* 2005, II, 282, with comment by Paone; Cass., sez. pen., June 26, 2002. *Impresa*, 2003, 117; Cass., sez. pen., February 12, 2003. *Rivista penale*, 2003, 866; Cass., sez. pen., April 12, 2002. *RivistAmbiente*, 2003, 71.

65 *Kigura* v. *Kasaoka*, D. Ct. of Kyoto, December 19, 1978. The decision is translated and reported in Milhaupt, Ramseyer, West 2006: 327 ff.

activity such as cooking blowfish liver. The circumstance that a city ordinance prohibited the serving of this part of the fish played an important role in the court's finding, since its violation constituted a kind of negligence *per se*.[66] The reference to the particularly high degree of care required by the seller, along with the aspect of negligence *per se*, seems to disguise a form of strict liability. A second case which also occurred prior to the enactment of the product liability law concerned *tofu* eggs contaminated with salmonella.[67] Here the court exceptionally applied the contractual remedy provided under art. 415 of the *Minpo*, overcoming the privity barrier and holding the seller strictly liable for the damages suffered by the consumers. Both the cases, although resorting to different legal solutions (tortious in the first case, contractual in the second), have *de facto* made use of a strict liability rule, imposing on the seller a type of absolute warranty as to the safety of the product. A third case, mentioned before, concerned food poisoning caused by E. coli, which occurred in an elementary school: the judges, using the language of negligence, sustained that the defendants violated the basic standards of due diligence.

A richer and more variegated body of case law exists in American legal experience. There have been several occasions when courts have had to decide cases in which an agricultural product, originally tainted by some kind of natural agent, caused injury to the consumers. The results, as we will see, do not offer a clear-cut answer to whether the US system holds the producers strictly liable in the event of a defective primary agricultural product. Indeed, solutions vary according to the state concerned and to the natural agent responsible for the contamination. It should be further noted that, when we speak of the strict liability rule, we are referring to liability for manufacturing defects. Only with regard to these defects, as we have seen before, it is possible to speak of *strict* liability: in the case of design and warning defects, the judges tend to apply a negligence-based liability rule. The remark is important to fully appreciate the division I am introducing between cases in which the producer has been held strictly liable or not. Then, the fact that a case is included in the group in which the manufacturer has incurred liability only means that she has not been held responsible for a manufacturing defect, but it does not indicate that she has not been found liable in negligence (for example, for failure to warn).

One group of cases admits the possibility of applying a strict liability rule for defects, depending on which natural elements have contaminated the food. Most of the cases concern raw oysters infected by bacteria or beef contaminated by salmonella or E. coli. There are various theories used to justify this solution. In the majority of cases, the consumer expectation test is applied: the courts rule

---

66   The defense of both the chef and the restaurant pointed to the fact the customer was informed and aware of the risks in consuming blowfish liver and that, consequently, he accepted the risk.

67   See *Kanmaki* v. *Ohashi*, D. Ct. of Gifu, December 27, 1973, reported in Kitagawa 2006: § 4, 21–2.

that, even if the contaminant agent can be considered as occurring naturally in the product, nevertheless the average consumer could not reasonably expect its presence.[68] No attention seems to be paid to whether the producer/seller could have detected the agent. The decisions envisage a regime under which liability is absolute, probably paying tribute to the historical antecedents of product liability law, descending as it does from the (contractual) warranty of fitness. In this regard, courts often refer both to tort and contract in finding the producer strictly liable.[69] This depends in part on the fact that, in many cases, the producer is, at the same time, also the direct contractual counterpart of the victim; but, on the other hand, it is a consequence of the hybrid nature of US products liability. Contractual and tort actions, therefore, often coexist within the same decision. In a limited number of cases, the producer/seller has been held liable through a species of negligence *per se*.[70] The marketing of contaminated foodstuffs has been interpreted as a violation of the statutory provisions prohibiting the sale of adulterated products to the public. The rationale supporting this solution seems to be similar to that underlying the breach on an implied warranty of merchantability, that is, to make the producer the absolute guarantor of the food's fitness for consumption.

In the second group of cases, the courts have negated the proposition that an agricultural product which is already tainted in its original state, can be considered as affected by a manufacturing defect and, consequently, have refused to apply strict liability.[71] The common rationale behind the decisions is that the defect is neither created by the manufacturer nor is she able to detect it through reasonable means

---

68 *Wachtel* v. *Rosol*, 271 A.2d 84 (Conn. S. Ct. 1970); *O'Dell* v. *DeJean's Packing Co., Inc.*, 585 P.2d 399 (Okla. Ct. App. 1978); *Battiste* v. *St. Thomas Diving Club, Inc.*, 15 V.I. 184 (V.I. D. Ct. 1979); *Cain* v. *Sheraton Perimeter Park South Hotel*, 592 So.2d 218 (Ala. S. Ct. 1991); *Kilpatrick* v. *The Superior Court of the City and County of San Francisco*, 233 Cal. App.3d 233 (Cal. Ct. App. 1991); *Koster* v. *Scotch Associates and Charlie O's, Inc.*, 640 A.2d 1225 (N.J. S. Ct. 1993); *Ayala* v. *Bartolome*, 940 S.W.2d 727 (Tex. Ct. App. 1997).

69 *O'Dell* v. *DeJean's Packing Co., Inc.*, cit.; *Battiste* v. *St. Thomas Diving Club, Inc.*, cit.; *Cain* v. *Sheraton Perimeter Park South Hotel*, cit.; *Kilpatrick* v. *The Superior Court of the City and County of San Francisco*, cit.; *Koster* v. *Scotch Associates and Charlie O's, Inc.*, cit.

70 The cases are quite old and concern pork meat contaminated with trichinae: *Troietto* v. *Hammond Co.*, 110 F.2d 135 (6th Circ. Ct. App. 1940); *Kurth* v. *Krumme*, 56 N.E.2d 227 (Ohio S. Ct. 1944).

71 *Bronson* v. *Club Comanche, Inc.*, 286 F. Supp. 21 (V.I. D. Ct. 1968); *Hoch* v. *Venture Enterprises, Inc.*, 473 F. Supp. 541 (V.I. D. Ct. 1979); *Winstead* v. *Ed's Live Catfish & Seafood, Inc.*, 554 So.2d 1237 (La. Ct. App. 1989); *Simeon* v. *Doe*, 602 So.2d 77 (La. Ct. App. 1992); *Simeon* v. *Doe*, 618 So.2d 848 (La. S. Ct. 1993); *Clime* v. *Dewey Beaches Enterprises, Inc.*, 831 F. Supp. 341 (Del. D. Ct. 1993); *Porteous* v. *St. Ann's Café & Deli*, 713 So.2d 454 (La. S. Ct. 1998); *Edwards* v. *Hop Sin, Inc.*, 140 S.W.3d 13 (Ky. Ct. App. 2003); *Woeste* v. *Washington Platform Saloon & Restaurant*, 836 N.E.2d 52 (Ohio Ct. App. 2005).

of inspection. The issue of being able to use reasonable means of detection of the contaminating agent is particularly common in the case of oysters contaminated with the *vibrio vulnificus* bacteria. To be sure that the oysters are free from the bacteria, each of them should be tested: but the testing involves their destruction. On the other hand, random testing of some of the products in a batch also proves unfeasible, since the same batch can contain both contaminated and perfectly safe oysters. Being aware of these difficulties, the courts have decided that strict liability does not provide a reasonable solution to the problem and have preferred to apply a negligence rule.

This conclusion receives further support from another aspect, linked to the characteristics of the *vibrio vulnificus* bacterium. This agent, in fact, does not pose a danger to the health of all consumers, but only to the ones who are already immune-deficient or have liver problems. In other terms, the risk of health problems deriving from the consumption of food contaminated with *vibrio vulnificus* affects a very specific category of customers. The courts have decided that, given the limited danger to general public health, a duty to warn was more appropriate than holding the manufacturer strictly liable. Negligence, as mentioned before, is the standard by which compliance with this duty is judged: the courts assess whether it was reasonable to impose such a duty on the defendant and whether the warning was reasonably clear and understandable for the average customer. Moreover, in the states where the consumption of raw oysters can be regarded as traditional, the Department of Health has issued specific regulations requiring warnings to be placed in menus or close to locations where oysters are served.[72] If the warning is properly displayed, the consumer is considered to assume the risk of injury that could be caused by the ingestion of contaminated shellfish.

The judges appear to implement a rule of bilateral prevention, imposing a duty on both the seller and the customer to act with care to prevent the damage. In the same vein are the few decisions dealing with pork which is already infected, in its original state. In this instance, the contamination depends on parasites (trichinae) which can cause trichinosis, a disease which is occasionally fatal. The presence of this parasite cannot be easily detected; on the other hand, proper cooking kills the agent, preventing any damage. The courts have thus ruled that the manufacturer or seller of meat contaminated with trichinae is not strictly liable for any consequent injury sustained by the consumer, since the latter was under a duty to thoroughly

---

72   This is the case of Louisiana, for example, where in February 1991 § 23:006-4 of the sanitary code was amended. The actual version of the section provides: "All establishments that sell or serve raw oysters must display signs, menu notices, table tents, or other clearly visible messages at point of sale with the following wording: 'There may be a risk associated with consuming raw shellfish as is the case with other raw protein products. If you suffer from chronic illness of the liver, stomach or blood or have other immune disorders, you should eat these products fully cooked.'" Two other states requiring such warnings are Ohio (§ 2307.76 of the Rev. Code Ann.) and Texas (§ 229.164(r) of the Adm. Code).

cook the meat.[73] As to the duty to warn customers of possible contamination, the decisions do not impose any obligation in this sense. The fact that the meat must be properly cooked is a matter of common knowledge: consumers do not have to be warned against risks which are open and obvious.

Along with these two major groups, there is a third class of decisions which can be viewed as tangential to them. In these cases, the courts were asked to assess whether it was possible to find a public institution (usually local departments of health) liable for having neither imposed a duty on the sellers of shellfish to warn the customers of the health risks that consuming raw shellfish could pose, nor having checked that such warnings were effectively displayed. What is asserted by the plaintiffs here is not that the institution is strictly liable, but that it negligently omitted to act, breaching the duty to protect public health through public intervention. The legal doctrines and conceptual problems that this kind of lawsuit involves will be more thoroughly analyzed in the second part of the chapter: the attention here is focused only on the solutions that the courts have provided in adjudicating these claims.

The claims can be divided in two different classes. On the one hand, we have plaintiffs alleging that the departments of health had a duty to issue regulations obliging the sellers to post warnings about the risk of consuming raw shellfish. In these cases, the courts have not accepted that public bodies are to be held liable, since the option as to whether to issue such regulations falls within their discretionary powers and cannot be scrutinized by the courts.[74] On the other hand, there are cases in which the public bodies have simply failed to enforce regulations imposing such warnings. The local department of health has a specific obligation to send officers to inspect restaurants, and so on, for compliance with the requirements prescribed in the relevant regulations. If the department certifies such compliance and then evidence is brought that this is not the case, the public body can incur liability. Two decisions delivered in Louisiana serve to illustrate this event. The courts ruled that the duty of a public body to control the effective compliance with statutory provisions is not a discretionary function; in these cases, the margin for action of the public body are narrow and are subject to the scrutiny of the courts. The consequence was that the department of health was found liable in both the decisions for having negligently failed to enforce the statutory provision making it obligatory to display warnings about the risk of consuming raw shellfish.[75]

---

73   *Clouser* v. *Shamokin Packing Co.*, 71 Pa. D. & C.2d 785 (Pa. Common Pleas Ct. 1975); *Scheller* v. *Wilson Certified Foods, Inc.*, 559 P.2d 1074 (Ariz. Ct. App. 1976).

74   *Simeon* v. *Doe*, 602 So.2d 77, cit.; *Simeon* v. *Doe*, 618 So.2d 848, cit. As we will see more in detail in the following pages, the legal doctrine used by the courts to deny the plaintiff's claim is the so-called "discretionary function exemption."

75   *Gregor* v. *Argenot Great Central Insurance Company*, 817 So.2d 152 (La. Ct. App. 2002); *Gregor* v. *Argenot Great Central Insurance Company*, 851 So.2d 959 (La. S. Ct. 2003). In *Vargas* v. *Continental Cuisine, Inc.*, 900 So.2d 208 (La. Ct. App. 2005), the court recognized in principle that the Department of Health violated its duty to enforce

A fourth group of cases which is worth mentioning does not concern tort liability, but the interpretation of the word "adulterated" as found in the Federal Meat Inspection Act. In particular, the question was whether raw, unprocessed meat contaminated with salmonella could be considered adulterated and, therefore, be removed from circulation. Two federal courts of appeals held that, to constitute adulteration, the contaminant must have entered the product during the processing phase. Since salmonella occurs naturally in most meat, independent of the processing carried out by the producers, no state of adulteration could be found in the cases under scrutiny (Johnson 2004).[76] Applying the rationale of these decisions to the realm of liability for primary agricultural products, it is highly probable that producers would not be held liable where salmonella-tainted meat has caused injury to consumers. Clearly, these decisions run parallel to the cases where courts have refused to apply strict liability to agricultural products which are infected before any manufacturing process has taken place.

Some Preliminary Comparative Remarks on the Liability for Contaminated Foodstuffs

The analysis conducted so far permits some preliminary conclusions to be drawn on the role played by food liability in the different legal systems considered. The US is by far the country with the most active food liability system. This is in line with the more general trend by which tort law is frequently used as a way of apportioning risks between the different parties involved in an activity. The ample case law attests to the pivotal role that food liability has played in the evolution of the concept of food safety, shaping the attitudes of both producers and consumers with regard to production modalities, the sanitary state of facilities, and warnings on products. In addition, liability for foodstuffs has historically been a pioneer, preceding the formulation of many of the solutions adopted in the wider field of product liability.

The importance of the case law goes beyond the specific realm of the decisions forming it, to embrace and address a whole assembly of bargains that are traded, taking account of the relevant judicial decisions. Indeed, the extent of the case law implies, as a consequence, its ability to create incentives for and have a modifying influence on settlements between consumers and food producers. It is of course difficult, if not impossible, to quantify the number of cases which are settled instead of proceeding to trial and a judicial decision: producers and insurance companies are highly motivated not to disclose such data, in order to

---

the relevant section of the Louisiana sanitary code imposing the health warning, but then dismissed the plaintiff's claim, having failed to find a causal link between the negligent conduct of the department and the damage suffered by the victim.

76   *Supreme Beef Processors, Inc.* v. *United States Department of Agriculture*, 275 F.3d 432 (Ct. App. 5th Circ., 2001); *American Public Health Association* v. *Earl Butz, Secretary of Department of Agriculture*, 511 F.2d 331 (Ct. App. Columbia, 1974).

avoid bad publicity which might adversely affect consumer confidence. But even without certain data, we can take note of the abundant news coverage reporting settlements concerning food safety issues; a quick survey bears out the frequency of this practice.[77] The combined effect of litigation and out-of-court settlements is important in addressing food safety issues and stands on an equal footing with administrative regulation. In this respect, it could be said that the US is being driven by the twin engines of regulation and precedent.

In Europe, food liability has traditionally played a marginal role. This holds true both before and after the enactment of the product liability directive. It is also valid in relation to the common law–civil law divide, since England has not experienced the same developments that have occurred in the US. The importance of liability for food safety is, thus, a US phenomenon and not a general, characteristic feature of common law.

In contrast to the American experience, food safety is mostly promoted through administrative regulations, which represent the main reference point for food market operators. It should be added that, at least with regard to the civil law systems, an important role is played by criminal law. Criminal sanctions are often used to support the regulatory provisions adopted at administrative level. However, the use of criminal law does not have an equivalent importance to tort liability for foodstuffs in the US. While the latter participates in the process of setting the safety standards to be followed, criminal law enforces the regulatory norms already in place.

The minimal role of food liability in Europe, with respect to the US, can be explained by different factors. In large measure, it probably depends on the different institutional settings which characterize the two geographical areas. The presence of a publicly funded system of health insurance and the high costs of gaining access to courts are general features of the European systems that have induced a less frequent recourse to tort law (Reimann 2003b). In addition to this, the European experience lacks (or at least lacked until recent times) the legal tools which have further encouraged the widespread use of tort litigation in the US: I am referring here to strict liability, in the first instance, but also to class actions, pre-trial discovery, contingency fees, and so on.[78]

---

77 The spectrum is wide and covers cases ranging from meat contaminated with salmonella (the so-called "Jack in the Box cases," for example) to (alleged) allergic reactions following the consumption of genetically modified corn (the StarLink case); see, respectively, Manoukian 1994 and Uchtmann 2002.

78 With regard to class actions in the US, their role seems to be minimal in the specific context of food liability, unlike other areas of product liability. This might be determined by the fact that in most cases potential mass litigation is settled out of court. Some mass tort class actions have been certified in cases of food poisoning occurring during cruises, for example, *Hernandez* v. *Motor Vessel Skyward*, 61 F.R.D. 558 (Fla. D. Ct. 1974); *Bentkowski* v. *Marfuerza Compania Maritima*, 70 F.R.D. 401 (Pa. D. Ct. 1976).

The Japanese system offers a different account of the relationship between litigation, regulation and food safety. The body of case law is modest, equivalent to Europe in dimension, but its qualitative impact puts it in a different position with respect to Europe. The fact that food liability cases have traditionally concerned mass injury events, together with the large amount of publicity associated with this particular feature and the involvement of the government as a defendant, has ensured that it has a more far-reaching effect on the legal and economic contexts of food production. The firms operating in this sector have traditionally been very sensitive to the potential exposure to tort liability and have reformed their production processes to prevent this danger. The recent enactment of the product liability law has been interpreted as a further incentive to raise the standards of food safety and important financial investments have been made in this direction (Rothenberg 2000: 491–2).

The Japanese experience shows another important differentiating feature. Many cases of food contamination are dealt by the consumer information centers which, although formally independent, are emanations of the government (Nottage 2004). Public institutions are thus also able to maintain some measure of control over disputes that normally would go unnoticed in the European and American legal systems (Upham 1987). This kind of indirect control is reinforced by the activity of information counseling previously noted, which has an important role in influencing both consumers' and producers' behavior. Summing up, food litigation (or para-litigation) appears to have been a more prominent feature of the Japanese legal landscape than is the case in the European one. This outcome is determined not by the number of food cases, but rather by their salient profile: this therefore results in a reinforcement of the deterrent effect, in comparison to the European experience.

Which Liability Rule for the vCJD Victims?

In this second section, I will try to assess the practical feasibility of applying different liability rules to the BSE context and the theoretical implications involved in doing so.[79] The particular nature of vCJD, the uncertainties underlying the emergence and development of the disease, the role that private enterprise and public bodies have played during the BSE crisis, are all factors posing fundamental challenges to a legal system seeking to compensate the victims. The role of tort law is not confined merely to the compensatory aspect, but also concerns its ability

---

79 The possibility of using the tort regime to compensate the victims of defective foodstuffs is a problem which does not relate exclusively to the BSE case. Growing concerns have been expressed, for example, with regard to genetically modified food and the potential detrimental effects it can have on the consumer's health (Burk, Boczar 1994; Davies, Levine 2000; Prati, Massimino 2001; Van Tassel 2004). For a first case of an (alleged) allergic reaction to genetically modified corn, see Uchtmann 2002.

to manage risks through *ex post* monitoring of the activity generating the risks. This control technique allows tort law to display its deterrent effect, preventing the occurrence of the same risks in the future. The analysis must look at both sides of the coin, in the effort to design an operational rule which embodies both compensation and deterrence.

The Tort System as an Ex Post *Tool of Risk Management*

Tort law is not only a means for compensating the victims of an accident, but it is also intended to deter future harmful actions. The function of tort law in this regard is similar to that of safety regulation: both share the goal of minimizing the social costs associated with risky and/or damaging activities. The main difference between them clearly relates to the temporal framework within which they both operate.

Tort law operates *ex post*, that is, only after an accident has occurred. The court is called upon to judge the legitimacy of the activity which caused damage, assessing whether the activity was permitted and whether it was diligently performed. While in the specific case such an evaluation is linked to the award of compensation for the victim, at the same time it also takes on didactic meaning for those intending to perform that same activity in the future. They will be under an incentive to make their behavior conform to the indications provided by court judgments: failure to do so could expose them to an obligation to compensate the victims for damages caused by their wrongful actions.

On the other hand, safety regulation operates *ex ante*, setting the requirements that all those intending to perform the regulated activity must follow. It is detached from single, specific events, being aimed at regulating general classes of cases by reference to a command and control framework. Moreover, the goal of safety regulation is not compensation: violation of its provisions typically involves administrative sanctions.

Ex ante safety regulation and *ex post* tort liability are not two separate spheres: indeed, they blend, to create a comprehensive framework in which both interact (Shavell 1984a, 1984b; Viscusi 1988; Kolstad, Ulen, Johnson 1990; Rose-Ackerman 1991; Burrows 1999; Schwartz 2000; Faure 2002; Hiriart, Martimort, Pouyet 2004; Izzo 2004). In other words, no legal system makes exclusive recourse to only one of the two: on the contrary, they tend to allow the contemporaneous use of both. Such an outcome is the result of a basic, and in some respect banal, consideration. Neither safety regulation nor tort law are perfect tools in managing risky activities: both demonstrate shortcomings that weaken their ability to prevent future accidents effectively.

Safety regulation is affected by two main problems. The first concerns the enforcement of its provisions. The enforcement of administrative requirements can be very costly and depends heavily on the quantity of resources that the regulator is willing to invest in this activity. Financial constraints can severely undermine the enforcement side of safety regulation: the public institutions have, thus, to find a way to balance such costs with the need for an effective and thorough implementation of the regulation. The final result is often one of under-enforcement.[80]

The second problem relates to the presence of potential inefficiencies within the regulation itself. There are several sources of inefficiencies. First, a regulation may be inefficient due to gaps in its provisions; particularly in areas where technology has made fast progress, regulators cannot keep abreast of all the problematic aspects of a given activity. In addition, technical standards rapidly become obsolete: if the regulators do not update such norms frequently, new gaps can occur. A regulatory agency may sometimes fail to address these omissions in an adequate or timely way: there are many examples where the failure of the competent agency to react to a situation has prolonged, if not worsened, its state of inefficiency.[81] Second, agency capture can affect the efficiency of a regulation. Such capture is part of the wider phenomenon of lobbying, by which interest groups tend to influence legislators and regulators in order to obtain favorable norms. The lobbying process can be seen as a form of competition between different groups: there is a dynamic interaction among the groups, each of them trying to capture the regulator by discrediting the actions of the others (Becker 1983; von Wangenheim 1999; Stiglitz 2000: 189). The economic analysis of law predicts that small, well-organized groups with high stakes are the most effective in lobbying politicians or technocrats, thus prevailing over other competitors. Looked at from the regulators' standpoint, they appear to be particularly sensitive to pressure from special interest groups, especially when their appointment depends (formally or informally) on political choices. Indeed, in order to be elected (or re-elected) they need to obtain support from those who can sponsor their candidacy. Depending on which pressure group wins the competition, the result will be an inefficient regulation, caused by the lack of a careful balance between all the interests involved.[82]

80　The extent of the under-enforcement is, of course, a variable of the quantity of resources the public institutions have invested in it, but also of the overall efficiency of the administrative system, that is, of its ability, to a greater or lesser extent, to employ the resources obtained efficiently.

81　The technical standards relating to the production of animal feed and the inability of the regulatory agencies to review them once the BSE crises had emerged is a good example of inefficiency, but it is not the only one. The HIV epidemic is another case illustrating the lack of timely reaction that can affect an agency. For a comparative account of the management of this crisis, see Feldman, Bayer 1999. The reprocessing of single-use medical devices (or SUDs) provides a third and more recent example of regulatory void; see Hogan, Colonna 1998; Izzo 2004.

82　Not all the law and economics literature support the idea that lobbying determines inefficient regulation. For example, Schwartz (2000: 44) questions the link between lobbying and inefficient regulation, underlining that lobbies can provide useful information, otherwise unavailable to the regulators and support the withdrawal of existing, inefficient regulations sponsored by other interest groups.

Tort law can provide a partial corrective to many of the problems mentioned so far. The costs of the tort system are not entirely on the shoulders of the public administration, but are in part borne by the private parties paying court fees, attorneys, experts, and so on.[83] Moreover, tort law can be considered as a form of privately induced regulatory compliance, in the sense that plaintiffs, by suing the wrongdoer for having failed to comply with regulatory requirements, contribute to enforcing indirectly such requirements. It should be noted that the failure to comply with safety requirements constitutes a case of negligence *per se*, thus confining the defendant in a strict liability position. This remark highlights the enforcement strength of tort law with respect to safety regulation, since the wrongdoer has very narrow margins for escaping liability. On the other hand, the ability of tort law to facilitate an indirect enforcement effect such as this should not be overemphasized. The victim does not always bring a suit against the wrongdoer for having failed to comply with the required standards: difficulties in proving causation, high court fees, the need to pay the lawyer's fees, the prospect of low awards, the costs of obtaining scientific expertise, are all potential factors preventing potential plaintiffs from suing. Tort law provides a contribution to enforce safety regulation, but its actual importance depends on several institutional factors.

Tort liability can also lessen some of the potential inefficiencies plaguing safety regulation. The flexibility tort actions offer can counteract the abovementioned risk of gaps and obsolescence. Courts normally react more quickly than agencies to new legal challenges arising in social or scientific contexts. In this respect, courts can be viewed as being at the forefront of many areas of the law.[84] Regulators usually intervene at a subsequent phase, after the courts have begun to struggle with the new legal issues and have provided some preliminary, partial solutions. The courts can also be an additional source of scrutiny with regard to the safety standards set out in the regulation. If the risk is that these standards are biased in favor of the most effective interest group, tort actions can provide a different forum in which to review inefficient standards.

The problem is closely intertwined with the defenses of statutory preemption and regulatory compliance. Some US federal safety regulations contain a provision forbidding the states or their subdivisions to establish requirements which differ from, or are additional to, those provided for in the regulation itself; such provisions are called "preemption clauses." It is uncertain whether courts can be considered as a subdivision of a state and, consequently, can set additional or different requirements through their decisions. The case law is mixed in this regard, providing different solutions based on the types of different/additional

---

83 The costs associated with tort law are incurred only once an accident happens, while the administrative costs are sustained regardless of such occurrence.

84 New technologies might improve the ability of the administrative agencies to react quickly to new challenges. For example, great emphasis has been posed on the possibility that the so-called "e-rulemaking" could improve citizen participation in, and the final result of, the regulatory process (de Figueiredo 2006).

requirements established by the courts or on the history of the specific preemption clauses.[85] Such clauses are peculiar to the federal structure of the American system and, for this reason, do not exist in Europe and Japan.

A problem common to all three legal systems concerns the regulatory compliance defense. While preemption clauses operate at the procedural level, preventing a lawsuit from being brought, the regulatory compliance defense aims at blocking a legal action which does not face any procedural obstacle. The defendant's argument is that no negligence can be found against her, since she has complied with all the norms laid down by the regulation. Even if such a defense is frequently raised, the tendency of most courts is not to allow it (Faure 2002; Monateri 1998: 95–6). The judges usually interpret the regulatory requirements as minimum ones: compliance with them does not exempt the defendants from liability when specific circumstances or scientific innovations require the adoption of stricter standards.

If tort law can alleviate some of the problems of regulation, on the other hand it presents deficiencies of its own. The first of them concerns the gathering of information. Regulation is much better equipped than tort law in this regard. The information gathered during a trial is fragmented and linked to the features of the specific case: the institutional constraints of the judicial process do not allow a body of data to be collected which is either of general significance or complete. Additionally, the use of tort law for getting information entails a waste of resources: each court acts in an isolated way and the same information can be collected several times by different courts, with a consequent duplication of costs. Gathering general information would be beyond the goal of the tort process, which has the more limited aim to provide (or deny) compensation to the victim of an alleged, specific wrongful act. On the contrary, regulation is particularly well suited to the task of consolidating information. In fact, this is one of its main goals: collecting a comprehensive set of data is the first step of any regulatory action. This is a consequence of its nature and scope: while tort law exists to resolve a specific dispute, regulation provides general norms designed to cover the largest number of cases. Economies of scale play an important role in this context: they conserve resources by coordinating the efforts of the different subjects involved in the activity.

---

85   For example § 360k(a) of the Medical Device Act prohibits states, or subdivisions of the states, to set requirements with regard to medical devices which are additional to or different from those established in the same statute. In *Medtronic Inc.* v. *Lohr*, 116 S. Ct. 2240 (S. Ct. 1996), the Supreme Court interpreted § 360k(a) as allowing suits to be brought in common law against the producers of medical devices, although the claim is based on negligence and could potentially set additional or different safety requirements. In other contexts, courts have preempted only some types of claims, while allowing others. Recently, the Supreme Court found that FDA regulations concerning drug labeling do not preempt state product liability claims; see *Wyeth* v. *Levine*, 129 S. Ct. 1187 (S. Ct. 2009).

A second deficiency of the tort system is connected to the processing of the information obtained. The point is an extension of the previous remark concerning the gathering of data. In this case, too, the institutional constraints of the tort process prevent a complete and thorough treatment of the information. This is in part due to problems mentioned before: the focus of tort law on a specific case, the isolated way courts operate, the fragmented nature of the data obtained. Expertise is an additional problem in this context. The elaboration of data requires the contribution of experts, especially in technical areas where the layperson has limited knowledge. Economies of scale play an important role also in this regard, permitting the knowledge obtained through long-term investments and specifically dedicated infrastructures to be shared. The amount of resources and investments that complex scientific information assessments require is hardly compatible with the tort process. Moreover, private parties embarking on such investments might not be able to enjoy all the benefits deriving from them: they therefore have few incentives to provide the necessary resources.

Third, partly because of the deficiencies described so far, tort law seems also to be ill-equipped for achieving a careful balance between the risks and benefits an activity entails. The impossibility of making a thorough collection and analysis of the data hinders the full appreciation of all the benefits and costs involved. In addition, such a balance implies an important component of political discretion, in the sense that it must be based on choices which are not purely technical. Such discretion is better placed in institutions, as regulatory agencies, which are more politically accountable than courts and which can provide a more appropriate forum where all affected interests can be considered (Viscusi 2002; Calfee 2002).

The last problem concerns uncertainty. While the scope of regulation is primarily to set norms and standards which are applicable to the largest number of cases possible, we have already noted that tort law produces standards which are case-dependent. This has an important consequence from the perspective of potential defendants. They will indeed be uncertain as to whether the particular standard or rule which emerges from a decision will be applied to their case. Such an evaluation not only requires them to assess whether their case is identical to the one in which the standard was set, but also, in the case of divergence, whether these differences are significant enough to recommend the adoption of a different standard. The lack of certainty is further compounded by the possibility that different courts set different standards for analogous cases. To be clear, regulation is far from immune from these kinds of difficulties: different interpretations of regulatory provisions can lead to uncertainty as well. But the problem in the latter case seems to be less severe than with tort law. First, the presence of a generally applicable rule provides a more certain point of reference than case law does, since the latter can be chaotic and contradictory. Second, at least when it appears clear from the rule that the regulator expressed a political preference with regard to the desirability of a given activity, courts are usually reluctant to intrude on the discretionary choice which has been made.

Given the mutual deficiencies that regulation and tort law demonstrate and their reciprocal ability partially to overcome them, it is not surprising that all the legal systems rely on a combination of both instruments. The extent of the overlap, as well as their reciprocal boundaries, varies according to the system and the specific area of law considered. Taking up once again the considerations expressed at the end of the comparative overview on foodstuffs liability, the mix appears to be more balanced in the US, where tort liability has played an important role in developing a food safety system. Japan and Europe seem to be more regulation-driven, even though Japan historically has had high-profile cases.[86] On the other hand, it is true that, whichever legal system is considered, the food industry is one of the most heavily regulated sectors. This is an important comment, so far as the US is concerned, moderating the current importance of food liability there. While it has assumed an important role when compared to Europe and Japan, the same cannot be said if we contrast it with the liability affecting other industries, especially in modern times. Litigation for other types of products (for example, medical devices, pharmaceuticals, cars, and so on) has a much higher impact nowadays on the relevant industries than litigation concerning foodstuffs. In the past, the area of food liability offered both extensive case law and innovative legal theories to deal with the problems raised by the cases. Today, a plateau seems to have been reached, a quiet point from which routine litigation proceeds. The remark helps us to assess the extent of the mix between tort law and safety regulation in the US food safety system: more tort law oriented than Europe and Japan, but, at the same time, more regulation-driven than other US industries.

Having described how tort law can be considered an (*ex post*) tool of risk management, interacting with (*ex ante*) safety regulation, we can now analyze which rule appears to be more suitable in compensating the victims of vCJD.

The Problem of Uncertainty

The scientific features characterizing both BSE and its human variant, vCJD, produce an indeterminate situation with regard to several components of tort liability. Such indeterminacy has inherent paralyzing effects which, as I will note, severely undermine any possibility of claiming damages for injury and loss caused by vCJD, regardless of whether negligence or a strict liability rule is applied.

Causation   The first problem concerns causation. As noted in Chapter 2, BSE/vCJD has a very long incubation period, ranging from five to fifteen years. There are no means of testing whether the infection developed before the onset of clinical symptoms. This has important consequences for the ability of potential plaintiffs

---

86   It should be mentioned that art. 21 of European Regulation 178/2002 has stressed a mixed approach to food safety, by providing that the administrative framework set in the regulation will not affect the applicability of the product liability directive.

to prove a causal link between vCJD and a specific, contaminated product.[87] Let us imagine a hypothetical case in which the relatives of a vCJD victim decide to consult an attorney to obtain some redress for their loss. The first problem that the attorney must consider is the identification of the potential defendant. Probably the victim had beef at home, hamburgers with her friends and sometimes steaks for dinner in restaurants. The potential sources of contamination are countless. Given the length and variances in the latency period, it is scientifically impracticable to trace back the single piece of meat which was infected.

Identification of the producer could be even harder. The principle of traceability has been only recently established: without it, it may be almost impossible to trace the original producer. But also imagining that such a principle could be applicable to a BSE case, it is hard to conceive that the consumer would be able to retrace every individual purchase from which her disease could have originated.

The problematic relation between causation and factual uncertainties is neither novel, nor peculiar to vCJD. In the past, the same problem has emerged in relation to other products, such as pharmaceuticals and, more recently, lead paints. In these cases, too, it was impossible to determine the exact product or producer which caused the damage. Some courts tried to develop a solution that could bypass the traditional way of establishing the causal link, by creating a new rule, referred to as "market share liability."[88] According to this, when it is clear that a determined type of product is the origin of certain injuries but it is impossible to identify the specific manufacturer which marketed it, all the producers of that type of product can be sued. The producers become severally liable according to their respective shares in the market, except where they can prove that their specific product was not the cause of the harm. The award each producer must pay to the victim is a fraction of the total damage suffered, calculated on the basis of its share in the product market. The rationale of the new rule is clearly to counterbalance the profits the producers gain from marketing a dangerous product by making them proportionally accountable for the harm they cause.

---

87   The difficulties that a potential plaintiff must overcome with regard to causation in vCJD cases flow from factual uncertainties. Scientific uncertainties are not at stake here, since the scientific mechanism, by which the consumption of BSE-infected meat causes vCJD, is quite clear.

88   The leading precedent is *Sindell* v. *Abbott Laboratories*, 607 P.2d 924 (Cal. S. Ct. 1980), a case concerning a pharmaceutical product, called DES, prescribed to women to prevent miscarriages during pregnancy. The drug proved to cause cancer in the daughters of the women who took it and its marketing was prohibited. The lawsuits filed by the victims had a difficult time, since it was almost impossible to determine who the specific producer was of the drug that had been taken, given the time which had elapsed and the fact that many producers manufactured the same kind of drug. The Californian Supreme Court reversed the burden of proof with regard to causation, imposing on the defendants the burden of proving that they did not produce the specific pill that caused the damage to the plaintiff. Those failing to discharge this burden would be held liable in proportion to their market share (Owen 2005: 747 ff.).

The market share liability rule has been adopted by only a few courts, mainly in decisions concerning pharmaceuticals and more rarely in asbestos and lead paint cases.[89] But most courts have rejected such a form of liability, especially in recent times (Gifford, Pasicolan 2006; Geistfield 2006; Damron 2006).[90] The reasons behind this refusal are worth analyzing, since they can also be largely applied to the (potential) vCJD litigation (Owen 2005: 749). The first reason concerns the practical feasibility of determining the market shares of each producer. Even if a product is manufactured by few companies, it could be difficult to ascertain the quotas of each of them. Indeed, the retailer should maintain a register where they report the number of products they have sold; moreover, such registers should be kept for a long time, with consequent conspicuous costs (Fischer 1981).

Moreover, there are goods which are manufactured on a large scale by several different producers. The greater the number of producers, the more difficult it becomes to determine their respective shares in the market. The viability of the theory seems, therefore, to be severely limited on a practical level. The second problem with market share liability concerns its compatibility with the traditional theories of causation. The core of the objection in this regard is that such a theory seems to go too far, deviating excessively from the element of causation. Indeed, what we have here is only hypothetical causation, created by imposing on the defendant the burden of proving that its specific product was not the cause of the damage incurred by the plaintiff. In this way, the courts have created a mechanism

---

89   *Collins* v. *Eli Lilly and Co.*, 342 N.W.2d 37 (Wisc. S. Ct. 1984); *Abel* v. *Eli Lilly and Co.*, 343 N.W.2d 164 (Mich. S. Ct. 1984); *Morris* v. *Parke, Davis & Co.*, 667 F. Supp. 1332 (Fla. D. Ct. 1987); *Hymowitz* v. *Eli Lilly and Co.*, 73 N.Y.2d 487 (N.Y. Ct. App. 1989); *Conley* v. *Boyle Drug Co.*, 570 So.2d 275 (Fla. S. Ct. 1990); *Ray* v. *Cutter Laboratories, Division of Miles, Inc.*, 754 F. Supp. 193 (Fla. D. Ct. 1991); *Smith* v. *Cutter Biological, Inc.*, 823 P.2d 717 (Haw. S. Ct. 1991); *Jackson* v. *Glidden Co.*, 647 N.E.2d 879 (Ohio Ct. App. 1994); *Richie* v. *Bridgestone/Firestone, Inc.*, 22 Cal. App. 4th 335 (Cal. Ct. App. 1994).

90   *Celotex Co.* v. *Lee Loyd Copeland*, 417 So.2d 533 (Fla. S. Ct. 1985); *Cummins* v. *The Firestone Tire & Rubber Co.*, 495 A.2d 963 (Pa. S. Ct. 1985); *Tirey* v. *Firestone Tire & Rubber Co.*, 513 N.E.2d 825 (Ohio Com. Pl. 1986); *Goldman* v. *Johns-Manville Sales Co.*, 514 N.E.2d 691 (Ohio S. Ct. 1987); *Bixler* v. *Avondale Mills*, 405 N.W.2d 428 (Minn. Ct. App. 1987); *York* v. *Lunkes*, 545 N.E.2d 478 (Ill. Ct. App. 1989); *Kinnett* v. *Mass Gas & Electric Supply Co.*, 716 F. Supp. 695 (N.H. D. Ct. 1989); *Leng* v. *The Celotex Co.*, 554 N.E.2d 468 (Ill. Ct. App. 1990); *Lee* v. *Baxter Health Care Co.*, 898 F.2d 146 (4th Ct. App. 1990); *Santiago* v. *Sherwin Williams Co.*, 3 F.3d 546 (1st Ct. App. 1993); *Setliff* v. *E.I. Du Pont de Nemours & Co.*, 32 Cal. App. 4th 1525 (Cal. Ct. App. 1995); *Bly* v. *Tri-Continental Industries, Inc.*, 663 A.2d 1232 (D.C. Ct. App. 1995); *In the Matter of New York State Silicone Breast Implant Litigation*, 631 N.Y.S.2d 491 (N.Y. S. Ct. 1995); *Jefferson* v. *Lead Industries Association, Inc.*, 106 F.3d 1245 (5th Ct. App. 1997); *Brenner* v. *American Cyanamid Co.*, 699 N.Y.S.2d 848 (N.Y. S. Ct. 1999); *Black* v. *Abex Co.*, 603 N.W.2d 182 (N.D. S. Ct. 1999); *Hamilton* v. *Beretta U.S.A. Co.*, 750 N.E.2d 1055 (N.Y. Ct. App. 2001); *Spencer* v. *Baxter International, Inc.*, 163 F. Supp.2d 74 (Ma. D. Ct. 2001); *Lewis* v. *Lead Industries Association, Inc.*, 793 N.E.2d 869 (Ill. Ct. App. 2003); *Ferris* v. *Gatke Co.*, 107 Cal. App. 4th 1211 (Cal. Ct. App. 2003).

which is similar to a form of collective insurance; but insurance mechanisms are conceptually different from tort remedies. Tort law has always been conceived of as a tool for making a specific party liable for a particular course of conduct which has caused an identifiable harm. Eliminating the element of specificity seems to do away with one of the characterizing features of tort law.

The vCJD litigation highlights the difficulties with market share liability mentioned so far. The number of farmers and feed producers potentially involved is huge, with the consequential problems in ascertaining the market shares for each of them. The complete lack of records makes the problem even worse than in the case of pharmaceuticals.[91] The causation element would be extremely stretched, since the high number of producers involved would accentuate the hypothetical nature of market share liability, at the same time weakening the specificity element of tort law.

There is a further problem differentiating the vCJD litigation from other cases where market share liability has been used. While in the existing case law, all the defendants acted negligently, this is not the case with BSE-tainted meat. Not all the meat produced in the years from the 1980s to the mid-1990s was infected with BSE; therefore, there are producers who did not market defective meat. On the other hand, all paints containing lead, or all pharmaceuticals with a given chemical composition, could be considered defective. This implies that all the producers could be deemed liable with regard to their conduct, since they all marketed a product which contained flaws; the uncertainty related only to which specific product caused the damage. In the vCJD litigation, uncertainty concerns not only causation, but the wrongfulness itself of the defendant's conduct. The two set of cases are, therefore, different. Extending market share liability to vCJD litigation would mean making a double blind guess: not only might the product have caused the damage, but the product might also have been defective. If the "traditional" market share liability stretches the operational rules of tort law, this stretching would be even further accentuated in the case of the vCJD litigation.[92]

Prescription A second element of uncertainty deserves attention. The scientific ambiguities and the long latency period characterizing vCJD have an obvious effect

---

91 In Europe, the system of traceability for food products was created only after (and as a response to) the mad cow crisis, through the enactment of Regulation no. 178 of 2002. In Japan, a similar (albeit partial) system was implemented in 2003, while there is no such provision at all in the US.

92 The problem of using tort law in cases where uncertainty concerns both causation and conduct has emerged not only with regard to market share liability, but also in connection with so-called "evidential damage" (Porat, Stein 2001). Evidential damage is an operational rule by which, in cases where the uncertainty is determined by a lack of evidence due to the negligence conduct of the defendant, the burden of proof is shifted from the plaintiff to the (alleged) wrongdoer. But in cases in which it is impossible to determine whether the defendant acted wrongfully, the proponents of the evidential damage admit that such theory cannot be applied (Porat, Stein 2001: 187).

also on the limitation period on the right to sue the wrongdoer. In order to prevent the economic and social costs that an indefinite exposure to liability entails, all the legal systems contain provisions barring a cause of action after a certain time has elapsed without an intention to act being expressed. The legal hurdle concerning potential vCJD litigation would concern the time from which the limitation period begins to run. It is clear that if the time runs from when the infection occurred, the possibility for the victim to sue the producer becomes reduced.

With regard to Europe, we must consider both the provisions contained in the product liability directive and the other general norms regulating prescription. Art. 10 of Directive 85/374 provides for a limitation period of three years that "shall begin to run from the day on which the plaintiff became aware, or should reasonably have become aware, of the damage, the defect and the identity of the producer." Art. 11 adds that the right to compensation will not be actionable after the elapse of ten years "from the date on which the producer put into circulation the actual product which caused the damage."[93] The first provision does not pose particular problems: the three-year period will run, in the case of vCJD, from the day in which the pathologist discovers that the cause of death is related to that particular disease.[94] The norm expressed in art. 11 is more problematic. Here, the time runs from the date in which the BSE-tainted meat was marketed. The first problem is practical. In order to determine the date in which the limitation period begins to run, we must single out the specific piece of meat which caused the infection. But, as noted, this is almost impossible in the context of the BSE/vCJD. The second problem is legal: even if we are able to ascertain the specific date in which the infection occurred, the disease could have manifested fifteen or twenty years from such date. Given the uncertain latency period, some of the claims could be barred, while others not. More worrisome from a legal point of view, the bar might be due not to the victim's failure to act promptly, but only to the fact that her disease took more time to manifest itself.

The provision does not seem to leave space for interpretations postponing the point from which the limitation period begins to run. The distinction between the three-year and ten-year periods reinforces such a conclusion: art. 11 provides an ultimate and absolute barrier protecting producers from possible future damages claims. On the other hand, such a provision is neither in line with the case law of the individual Member States nor with the operational rules followed in Japan and the US. With regard to the first discrepancy, courts have generally interpreted limitation periods in cases of latent damages in a way that favors the victims. The operational rule emerging from a comparative overview is that prescription begins

---

93   On the notion of "put into circulation," see *O'Byrne* v. *Sanofi Pasteur MSD Ltd*, European Court of Justice February 9, 2006 (C-127/04), *European Court Reports* 2006, I-1313.

94   It is actually impossible to determine the presence of the infective prions causing the vCJD while the patient is still alive. Absolute knowledge as to the cause of death can, thus, be obtained only through a post-mortem examination.

to run from the moment the victim had, or could have had using reasonable care, actual knowledge of the existence of the damage (Bona 2004; Hondius 1995). The rule closely resembles art. 10 of the product liability directive, determining the limitation period on a case-by-case basis, depending on the victim's factual knowledge.[95]

In this regard, a possible escape route from the rigidity of art. 11 could be to turn to the more pro-consumer national regimes. Art. 13 of the 1985 directive allows an injured person to have recourse to other "rules of the law of contractual or non-contractual liability." If the claim advanced under the product liability directive is time barred, then the plaintiff could resort to national liability norms in order to avoid the problem of limitation.[96] As noted, it is highly probable that national courts would consider as the starting-point for limitation the time in which the plaintiff could have had knowledge of the damage. Nonetheless, such an option might turn out to be merely theoretical, since the recent case law of the European Court of Justice shows that it has adopted a restrictive interpretation of art. 13.[97]

Art. 11 also departs from the solutions implemented in non-European legal systems, such as Japan and the US. With regard to the former, art. 5 of the 1994 product liability law provides for three different limitation periods. The first is a three-year period running from the time the injured person has actual knowledge of the injury and the producer's identity. The second is a ten-year period which starts from the date of delivery of the product. These two provisions mirror articles 10 and 11 of the European Directive. The third period concerns only those injuries "caused by substances which are harmful to human health when they remain or accumulate in the body, or where the symptoms of such injury appear after a certain latent period." In such an event, the ten-year period will run from the time the injury arises. The Japanese statute has, thus, assumed a more resolute pro-consumer slant, carving out a special regime that would favor the plaintiffs in potential vCJD litigation. The solution is in line with the pre-1994 case law, in which the Japanese courts had already stated that prescription begins to run only

---

95   The distinction between two different limitation periods introduced in the 1985 directive does not correspond to any Member State's statutory provision concerning the limitation period for tort actions. Hence national courts have dealt with a unitary concept of limitation period and have developed an operational rule which is able to provide some elasticity to it. The tension between pro-consumer elasticity, on the one hand, and pro-producer need of certainty, on the other, has been solved by the European law-makers by creating two different provisions, namely articles 10 and 11.

96   The solution is congruent with the policy rationale justifying art. 13, that is, to allow the consumer to resort to more favorable national, liability regimes than the one represented by the product liability directive.

97   In European Court of Justice January 10, 2006 (C-402/03), cit., the judges refused to allow a national rule establishing the extension of strict liability beyond the cases provided in directive 85/374. In the same vein, European Court of Justice April 25, 2002 (C-183/00), *European Court Reports* 2002, I-3901; April 25, 2002 (C-154/00), *European Court Reports* 2002, I-3879.

after the victim has knowledge of the damage and the identity of the wrongdoer (Kanayama 1995: 238–40).[98]

In the US, the point from which time begins to run is firmly linked to procedural problems, and in particular to the discovery rule. The operational rule is similar to the one already described; the limitation period runs from the moment in which the victim has, or could have had, using reasonable diligence, knowledge of the existence of an injury and of the identity of the wrongdoer. The difference here is that the rule is phrased in procedural terms. Courts speak of "accrual of the cause," meaning the time when the claim becomes enforceable before a court. This coincides with the moment in which the victim "discovers certain facts that will enable him to file a suit" (Levy 1987: 186; Green 1988; Corman 1991: 533 ff.; Gerstenblith 1995: 360–61).[99]

In the Japanese and American legal systems, the relationship between uncertainty and time seems to be less problematic than in the European context. With regard to the first, limitation is a hurdle which can be overcome through an elastic interpretation of the time when the limitation period begins to run. This interpretation presents stricter constraints in the European experience, *vis-á-vis* the rule envisaged in art. 11. But, as noted, margins exist to allow the norm to be bypassed, by resorting to the general provisions governing the time-barring of tort actions. The real, insurmountable problems concern the uncertainties surrounding the causation and wrongfulness elements. Here, the peculiarities of vCJD, coupled with the legal restraints governing tort law, make it very difficult to assert that a suit has any chance of success.

Development Risk Defense   A last, potential legal hurdle deserves a quick mention. A common feature of all the legal systems analyzed is the presence of a rule shielding the producers from liability when the product's risks were unknowable or unpreventable at the time it was marketed. It is the so-called "development risk defense" or state-of-the-art defense. Europe and Japan have codified the norm in their product liability laws (Stapleton 1994: 236 ff., Cerini 1996, Nottage 2004),[100] while in the US, the corresponding rule was elaborated by the courts and

---

98   In the Minamata case, the court addressed the problem of time limitation. The judges stated that the period began to run from the publication of the Health Minister's statement concerning the causes of the mysterious disease. See *Watanabe* v. *Chisso K.K., Kumamoto D. Ct.*, March 20, 1973: the decision is translated in English in Gresser, Fujikura, Morishima 1981: 86 ff. (in particular, 102 with regard to the limitation period).

99   *Urie* v. *Thompson*, 337 U.S. 163 (US S. Ct. 1949); *Harig* v. *Johns-Manville Products Corp.*, 394 A.2d 299 (Md. Ct. App. 1978); *Stoleson* v. *United States of America*, 629 F.2d 1265 (7th Circ. Ct. App. 1980); *Fusco* v. *Johns-Manville Products Corp.*, 643 F.2d 1181 (5th Circ. Ct. App. 1981); *Wilder* v. *Amatex Corp.*, 336 S.E.2d 66 (N.C. S. Ct. 1985); *Vispisiano* v. *Ashland Chemical Co.*, 527 A.2d 66 (N.J. S. Ct. 1987).

100   See art. 4(1) of the Japanese product liability law and art. 7(e) of the 85/374 European directive on product liability. In putting into force the 1985 directive, Spain is the only Member State to have provided that the development risk defense is not applicable to food producers.

then translated into statutes in some states (Vandall 1994; Cupp 1994; Schwartz, Tedesco 2003; Owen 2005: 675 ff.).[101]

Perplexities and hesitations have characterized the application of this exemption from its very beginnings. First, the state-of-the-art defense allows the courts to assess whether the defendant should have known the existence of risks associated with its product: an evaluation close to the negligence paradigm, which could cause a crisis in the strict liability rationale characterizing product liability.[102] The second problem concerns the issue of what constitutes the "state of the art." Different opinions have been expressed in this regard, ranging from the customary practices followed by the industry to the highest level of scientific and/or technological progress available at the time (Owen 2005: 678). Most of the courts have disregarded both these extremes, preferring to adopt a middle-ground approach. The adoption of simple, customary practices does not exempt manufacturers from liability; on the other hand, the courts have devoted attention to the availability of the latest scientific and technological developments for the producers. Nowadays, considered from the comparative perspective, the predominant rule tends towards holding the manufacturer liable if it failed to adopt not the best *existing* technology, but the best one *reasonably available*.[103]

---

101   Up to now, sixteen states have enacted statutory provisions introducing different forms of state-of-the-art defense.

102   For US decisions refusing to apply the state-of-the-art defense because contrary to the strict liability rationale, see *Elmore* v. *Owens-Illinois, Inc.*, 673 S.W.2d 434 (Mo. S. Ct. 1984); *Johnson* v. *Raybestos-Manhattan, Inc.*, 740 P.2d 548 (Haw. S. Ct. 1987); *Spieker* v. *Westgo, Inc.*, 479 N.W.2d 837 (N.D. S. Ct. 1992). Nowadays, most of the US courts apply the state-of-the-art defense, at least with regard to defective and warning defects. With regard to warning defects, see *Feldman* v. *Lederle Laboratories*, 479 A.2d 374 (N.J. S. Ct. 1984); *Borwn* v. *The Superior Court of the City and County of San Francisco*, 751 P.2d 470 (Cal. S. Ct. 1988); *Owen-Illinois, Inc.* v. *Zenobia*, 601 A.2d 633 (Md. Ct. App. 1992); *Young* v. *Key Pharmaceuticals, Inc.*, 922 P.2d 59 (Wash. S. Ct. 1996); *Wagne* v. *Roche Laboratories*, 671 N.E.2d 252 (Ohio S. Ct. 1996); *Vassallo* v. *Baxter Healthcare Co.*, 696 N.E.2d 909 (Mass. S. Ct. 1998); but apparently against this trend, see *Green* v. *Smith & Nephew AHP, Inc.*, 629 N.W.2d 727 (Wisc. S. Ct. 2001); *Golonka* v. *General Motors Corp.*, 65 P.3d 956 (Ariz. Ct. App. 2003). As to design defects, see *Penick* v. *Christensen*, 912 S.W.2d 276 (Tex. Ct. App. 1995); *Potter* v. *Chicago Pneumatic Tool Co.*, 694 A.2d 1319 (Conn. S. Ct. 1997); *LaBelle* v. *Philip Morris, Inc.*, 243 F. Supp.2d 508 (S.C. D. Ct. 2001); *Falada* v. *Trinity Industries, Inc.*, 642 N.W.2d 247 (Iowa S. Ct. 2002). The scandals relating to the side-effects of drugs such as thalidomide seem to have conditioned the Japanese and European legal landscape by focusing the attention of legislators on the possibility of being aware of such risks. The result has been the adoption of the development risk defense, whose purpose is, in fact, to regulate liability for unknown dangers. As Jane Stapleton (2002: 1245 ff.) notes, such provision seems to be quite paradoxical given the starting-point, that is, the protection of consumers.

103   With regard to the US, see *Chown* v. *USM Co.*, 297 N.W.2d 218 (Iowa S. Ct. 1980); *Crispin* v. *Volkswagenwerk AG*, 591 A.2d 966 (N.J. S. Ct. 1991); *Indianapolis Athletic Club, Inc.* v. *Alco Standard Co.*, 709 N.E.2d 1070 (Ind. Ct. App. 1999). The states

The uncertainties surrounding vCJD could fit into this defense (Mazzo 2007: 171). Determined in part by the evasive conduct on the part of the public authorities in dealing with the first signs of the crisis, for a long time the producers were in a state of ignorance about the risks that the meat they were marketing posed for human health. Similar considerations can also be made with regard to the feed producers. In such a context, their role in adopting risk-reducing strategies was minimal. The doubts as to the very existence of prions, not to mention the means of inactivating them, testifies to the difficulties faced by the producers. They could successfully claim to be exempted from liability, given the impossibility of knowing the dangers. The state-of-the-art defense thus becomes a further obstacle along the course upon which vCJD victims must embark, in order to obtain compensation.

Is Strict Liability the Right Answer for the vCJD Victims?

One of the first legislative reforms enacted in Europe in the wake of the mad cow crisis was the amendment of the 1985 product liability directive. Strict liability was extended to primary agricultural products by Directive 1999/34: the main purpose of this enactment was to provide a more effective means of protection to the growing number of vCJD victims. The legislative history accompanying the amendment is clear in this regard. The final report on the mad cow crisis recommended, among other reforms, extending strict product liability to primary agricultural products (Medina Ortega 1997; Mazzo 2007: 142 ff.). The amendment of the 1985 directive was the first of the suggested changes to be implemented. Other documents indicate that the first concern in amending the products liability directive was to provide the potential victims of vCJD with an expeditious remedy and to restore consumer confidence in the safety of agricultural products.[104] The fact that the European legislators have chosen a specific strategy for dealing with potential vCJD litigation, a strategy reasserted a few years later by art. 21 of Regulation 178/2002,[105] compels us

---

that have codified the state of the art defense have adopted the same kind of definition: see Neb Rev. Stat. § 25–21, 182; Mo. Rev. Stat. § 537.764; Ariz. Rev. Stat. § 12–681. As to Europe, see European Court of Justice May 29, 1997 (C-300/95), *European Court Reports* 1997, I-2649 (Ponzanelli 1997; Hodges 1998). The commentary to the Japanese product liability law does not make clear what is the level of knowledge required, referring generically to the "highest level of knowledge available at the relevant time" (Aa. Vv., 1996: 320).

104   For example, the official website of the European Union, reporting the summaries of the legislation concerning consumer safety, links the 1999/34 Directive to the mad cow crisis; see <http://europa.eu/scadplus/leg/en/lvb/l32012.htm>. Recital number (5) of Directive 1999/34 states that one of the main purposes of the extension of strict liability to primary agricultural products is to "restore consumer confidence in the safety of agricultural products," confidence deeply shaken by the BSE affair.

105   Art. 21 of Regulation 178/2002 provides: "The provisions of this Chapter shall be without prejudice to Council Directive 85/374/EEC of July 25, 1985 on the approximation

to investigate the soundness of the choice, with regard to the conceptual and economic premises of a strict product liability regime.

Before exploring such a failed strategy, I should put in a caveat with regard to nomenclature. When I refer to producers, I mean the cattle farmers and the feed producers. Other entities are, of course, involved in the production of beef for human consumption. Among them, slaughterhouses deserve a particular mention. Can they be considered as producers? Many problems could apparently be solved by holding them liable: they are usually large, with deep pockets, and able to invest resources in new technologies. The reason for rejecting such a conclusion is legal. They cannot be considered beef producers because the meat reaches them already as a final (defective) product. They do not produce the meat, in other words, but simply receive and resell it.[106] The defect in the beef preexists (and it is in unrelated to) their activity: they are only a way station for the BSE-tainted meat. Furthermore, we will see that the same problems I will underline with reference to cattle farmers also plague those running slaughterhouses.[107]

---

of the laws, regulations and administrative provisions of the Member States concerning liability for defective products" (Albisinni 2003b; Prosperi 2003).

106 Stella (2006: 1593) asserts that the final producer may also be considered liable in cases in which the defect is entirely due to one component of the final product. The example the author provides regards the use of (defective) gammaglobulines in the manufacture of pharmaceutical products: here the final producer (that is, the pharmaceutical company) is liable even if the defectiveness of the product depends uniquely on the gammaglobulines. Using the same kind of reasoning, it might be argued that the slaughterhouses, as final producers, can be deemed liable for the defect (prions) present in the meat. The extension is unconvincing for two reasons. First, the manufacture of drugs is very different from that of meat. Whereas in the first case, the final product is a complex one, requiring considerable intervention by the final producer, when the meat reaches the slaughterhouses it is already a complete product, which needs only to be butchered. Second, an excessive expansion of the liability of the final producer contradicts the original rationale behind product liability, raising conceptual and economic difficulties I will be underlining in the following pages.

107 It should be noted that art. 3 of the European Product Liability Directive provides that "Where the producer of the product cannot be identified, each supplier of the product shall be treated as its producer unless he informs the injured person, within a reasonable time, of the identity of the producer or of the person who supplied him with the product." Theoretically, therefore, the slaughterhouse could be held liable in lieu of the producer, if it is unable to indicate the name of the specific farmer who sold it the meat. Such form of liability is nowadays reinforced by the provisions contained in Regulation 178/2002 relating to traceability, since the supplier has the duty to keep records of the producers who supplied him. Furthermore, the kind of liability which could arise at this regard is closely related to Porat and Stein's idea of evidential damage (Porat, Stein 2001). But holding the supplier liable according to the considerations above mentioned is troublesome in the BSE context for two reasons. First, the problem of causation stops any attempt by the victim to obtain compensation from the slaughterhouses as well. Second, the traceability duty cannot be applied to the BSE context, since Regulation no. 178 was enacted after the occurrence (and as a consequence of) the mad cow crisis. Nonetheless, the supplier's liability for

The Conceptual Failures of Strict Liability

Product liability is based on specific conceptual premises which justify the adoption of a stricter rule than that existing in other areas of tort law. The core of these premises is that the manufacturer must be held accountable for the risks he creates through his production activity. If the risks are converted into injury or loss, then the producer will be considered liable for them. This core concept has two implications. First, the risk must be generated within the sphere of the producer's activity; second, the producer must maintain control over this sphere. Only if these two intertwined corollaries are respected does the core condition hold true, namely that the risk is generated through the producer's activity. The evolution of product liability demonstrates the validity of this comment. Even when applying contractual warranties, as in the early evolutionary stage of US products liability, courts have always held the producer liable when they perceived the producer had some kind of control over the production process.

This is also true with regard to manufacturing defects, where the manufacturer's conduct is apparently irrelevant. Indeed, the courts have applied strict liability for manufacturing defects only when they thought that the producer had some kind of control over the processing and could have prevented the damage. The manufacturing defect is typically one arising from a deviation from a certain standard of production, that is, a defect occurring in individual, specific goods, which depart from the generality of the products belonging to the same series. The producer can, in abstract terms, prevent such a defect by improving the manufacturing processes or the quality controls on individual items. It will halt the improvement process when the costs of maintaining it exceed the compensation due as a result of the defect. It is with regard to this head of damages that product liability has been created: damages, in other words, that would exist anyway because of the economic calculation made by the producer. The producer is not liable for damages arising out of "defects" due to factors beyond his control, such as natural and unavoidable elements present in raw materials used to manufacture the final product (Stapleton 2002: 1232–4; Izzo 2004: 424).

The US case law concerning primary agricultural products largely confirms this observation. Few courts have been willing to create a sort of absolute liability against the manufacturer, also covering defects which are out of her control. On the contrary, most of them have preferred to avoid venturing into the perils of manufacturing defects, resorting to information defects and/or to the consumer's role in avoiding the damage.[108] This is also one of the reasons why the original version of the European product liability directive (and the current version of the

---

defective primary agricultural products might assume an important role in the future, given the traceability system implemented by Regulation 178/2002.

108   The case law concerning infected oysters has stressed the importance of informing customers of the potential presence of noxious bacteria, at the same time refusing to equate bacteria presence to manufacturing defects. The case law concerning infected meat, on the

Japanese law) exempted primary agricultural products from strict liability: a natural product cannot be considered defective, because there is no human intervention.

What kind of defect would be plaguing BSE-tainted meat? Let us start with the design defects. The first impression is that primary agricultural products are not designed, as such. Therefore, the design defects category could apparently be ruled out. The point seems to be confirmed by comment (b) to § 7 of the third Restatement on product liability, according to which most food does not have a design. This is in part true for meat, since the infective agents called prions have not been "planned" to be present in the final product. But it is possible to advance an alternative interpretation of the design defect category, which takes into account the modern production techniques used in the agricultural sector. As we know, the spread of mad cow disease was due to the practice of feeding cattle on meat and bone meal products (MBMs). The use of MBMs, instead of regular meal, could be viewed as a design choice made by the feed producers, which changed their product's composition in order to improve its nutrient qualities. The change in the design of the feed has introduced a new risk in the food chain which, in turn, has led to the outbreak of BSE/vCJD.[109] From this perspective, feed producers could be held liable for having marketed a product (the MBMs) with a design defect. The kind of liability which could arise is analogous to that of the supplier of (defective) raw materials.[110] The practical feasibility of pinning liability on the feed producer is jeopardized by the same considerations that I have grouped under the "uncertainty problem" label. Indeed, in this case, too, causation, limitation and the development risk defense can hamper the victim's ability to obtain a remedy. Nonetheless, the idea that modern agricultural techniques can be conceived of as design defects opens a new window for the future, allowing the victims to be compensated for the (risky) innovative choices made by the producers.

With regard to information defects, at first glance it is hard to imagine labels warning that the meat we are buying might be contaminated with BSE. Indeed no public authority, anywhere in the world, has taken such a step, preferring to forbid the marketing either of the potentially infected meat or of parts of the animal considered particularly at risk. On the other hand, there are no compelling conceptual reasons to rule out such a category of defects. From a purely legal point of view, if a cattle farmer knew of the risks of contracting vCJD from BSE-tainted beef and marketed it without making consumers aware of them, he could be held

---

other hand, has highlighted, in most of the decisions, the importance of an active role by consumers/restaurants in cooking the food properly.

109　The idea was first suggested me by Umberto Izzo, who makes the point that to feed the cattle with meat and bone meals could be conceived of as a design choice, inserting a new risk factor into the final product (the meat).

110　It might be objected that conceiving of the feed as a raw material with respect to the meat (that is, the final product) could be rash, since the feed is digested and chemically transformed by the animal. But the risks (prions) it presents persist, despite this transformation process.

liable for failure to warn. The practical difficulty in making a manufacturer liable for failure to inform is due more to the peculiarities of information gathering and production in the beef market than to legal hurdles. This point will be explored in the next section, devoted to the economic failures. Moreover, as noted previously, the standard used by the courts for information defects is closer to the negligence paradigm than to a strict liability rule. The protection offered to the consumers would be, thus, less effective than that resulting from the presence of a manufacturing defect.

On the other hand, considering BSE-tainted meat as affected by a manufacturing defect can be conceptually difficult (Stapleton 2003). A manufacturing defect is one arising during some kind of processing. This is not the case with BSE: the prions pre-exist the manufacturing.[111] They infect the meat independently of the conduct of the cattle farmers. It is something analogous to the exemption from liability when the defect was due exclusively to imperfections in the raw material used in the manufacturing and the producers could not detect or eliminate such imperfections. Here the imperfection (the prions) is present in the animal feed used to nourish the cattle. Are the producers of animal feed thus liable for a manufacturing defect? I am inclined to reject such a conclusion. The animal feed producers can invoke the same conceptual hurdles advanced with regard to the beef producers. The contamination of their final product (that is, the animal feed) is due to imperfections present in the raw material used to manufacture it, namely the carcasses of cows and other animals infected with BSE. In such a case, the cattle farmers again become liable, this time as the producers of the raw material. The same kind of reasoning can be repeated again and again, generating an endless circle in which no one is liable. The reasoning is different with regard to design defects, as noted. In this case, the fact of producing feed using the carcasses of dead animals is a design choice which can be attributed uniquely to the feed producers. If it is conceptually hard to imagine a manufacturing defect with regard to these producers as well, the same conceptual difficulties do not arise with regard to design defects.

The conceptual hurdles highlighted so far apparently apply only to the US context, given our reference to the tripartition in manufacturing, design and information defects. Indeed, both the European directive and the Japanese law on product liability do not make any reference to such a distinction. But, beyond the partitions used, the conceptual rationale of these laws is the same as the US product liability regime. From a legal point of view, they are the offspring of that regime and are based on the same conceptual premises. Consequently, it is not problematic to extend the conceptual failures noted with regard to the US system to the other two legal systems.

---

111   This line of reasoning is very close to the one I have used to rule out the slaughterhouses as producers. Also in that case I stated that it is impossible to consider such entities as producers, since the defect in the product pre-exists their conduct.

The Economic Failures of Strict Liability

Closely intertwined with these conceptual premises are also economic justifications in support of strict product liability regimes. The first concerns risk spreading. The basic purpose of any liability system is to shift the costs associated with negative externalities from the victim to the party causing these externalities. In the context of product liability, the negative externality is represented by the damage caused by the defective product: the cost of the damage is transferred from the injured to the producer, through a strict liability rule. The producer has, thus, an incentive to take into account these additional costs as well, considering them as part of the production process. In order to pay for future awards, financial resources will be set aside or, more probably, an insurance policy will be taken out. In both instances, an increase in the product's price will cover the costs associated with these mechanisms. Thus, the risk that the product will cause damages to a person, which is quantified in the insurance premium to be paid, is spread among the consumers.[112]

Problems arise in the context of catastrophic damages. Risk spreading needs an accurate *ex ante* calculation of the probability that a given loss or injury will occur. The insurance premium, as well as the amount of financial resources to be accumulated, is determined by the expected number and amount of awards to be paid. In cases in which uncertainties prevent a forecast of the number and/or the amount of the awards, setting the premium becomes problematic and insurance companies tend not to insure these sectors (Kunreuther, Freeman 2001; Faure 2004b; Kunreuther, Michel-Kerjan 2007; Faure 2007).

In this regard, the BSE/vCJD context serves as a paradigm. The scientific uncertainties surrounding the pathologies have consequences, not only for legal components such as causation and wrongfulness. They also prevent a careful assessment from being conducted, in relation to the potential amount of damages to be paid. Given the long latency period and the impossibility of discovering the presence of infective prions before the death of the contaminated person, the main difficulty concerns the feasibility of predicting the precise number of vCJD cases. The hurdle is analogous to that existing for other types of risk, such as

---

112 In *Escola* v. *Coca Cola Bottling Co. of Fresno*, cit., 462, Justice Traynor noted: "The cost of an injury and the loss of time or health may be an overwhelming misfortune to the person injured, and a needless one, for the risk of injury can be insured by the manufacturer and distributed among the public as a cost of doing business." Fleming (1957) was one of the first authors to underline the ability of strict liability to promote what he calls "loss administration." The early stages in the evolution of products liability have emphasized such a rationale: Prosser 1960: 1120 ff.; Trimarchi 1961. One of the most complete and accurate examinations of the economic justifications for adopting a strict liability rule is in Shavell 1987. For a critical review of the relation between expansion of product liability and availability of insurance, see Epstein 1985.

earthquakes, typhoons, and so on.[113] And, as in such contexts, in the vCJD case too, the risk-spreading function also appears to be in jeopardy.

The second economic justification concerns deterrence. Strict liability is said to have the ability to influence the future behavior of the (potential) defendants by either discouraging them from undertaking too dangerous activities or providing incentives to adopt precautionary measures in order to minimize the risk of damage occurring. The deterrent effect of strict liability is considered greater than that of liability for negligence in cases of so-called unilateral precautions, that is, instances where only one subject can act to prevent the damage (Shavell 1980). Under the deterrence function, producers have an incentive to create research strategies aimed at developing new tools to minimize the chances of damage and/or its effects (Shavell 1992). This goal can be carried out through different means, such as devising new technologies capable of preventing future damage; implementing monitoring systems whose purpose is to uncover possible, unknown side-effects of the products, and producing and/or gathering scientific information which can be used for further scientific developments. An often-cited example concerns pharmaceutical companies which, under the stick of strict product liability, have a strong incentive to invest financial resources in their R&D departments (Pardolesi 2006: 21).

The BSE/vCJD affair seems to fit perfectly in the unilateral precaution category. The consumers cannot play any active role in avoiding the contamination: they have no means of inspecting the meat for prions, proper cooking does not kill the infective agents, and the noxious condition is not determined by the consumers' faulty storage of the meat. The only subject able to influence the existence and extent of the contamination risk appears to be the producer. On the other hand, attention should be paid to the peculiarities of the cattle industry. In this sector, economic power is concentrated at the slaughterhouse and processing plant levels, while the cattle farmers' world is more dispersed and fragmented.[114] This dispersion implies a detrimental effect on the deterrent strength of a strict liability rule. Only big industries have the economic resources not only to finance R&D departments, but also to set them up. For small and medium firms, it would simply not be feasible to commit resources in order to maintain the same course. Indeed, what usually happens is that these firms rely on third parties for both gathering scientific information and developing risk abatement technologies. Things are different with regard to feed producers. Here the size of the firms allows them

---

113   Kunreuther, Michel-Kerjan (2007) make some proposals to mitigate the insurability problem of catastrophic damages, developing economic models to determine the capital needed by insurers to fund unpredictable losses and claiming for a more proactive role of the government as reinsurer.

114   Pittman (2005: 6) observes that most cattle farmers operate on a small-scale basis. Roberts, O'Brien (2004: 4) note that cattle farmers cannot be considered as having deep pockets, since they have limited financial resources.

to invest resources in the R&D sector: therefore, strict liability can determine the deterrent effect mentioned.

There is also an additional aspect of the problem. Unlike industries traditionally and heavily involved in science and technology, cattle farmers conceive of their activity as being determined by nature rather than science. In other words, the pharmaceutical industry and the cattle industry, for example, have two different mindsets: the latter is not institutionally, so to speak, as attentive to scientific problems as the former. The problem then, is not only economic, but involves the entrepreneurial culture of different industry sectors. The point seems to be contradicted by the fact that modern agriculture relies heavily on technology, such as biotechnology or the production of animal feed itself: questions could be raised as to why the same mindset we note in the pharmaceutical sector is not present in the agricultural one. Beyond commenting that agriculture is conceived of as a natural activity, two further arguments can be advanced. First, the situation is changing, especially at the processing level. A new mentality, more attentive to the role of technology in guaranteeing food safety, is developing: the very adoption of the HACCP system testifies to improved sensitivity to these themes. The second comment concerns the separation between different industries in the agricultural sector. While the typical pharmaceutical firm represents a unit with regard to the design, production and marketing of a drug, the situation is much more fragmented in the field we are dealing with. The BSE crisis illustrates the point well. Here the production chain is represented by: 1) the firms producing the animal feed, 2) the cattle farmers, and 3) the meat packing industries. Each industry represents a unit, uncoordinated with the others. Such fragmentation brings with it a division in responsibilities: the "others" are the ones who should be paying attention to science and technology. One of the reasons for the different mindsets, then, could be due to the idea that other "units" have to care about the side effects in using technology in food production.

Due to the set of problems underlined so far, the deterrent ability of a strict liability system seems severely undermined in the vCJD context, at least with regard to the cattle farmers. The fragmented and multi-layered nature of the food industry forms a barrier to advocating the economic rationale successfully used in other production areas. In addition, the risk-spreading rationale is weak as well, as noted. The conclusion is quite clear: the adoption of strict liability with regard to primary agricultural products does not appear to be a satisfactory choice. The conceptual and economic failures point to an operational rule close to the negligence paradigm; in this sense, the solutions implemented in Japan and the US for unprocessed agricultural products are preferable. Again, a distinction must be made with regard to the liability of the feed producers. The conceptual and economic failures appear to be less convincing when applied to this industry. The strict liability rationale could actually be the incentive for feed producers to invest resources in risk-abating technologies; at the same time, the defect contaminating the feed can be conceptually conceived of as a design defect.

On the other hand, the legal hurdles highlighted before bring the entire tort system more radically into question. The problems of causation and wrongfulness touch any liability system, whether strict or negligence-based. It is the tort system as such that is failing. To be clear, such problems concern individual liability, that is, the responsibility of the individual person or entity toward the victim. An alternative path for vCJD victims could be represented by claiming that the government is liable for failure to act. The next section will be dedicated to the analysis of this different solution.

Tort Law and the Role of the Government

The preceding analysis highlighted some points worthy of further exploration. The fragmented nature of the cattle industry, the difficulty it has in producing and/or gathering information, the many uncertainties, both scientific and legal, surrounding diseases such as BSE/vCJD, create havoc for a liability model centered on the individual level. At this point, any legal system faces two possible alternatives. The first is to let the loss lie where it falls, that is, on the victim's shoulders. The second solution seeks to ascertain whether the government had a duty to intervene to protect public health and if it breached such a duty (van Boom, Pinna 2005). As we will see, there is also a third option, whose nature is in some way ambiguous with regard to the liability problem: that of the so-called "no-fault" compensation plans.

Government Liability for Failure to Act

Let us start off the analysis by considering the existence of a duty by the government to protect citizens. To be clear, the question is not whether the government has a duty to protect public health: obviously it has. Indeed, the question concerns the extent of the duty. How far does a duty to act, which lies on a public agency, a department, or a ministry, and so on, have to go, in order to protect the health of citizens? The problem concerns the degree to which courts can review whether or not the government performed such a duty correctly. The point is closely intertwined with historical considerations regarding the room for discretion to be attributed to public bodies operating their own functions: the wider the discretion conceded to the government, the narrower the margins of its liability.

The American Experience

US law protects the discretionary actions of public bodies closely. Up to the first half of the last century, the American courts applied the common law principle of sovereign immunity; consequently, the government had the benefit of total protection from any kind of tortious liability. Despite its historical origin, connected to the person of the King,[115] the justifications used by American courts and legal scholars for the existence of the immunity were founded not on conceptual theories, but on practical matters, such as the necessity to allow the performance of public duties without the threat of possible suits (Street 1948: 342–3). The practical angle from which sovereign immunity was observed and applied in the US was destined to have important consequences on the following stage of its evolution. In 1946, Congress passed the Federal Tort Claims Act, creating a general cause of action for tort liability against the government.[116] According to the new law, the United States would be subject to tort liability in the same way as any other private individual;[117] the provision seemed to put an end to the deployment of sovereign immunity in the US. But § 2680 provides for an array of exceptions limiting the applicability of such cause of action. The most notable is under letter (a): the so-called "discretionary function" exception. According to this, private individuals cannot bring a suit against the government when the action alleges a failure to perform a discretionary function or duty by a federal agency or any other governmental body.[118] The practical reasons which made sovereign immunity acceptable to American courts now provide the foundation for the discretionary function exception. The rule has thus been justified on several grounds: to respect the constitutional principle of separation of powers; to avoid the huge costs that a limitless cause of action would entail for the government; to permit the regulation of the private sector by the state without the threat of lawsuits (Goldman 1992: 852 ff.). State legislation has adopted the model set in the 1946 federal act, permitting a general action in tort against the states but, at the same time, providing for the discretionary function exception.

---

115   The principle of sovereign immunity originates in the idea by which "the King can do no wrong." Such an idea "had its roots in feudalism. Just as no lord could be sued in the court which he held to try the cases of his tenants, so the king, at the apex of the feudal system, could not be sued in the royal courts" (Street 1948: 341). Later, the principle was reinforced by the theories of absolute power associated with the state (Borchard 1926). A different view, rejecting the idea that the principle of sovereign immunity originated by the *dictum* "the King can do no wrong," is expressed by Jaffe 1963.

116   28 U.S.C. §§ 2671–80. On the legislative history of the Act, see Street 1948 (344–6).

117   28 U.S.C. § 2674: "The United States shall be liable, respecting the provisions of this title relating to tort claims, in the same manner and to the same extent as a private individual under like circumstances, but shall not be liable for interest prior to judgment or for punitive damages." 28 U.S.C. § 1346(b) provides that only federal district courts have jurisdiction in deciding tort claims brought against the government.

118   28 U.S.C. § 2680: "The provisions of this chapter and § 1346(b) of this title shall not apply to: (a) Any claim based upon an act or omission of an employee of the Government, exercising due care, in the execution of a statute or regulation, whether or not such statute or regulation be valid, or based upon the exercise or performance or the failure to exercise or perform a discretionary function or duty on the part of a federal agency or an employee of the Government, whether or not the discretion involved be abused."

Shortly after the enactment of the Federal Tort Claims Act, the Supreme Court had a chance to express its view on the interpretation of the discretionary function exception (Kaminiski 1952; Zillman 1995; Seamon 1997). In 1953, the court decided the case of *Dalehite* v. *United States*, which concerned the explosion of a deposit of ammonium nitrate located in the small town of Texas City.[119] The disaster caused the loss of many lives and a vast amount of damage to property: 8,500 plaintiffs claimed compensation from the federal government, which managed the deposit (Zillman 1995: 368). The Supreme Court stated that the government could not be found liable because its choices with regard to the location and the maintenance of the ammonium nitrate deposit were based on a policy judgment, as such protected by the discretionary function exception.

An important evolution in the interpretation of the exception occurred in 1988, with the Supreme Court decision *Berkovitz* v. *United States*.[120] The plaintiffs alleged that the negligent conduct of the Food and Drug Administration in licensing a polio vaccine was related to the onset of polio in their child, who had ingested the vaccine. The court introduced a two-step test to evaluate if the discretionary function exception was applicable to the case. First, the judges must assess whether the conduct was discretionary or not: conduct cannot be discretionary if that course of action is imposed by law, regulation, or other agency prescription. In the case that the conduct is discretionary, the second limb of the test must be verified. In such a case, the judges must assess whether the conduct involves the kind of discretion that was intended to be protected through the exception (Seamon 1997: 703–705). This is the case when the choices made by the governmental body are based on public policy considerations, such as balancing safety concerns with budgetary issues. In *Berkovitz*, the court focused mainly on the first part of the test, ruling that the discretionary function exception covers the choice of the criteria used to test the vaccine's safety, but if such criteria, once set, were violated, then the exception would not operate.

Three years later, in 1991, the Supreme Court gave a judgment clarifying the second limb of the test set out in *Berkovitz*.[121] According to the judges in *Gaubert*, the reasons behind the granting of discretion to a governmental body must be compared to the (discretionary) action taken by such a body. If the action is

---

119   *Dalehite* v. *United States*, 346 U.S. 15 (1953). In a case decided by the US District Court of Minnesota, the judge dismissed an action brought against the FDA by the heirs of a person who died as the result of an adverse reaction to a drug approved as safe by the Agency. The decision established that the decision of the FDA to approve the introduction of a drug in interstate commerce is covered by the discretionary function exception: *Gelley* v. *Astra Pharm. Prods. Inc.*, 466 F. Supp. 182 (Minn. D. Ct. 1979). See also *Forsyth* v. *Eli Lilly & Co.*, 904 F. Supp. 1153 (Haw. D. Ct. 1995); *Wells* v. *United States*, 851 F. 2d 1471 (Ct. App. Columbia 1988).

120   *Berkovitz* v. *United States*, 486 U.S. 531 (1988). *Berkovitz* was preceded by another Supreme Court decision, *United States* v. *S.A. Empresa de Viacao Aerea Rio Grande (Varig Airlines)*, 467 U.S. 797 (1984).

121   *United States* v. *Gaubert*, 499 U.S. 315 (1991).

justified in the light of the reasons given (expressly or implicitly) in the statute, then the discretionary function exception can shield the government from liability in tort.[122]

The cases mentioned previously with regard to the liability of American (local) authorities for the failure to warn the citizens of the risks arising from the consumption of raw oysters match with the analysis of the discretionary function exception outlined so far. Thus, courts have refused to hold states liable in cases where they decided to release no warning or only limited warnings. The judges have stated that such decisions were grounded on policy considerations and were covered by the discretionary function exception.[123] On the contrary, tribunals have found states liable when they failed to enforce existing regulations; this is the case, for example, when local inspectors did not check that the restaurants had displayed the warnings required by the regulation.[124] Here no discretionary action can be ascertained on behalf of the public authority. The discretionary power has been already exhausted with the enactment of the regulation: the government has the duty to guarantee the enforcement of the law, without any room for policy considerations.

The European Legal Systems

With regard to Europe, the discussion must differentiate between the British and the continental legal systems (Fairgrieve 2003). Britain started its legal evolution from an almost identical point as the American one. Indeed, the doctrine of sovereign immunity originated in this country and was then adopted in the US: we might, therefore, still expect the principle to be widely represented in current British case law. But an event occurred, parallel to the American Federal Tort Claims Act, to differentiate the paths followed by the two legal systems. In 1947, the Crown Proceedings Act was passed, providing that the Crown is subject to tort liability just as any other private individual.[125] The element of differentiation relates to the

---

122 Criticisms of the current interpretation of the discretionary function exception have been raised by Goldman 1992 and Hackman 1997. The authors point to the fact the exception (§ 2680(a)) has swallowed the rule (§ 2674) and that the test used by the courts is too confused.

123 It should be kept in mind that the discretionary function exception here is provided in state legislation. As we have noted before, however, state legislation has transposed the norms contained in the Federal Tort Claims Act into the local codes, included the discretionary function exception. For the case law, see *Simeon* v. *Doe*, 602 So.2d 77, cit.; *Simeon* v. *Doe*, 618 So.2d 848, cit. On the similar problem concerning the duty of the Environmental Protection Agency to warn about environmental hazards, see Jarvis 1993.

124 See *Gregor* v. *Argenot Great Central Insurance Company*, cit.

125 Crown Proceedings Act § 2: "Subject to this Act, (a) proceeding against the government by way of petition of right is abolished, (b) a claim against the government that, if this Act had not been passed, might be enforced by petition of right, subject to the grant of a fiat by the Lieutenant Governor, may be enforced as of right of proceeding against

discretionary function exception, present in the American statute but not in the British one (Street 1948: 353). The waiver of sovereign immunity thus seems more comprehensive in Britain than in the US, where traces of the old principle can be found in § 2680(a). The case law apparently confirms such an impression (Caranta 1992; Lazari 2005: 1 ff.). The British courts appear to have been more generous than their American counterparts in allowing tort claims against the government. According to British case law, the fact that the law attributes discretionary powers to a public body does not mean that such a body is exempted from any liability.[126] In the case *X* v. *Bedfordshire*,[127] the judges have

> ... identified three possible causes of action which might avail a plaintiff in a case against a public body. These were an action for breach of statutory duty *simpliciter*, without the need to prove any carelessness; an action for breach of a common law duty of care arising from the imposition of a statutory duty or from its performance; and misfeasance in a public office. (Craig 2003: 881; Nolan 2007: 887)

Our enquiry is focused on the second cause of action, that is, that centered on the breach of a statutory duty which requires proof of negligence.

The general declaration according to which public bodies are subject to liability is limited by the same decisions which offer it.[128] The courts state that not any form of negligence can determine the government's liability, but only the one consisting in the unreasonable exercise of discretionary powers (Craig 2003: 889). In particular, the courts refuse to assess what they call the policy area of the government's conduct, that is, the choices founded on policy decisions; on the contrary, a negligent action within the so-called "operational area" can determine whether the government is liable (Arrowsmith 1992: 170 ff.).[129] The difference with respect to the American solution is that, in the latter, even some operational decisions, if based on policy considerations, can successfully trigger the discretionary function defense: this does not seem to be the case in Britain. In addition, the most recent evolutions of British case law have also introduced some distinctions in connection with the policy area.

---

the government in accordance with this Act, without the grant of a fiat by the Lieutenant Governor, (c) the government is subject to all the liabilities to which it would be liable if it were a person, and (d) the law related to indemnity and contribution is enforceable by and against the government for any liability to which it is subject, as if the government were a person."

126   *Home Office* v. *Dorset Yacht Co. Ltd* [1970] 2 All ER 294; *Anns and others* v. *London Borough of Merton* [1977] 2 All ER 492.

127   *X (Minors)* v. *Bedfordshire County Council* [1995] 2 AC 633

128   Fairgrieve (2003: 64 ff.) notes that in the recent years a new approach to state liability has begun, with less frequent recourse to policy considerations to shield the government from liability.

129   *Anns and others* v. *London Borough of Merton*, cit.

Following a different path, a recent line of authority leaves the possibility open to find public bodies liable in tort only in cases where the duties imposed upon them are structured in such a way to create a private law right of action on behalf of an individual (Bailey 2006: 172–3). But, if such a private right does not exist, it is not possible to imagine a parallel duty of care at common law which, if breached, can give rise to liability.[130] This seems to be the case when the public law duty is framed in broad terms: here, indeed, it is difficult to imagine a private right to sue, given the wide words used by the draftsperson. These cases prefer to use the contraposition between justiciable/non-justiciable decisions instead of the distinction between policy and operational areas (Craig 2003: 897; Nolan 2007: 892–3). Some of the decisions falling within the policy area can result in the liability of the public bodies. Exempted from liability are only those discretionary decisions which are related to matters which courts are not suited to assess given their nature, or for which Parliament has excluded the possibility of a review by the judges: in other words, decisions which are justiciable (Bailey 2006: 169; Craig 2003: 891–2; Nolan 2007: 891–2).

Unlike the common law experience, the civil law systems have more frequently held the government liable in tort. This is the case for Italy. Traditionally, Italy had a similar principle to sovereign immunity, under which a public body could not be found liable in tort. But in the decades preceding the enactment of the 1948 Constitution, the situation was evolving and judges began to hold the government liable with regard to actions which were not the manifestation of a public power (Caranta 1993: 44 ff.; Follieri 2004).[131] A crucial evolution occurred in the 1990s, when the courts began to find governmental bodies liable for having failed to exercise careful control over activities subject to their supervision.[132]

---

130   *Gorringe* v. *Calderdale* [2004] 2 All ER 326. The Gorringe decision has been preceded by an array of cases that, even if departing from the policy-operational distinction, have nonetheless adopted different *rationes decidendi* (Bailey 2006): see *Phelps* v. *London Borough of Hillingdon* [2000] 4 All ER 504; *Barrett* v. *Enfield London Borough Council* [1999] 3 All ER 193; *Capital and Counties plc* v. *Hampshire County Council* [1997] 2 All ER 865; *Stovin* v. *Wise* [1996] 3 All ER 801.

131   The subject of government liability has been traditionally intertwined with the issue of compensation for the infringement of the so-called *interessi legittimi*, a legal phenomena protecting the interests of the citizen in relation to the correct action by the public authorities. The seminal decision by the Italian Corte di Cassazione, allowing compensation with respect to the *interessi legittimi* for the first time, was Cass., sez. un., July 22, 1999, no. 500. *Foro Italiano* 1999, 9, I, 2487, with commentary by Palmieri and Pardolesi.

132   An important recent line of decisions has concerned the liability of public bodies for having failed to carefully check the information provided by professional operators in cases of financial investments and stock exchanges: Cass. civ., sez. un., July 27, 1998, n. 7339. *Foro Italiano* 1999, 6, I, 2001, with comments by Palmieri and Cipriani; Cass. civ. March 3, 2001, n. 3132. *Foro Italiano* 2001, 4, I, 1139. For an analysis of the case law, see Palmieri 2001; Pesce 2005; della Cananea, Sandulli 2005; Scognamiglio 2006. In 2006,

Even if Italian judges are more generous than the American courts in compensating their citizens for wrongful actions of the government, it would be erroneous to believe that the tribunals check intrusively into the soundness of the discretionary choices made by the public bodies. In particular, there is a continuous struggle between the opposing needs to check the use of power by the government and to protect the sphere of discretion connatural to it. In this sense, even in the cases in which the courts intrude in the way public bodies exercised their power, they seem to be reluctant to interfere with their actions extensively. The operational rule emerging from the analysis of these decisions resembles the British approach. Although there is no formal distinction between policy area and operational area,[133] the Italian judges appear to hold the government liable mainly in cases in which it omitted to take positive steps to enforce an already existing and binding law, regulation, and so on.[134] On the contrary, they seem to refuse to consider the public authority responsible when its choices relate to pure discretionary policy considerations.[135] This means that, as is the case in Britain and as distinct from the American experience, discretionary choices connected to the way a law or regulation is enforced can determine the liability in tort of a public body.

Government liability in France has evolved in a particular way (Moreau 1986; Caranta 1993: 123 ff.; Flogaitis 2002; Le Tourneau 2004; Lazari 2005: 87 ff.; Rivero, Waline 2006: 403 ff.). This is mainly due to the fact that, while this area of

---

the Italian lawmakers introduced a special liability regime for public bodies performing functions of control in the financial sector: art. 4, third paragraph, letter *d)*, of the *Decreto Legislativo* December 29, 2006, no. 303, provides that such bodies are liable only in cases of malice or gross negligence (Carriero 2008).

133   In the early stages of the evolution of governmental liability, the distinction between policy and operational actions was known, although in subsequent years it has been abandoned (Caranta 1993: 10 ff.).

134   The liability of public bodies for misleading financial reports supplied to the public fits into this description. Here, liability arises because the public body omitted to control the completeness and veracity of the report, a duty imposed by law. Courts hold public bodies liable only in cases where they violated a specific duty imposed by a specific law; in the abovementioned example, the duty to check the veracity of every single financial report destined for the public.

135   The Tribunale of Napoli, for example, has refused to hold the Italian Minister of Health liable for having failed to enact regulations aimed at preventing the consumption of tobacco, stating that the choice whether to regulate a particular sector is a discretionary one, which cannot implicate any liability for the government: Trib. Napoli December 15, 2004. *Danno e Responsabilità* 2005, 6, 641, with comments by D'Antonio and Giacchero. See also Trib. Venezia June 6, 2008. *Danno e Responsabilità* 2009, 1, 82, with commentary by Lazari. It could be argued that a duty of protecting public health exists also with regard to the Minister of Health: liability could thus arise from proof that that the Minister has failed to fulfill it. The fact is that the duty to protect public health is a generic one, too vague to constitute the basis for a finding of liability against the government.

the law is normally within the ambit of the *juridiction de droit commun*, in France it has been attributed to the *juridiction administrative*.[136] But, despite the use of a different phraseology, the operational rules applied run parallel to the ones we have already seen with regard to Britain and Italy. At the initial stage of evolution, public bodies were completely shielded from any liability in tort (Lazari 2005: 94 ff.; Rivero, Waline 2006: 405 ff.). Starting from the second half of the nineteenth century, echoes of the initial solution can be traced in the dichotomy between actions of discretional administration and enforcement acts: only with regard to the latter could liability be founded. Although formally the distinction has now been abandoned, the rule by which the government is not liable for acts of so-called "high administration" (that is, policy choices) still holds (Caranta 1993: 139–40). What has changed is the liability of the public authority for the negligent control it exercised (or failed to exercise) over an activity which it had the duty to supervise. An array of decisions affirms the liability of the government in such instances.[137] But the same decisions introduce a limitation on liability. Public bodies are deemed to be liable only in cases of gross negligence (*faute lourde*), that is, cases in which the negligence was of exceptional importance (Caranta 1993: 224 ff.; Le Tourneau 2004: 121 ff.; Fairgrieve 2003: 106 ff.).[138] Courts tend to apply the gross negligence standard to cases in which the activity of the public body is particularly difficult, taking into account, for example, the complexity or the extent of such activity.[139]

French law has seen recent developments which seem to have opened up new space for affirming the liability of the state for failure to act (van Boom,

---

136 The leading cases are the decision *Blanco*, Tribunal des conflits, February 8, 1873, at <http://www.legifrance.gouv.fr/WAspad/UnDocument?base=JADE&nod=JCX8X 1873X02X0000000012>, and the decision *Pelletier*, Tribunal des conflits, July 30, 1873, at <http://www.legifrance.gouv.fr/WAspad/UnDocument?base=JADE&nod=JCX8X1873 X07X0000000035>.

137 The leading case is Conseil d'État March 29, 1946, at <http://www.legifrance. gouv.fr/affichJuriAdmin.do?idTexte=CETATEXT000007636299&dateTexte=>. See also Conseil d'État June 28, 1963. *Recueil Dalloz* 1963, 411; Conseil d'État February 14, 1973. *Recueil Dalloz* 1973, 141.

138 Conseil d'État, January 24, 1964. *Actualité Juridique. Droit Administratif* 1964, 187; Conseil d'État December 29, 1978. *Recueil Dalloz* 1978, 542; Cour administrative d'appel Paris, October 17, 1991. *Actualité Juridique. Droit Administratif* 1992, 171; Conseil d'État, November 30, 2001. *Revue Francaise de Droit Administratif* 2002.742. Rivero, Waline (2006: 429-430) and Le Tourneau (2004: 127), after having noted that the gross negligence standard is usually applied by administrative judges, report the so-called "*affaire du sang contaminé*," in which the court holds the government liable applying the normal negligence paradigm. As we will see, the different standard used in this context could have been determined by the fact that the government is in an ambiguous position with regard to the distribution of blood products, since it has a monopoly on it.

139 See, for example, Cour administrative d'appel Paris, December 19, 1995. *Recueil Dalloz* CE 1995, 671.

Pinna 2005: 9 ff.). In 2004, the *Conseil d'État* held the French government liable for having failed to protect the workers from the risks of exposure to asbestos.[140] In particular, the court stated that the government did not take prompt precautionary measures to protect the workers and that, therefore, it breached its duty of vigilance with regard to health and safety risks (van Boom, Pinna 2005: 12). This decision could mark a new path, increasing the chances of the victims of health risks to recover from the state, even if it is too early to speak of a jurisprudential *revirement* in the field.

A further area requiring some analysis concerns the liability of the European Union. As noted, the European institutions have played a pivotal role in the management of the public health emergency and many of the scandals associated with the mad cow crisis directly concern such institutions. Thus it is necessary to explore whether the European Communities can be found liable for having failed to exercise proper care in dealing with this new epidemic.

The European Union forms an autonomous legal system with respect to those of the member states: it has its own legal rules, concerning, among other things, tort liability as well. The treaties instituting the Community have specific norms providing for the liability of the European institutions. Nonetheless, given their generic formulation, these norms constitute a thin basis. It is not surprising, therefore, that the Community system of tort liability has evolved out of the decisions given by the European Court of Justice, which can be considered its ultimate creator. On the other hand, the Court of Justice has drawn inspiration for its creative process from the systems of the member states (Caranta 1993: 307 ff.). This is why the operational rules applied to cases of liability for omitted or negligent control closely resemble the solutions implemented in France (Caranta 1993: 331 ff.). The European Union can be judged liable only if the failure to perform the duties of supervision imposed by law consisted in gross negligence, also taking into account the complexity and discretion inherent in such duties (Gattinara 2005: 114; Lazari 2005: 251 ff.; Poto 2007).[141] But the Court adds a new element, making it more difficult to recover compensation for the damages suffered. The plaintiffs must prove, in fact, that the performance of the duties of supervision would have prevented the loss.[142] The burden of proof becomes very strict, barring most of the potential claims from recovery.

---

140   Conseil d'État, March 3, 2004. *Responsabilité Civile et Assurances* 2004, 234, with commentary by Guettier.

141   With regard to the case law embracing such principle, see Court of Justice, July 4, 2000 (C-352/98). *European Court Reports* 2000, I-5291; Court of Justice, July 10, 2003 (C-472-00). *European Court Reports* 2003, I-7541; Court of Justice, April 19, 2007 (C-282/05). *European Court Reports* 2007, I-1347; Court of First Instance, July 21, 2007 (T-351/03). *European Court Reports* 2007, II-2237.

142   Court of Justice, January 30, 1992 (C-363/88 and C-364/88). *European Court Reports* 1992, I-359. Along the same lines, a decision which rejected a claim by a group of cattle farmers asserting that the lack of intervention by the Community institutions during the

In 1994, the European Court of Justice was called upon to judge a case in which, *inter alia*, a request for compensation was advanced against the Commission for having failed to act promptly with regard to the enactment of rules concerning the radioactive contamination of foodstuffs.[143] Indeed, in the wake of the Chernobyl catastrophe, the Commission had delayed thirteen months between the Council's request to propose rules to deal with radioactive contamination of foodstuffs and the proposal of such rules. The Court refused to hold the Commission liable since, given the discretion it enjoys and the uncertainties surrounding the permissible levels of radioactive contamination in foodstuffs, the elapse of a thirteen-month period cannot be deemed unreasonable.[144]

The Court of First Instance has decided two cases concerning the liability of the European Union for having omitted to intervene to curb the spread of BSE.[145] In both lawsuits, the plaintiffs claimed that the lack of a prompt and radical intervention by the European institutions to prevent the spread of mad cow disease was at the origin of the financial losses suffered by the meat sector in the years following 1996. The judges rejected the compensation claims, noting that the plaintiffs had not proved the causal link between the failure to intervene and the damages suffered.[146]

The Japanese Case

With regard to Japan, it was only after the end of World War II that the idea that the government could be liable in tort emerged: before that time, public bodies could not be sued to recover tortious damages (Uga 1999).[147] In fact, Art. 17 of

---

mad cow crisis had provoked the dramatic fall in value of beef. The Court of First Instance refused to hold the European institutions liable, stating that the plaintiffs had not proved the causal link between the failure to intervene and the loss suffered: Court of First Instance, September 30, 1998 (T-149/96). *European Court Reports* 1998, II-3841 (Ambrosoli 2000). In both decisions, the impossibility of proving that, had the supervisory role been carried out, the damages would not have occurred, prevents any claim for compensation.

143 Court of Justice, September 15, 1994 (C-146/91). *European Court Reports* 1994, I-4199.

144 Court of Justice, September 15, 1994 (C-146/91), cit., paragraphs 76–8. In a case concerning wine, the Court of Justice refused to hold the Commission liable for having failed to enact proper regulations capable of preventing the marketing of adulterated wine: Court of Justice, July 4, 1989 (C-326/86 – 66/88). *European Court Reports* 1989, 2087.

145 Court of First Instance, September 30, 1998 (T-149/96). *European Court Reports* 1998, II-3841; Court of First Instance, December 13, 2006 (T-304/01). *European Court Reports* 2006, II-4857.

146 Court of First Instance, September 30, 1998, cit., points 116–18; Court of First Instance, December 13, 2006, cit., points 131 and 137.

147 The impossibility of suing the government when seeking tort damages was based on the strict division between public and private law. As the government was involved, public law had to be applied; moreover, only administrative courts had jurisdiction when

the 1947 Constitution states that any private citizen can seek compensation from the state for the illegal acts it carried out. The 1947 State Reparation Law has implemented this provision, establishing specific norms regulating procedures and limitation on the government's responsibility. Consequently, nowadays the State Reparation Law is the reference point for any tort claim brought against a public body, including claims concerning the omission to perform control duties imposed by law.

As has emerged in describing the case law relating to product liability, the plaintiffs have frequently chosen to sue the government as defendant, along with the manufacturers. The legal basis for such a strategy is the failure by the public authority to perform the careful checks required by law on the production activities which gave rise to the damages.[148] The rule created by the courts occasionally seems to go beyond the solutions described with regard to Europe. Not only does the failure to dedicate resources – as well as failing to create infrastructures and procedures for fulfilling a duty imposed by a specific law – constitute a valid basis to hold the government liable in tort; courts have also held the state liable in cases in which it failed to exercise its regulatory authority.[149] The case law is not clear on this last point, since there are also decisions refusing to hold public bodies liable in such circumstances.[150] Also, the cases concerning foodstuffs appear not to have taken a clear approach, sometimes establishing the liability of the government, sometimes negating it.

Moving to a general, comparative picture, the cases in which a public body has been held liable for the damages caused by the administration of HIV-tainted blood deserve particular mention.[151] These decisions apparently state that the government is liable if it fails to take preventive measures to minimize the risks associated with the blood. Adapting such reasoning to the BSE context, we might think that governments could be held liable for not having adopted the measures

---

a public body was party to a judicial proceeding. On the other hand, the pre-war law regulating administrative courts provided that these could not hear cases in which damages were sought against the government.

148   The choice of suing the government is a common feature with regard not only to the case law concerning foodstuffs, but more in general to all product liability cases (at least up to the enactment of the recent product liability law). For example, the cases concerning pharmaceutical products have seen the government involved as a defendant as well (Ottley, Ottley 1984).

149   See the Kumamoto Minamata Disease Case, cited in Uga 1999: 197.

150   See the Kyoto Minamata Disease Case, cited in Uga 1999: 198.

151   In England, see *A and others* v. *National Blood Authority and another* [2001] 3 All ER 289: for a comment Howells, Mildred 2002; in France Cass. 1er civ. April 12, 1995. *Juris classeur periodiques* 1995, II, 22467, with comment by Jourdain and Conseil d'État May 26, 1995. *Juris classeur periodiques* 1995, II, 22468, with comment by Moreau; in Italy Trib. Roma November 27, 1998. *Danno e responsabilità* 1999, 214 (Izzo 1999). On the HIV litigation in Japan and the settlements which brought it to an end, see Feldman 1999.

capable of reducing the spread of mad cow disease. But such a conclusion may be hurried. The element distinguishing the HIV-tainted blood case from the BSE epidemic is that in the former case, the public authorities have a monopoly on the collection of donated blood.[152] They were not only the body controlling the blood donation system, but also the ones managing it. This fact puts them in a different position with respect to the authorities responsible for meat inspection. Simply extending the solutions tried in one case to the other would mean overlooking this difference, since the degree of intrusion and control of public bodies in the food industry is inferior to that in the blood sector.[153]

We may now investigate the chances of success that an action would have, if brought against a public body for having failed to act during the BSE crisis. In the US, the possibilities would be close to zero. The discretionary function exception forms a formidable barrier to overcome, rigorously protecting public bodies from any intrusion into their discretionary choices. The protection provided by the exception is particularly wide, covering not only high-profile political choices, but ordinary ones as well. Only when an action is specifically dictated by law, some residual room for liability seems to exist. But this does not appear to be the case for BSE. The potential liability would precisely involve the choice to adopt laws mandating specific actions for dealing with BSE: a domain beyond the range of potential liability for American public bodies.

European countries seem to rely on the operational distinction between acts of high administration (or purely discretionary ones) and acts that, in implementing the former, maintain a limited space for discretion. Only with regard to the latter it is possible to imagine the government as liable. But most of the decisions taken in the BSE context can be considered purely discretionary. Indeed, they concern an emergency situation, where the elements of uncertainty outweighed other considerations; given these uncertainties, it was necessary for the national governments and the European Union to make choices as to how to use the (limited) resources available to tackle this potential crisis. It is obvious that deciding to deploy funds in this context would have meant subtracting the same funds from other areas of potential danger. The assessment of all these elements renders the choices made by the public bodies as ones of high administration: consequently, under the current legal regime in Europe, it is very hard to make the governments responsible for their decisions (or omissions).[154] A broader space for liability

---

152   For a comparison of the institutional setting characterizing the blood systems in US, France and Italy, see Izzo 2004.

153   On the other hand, it cannot be denied that the food industry is one of the most heavily regulated sectors in modern economies. In this sense, food and blood sectors are closer than other areas of production.

154   Van Boom, Pinna (2005: 7) concludes that: "If we reflect on how European legal systems deal with regulators' liability, the overall picture is one of utmost restraint." The same authors seem to think there are more possibilities with regard to the French system, taking into account the new decisions enacted by the Conseil d'État in 2004.

could exist in the case of Japan. Here, as noted, there have been successful cases with public bodies found liable for having failed to use their regulatory powers, also in highly discretionary contexts. If this is the case, then liability could be imposed on the Japanese government if the courts considered its regulatory action insufficient.

No-Fault Compensation Plans

There exists an alternative solution to the tortious liability of the government, which to some extent mirrors the other, namely the creation of no-fault compensation plans (Ponzanelli 1992: 101 ff.). These plans are usually set up either to tackle cases arising out of public health emergencies, or to address the fact that negative consequences associated with particular activities are unavoidable. An example of the first situation is the no-fault compensation plan provided for the victims contaminated with HIV-tainted blood (Feldman 1999: 68; Pontier 1992). The diffusion of the disease was, at least initially, largely unpredictable and created a situation of public crisis. In order to offer some relief to the victims of this new and unforeseeable disease, many countries have created indemnification plans. With regard to the second case, a good example is offered by the compensation programs set for vaccine-related injuries (Mariner 1986). Here, the possibility of health problems arising from the inoculation of the vaccine is foreseeable: yet the problems are, to a certain degree, unavoidable. Since the vaccination programs are considered particularly important for the protection of public health, but entail risks which cannot be evaded, many legal systems have deemed it equitable to compensate those who become the victims of the injury.

The advantages of these plans, if compared to tort law, relate to two main areas (Sugarman 1985; McEwin 2000; Liao, White 2002; Cohen, Dehejia 2004; Faure 2004a). First, they can benefit the potential plaintiffs by making their position easier. As we have seen in the BSE context, many legal hurdles can prevent the victims from obtaining reparation: proof of negligence, applicability of the concept of defect, causation, state-of-the-art defense, and so on. Compensation plans are able to circumvent many of these barriers. They are often the means of expressing the political will to provide relief to a specific group of victims, regardless of the complex legal problems surrounding their cases. The vCJD cases could provide a nearly perfect test in this sense. I have expressed many doubts on the possibility for a potential plaintiff to succeed in an action brought against either the manufacturers or the government. Despite the lack of legal arguments to support such an action, the political and moral responsibilities which emerged during the BSE scandal, coupled with the pressure from society requiring a prompt response, could persuade the authorities to adopt schemes for indemnifying the vCJD victims.

The second group of advantages concerns the costs of managing a no-fault compensation plan. Especially in cases where the litigation is complex and requires considerable financial resources and time, compensation schemes allow part of the costs to be cut by simplifying the procedures for obtaining payment for the damages suffered. If the litigated cases are repetitive, all presenting similar features, it might be more convenient to set up an administrative framework within which criteria for indemnification are defined.[155] In this case, too, the rationale behind the no-fault schemes fits the BSE case perfectly. There is no doubt that prospective litigation would not only be uncertain with regard to the results, but also expensive and time-consuming. On the other hand, the circumstances and problems characterizing it would be almost the same in all the cases. These characteristics would allow the adoption of an administrative framework tailored to the specific features of the BSE cases.

Also with regard to the adoption of no-fault compensation schemes, the US stands in a different position compared to the experiences of Britain, France, Italy and Japan. This finding is not surprising in the light of the analysis conducted in the preceding pages on the liability of public bodies. Compensation schemes can be considered, to some extent at least, as the other side of the coin of government liability. Systems prone to reject attempts to make public bodies liable will naturally be reluctant to set up administrative plans burdening the government's budget. Moreover, such systems tend to attribute great value to the enterprise of individuals, looking with suspicion upon institutions or solutions which place limits on it. Compensation plans have a strong social security flavor, which is at odds with a system focusing on the role of the individual.

This appears to be the case of the US. From a historical perspective, the American legal system has not always been averse to no-fault compensation plans. The welfare approach which characterized the first decades of the twentieth century in the United States produced legal reforms inspired by a philosophy of compensation. One of the first examples can be traced to the Worker's Compensation Acts, enacted by individual states between 1910 and 1920.[156] But, starting from the late 1960s, the cases in which both the federal government and the states decided to resort to compensation plans shrank dramatically.[157] Even

---

155   This is the case, for example, for compensation plans concerning the patients who contracted HIV or other diseases from blood transfusions. Here, the victim typically has to prove that 1) she is suffering of one of the diseases eligible for compensation according to the plan; 2) she received a blood transfusion; 3) the transfusion is probably the origin of the disease. These elements are assessed by a commission of experts and, if established, determine the right for the victim to obtain compensation.

156   For the current federal workers' compensation program, see 5 U.S.C. §§ 8101–52. One of the first schemes for compensating (federal) employees injured in service was enacted in 1916: 64 Cong. Ch. 458. For a historical account of the spread of the workers' compensation programs in the US, both at the federal and state level, and of their welfare matrix, see Fishback, Kantor 2000.

157   In the late 1960s and early 1970s, some states enacted auto-accident compensation schemes. In 1969, the Federal Coal Mine Health and Safety Act provided a compensation schemes for miners affected by the so-called "black lung" disease. The only example of a compensation scheme passed in the 1980s is the 1986 National Childhood Vaccine Injury

the most recent example, provided by the September 11 Victim Compensation Fund,[158] is considered more an exception than a sign of a no-fault compensation trend (Rabin 2002). The reason for the paucity of these schemes seems to be more political than based on a strict legal analysis.[159] The momentum for legal reforms inspired by broad ideas of social responsibility was lost in the second half of the 1970s; the Reagan administration may be considered as the turning-point, testifying to the birth of a more individualistic approach.[160]

The situation is quite different in Europe.[161] Here, ideas about social responsibility put down deeper roots than in the US and even nowadays, despite reforms in many states for reducing existing social security plans, they still play an important role in the political and social arenas. This different perspective makes compensation schemes more acceptable to the European countries than to their American counterparts. A survey of the solutions adopted in Britain, France and Italy confirms this impression. Systems of indemnification for the victims of particular accidents or diseases have been implemented since the end of the nineteenth century, with particular regard to injuries occurring in workplaces (McEwin 2000: 736).

The trend in using compensation schemes has not lost momentum in Europe, even in recent times. These plans appear to be a powerful political tool in the hands of national parliaments, allowing them to tackle emergency situations and offering a prompt response to the demand for action coming from the citizens. The long-standing tradition of compensation plans creates expectations in the countries' citizens, who look to them as a sort of natural answer that the government provides in managing a crisis. At the same time, the availability of these schemes offers a tried and tested model to legislators when faced with a new emergency. These two elements, together with an institutional background in which the states intervene, sometime intrusively, in economic and social matters,

---

Act. For a careful analysis on the history of no-fault compensation plans in the US, and the economic, legal and political reasons behind them, see Sugarman 1985: 627 and Rabin 1993.

158   The fund is contained in the Air Transportation Safety and System Stabilization Act, enacted in 2001.

159   The legal justifications for adopting compensation schemes rest more on the shortcomings of the tort law than on an analysis of the real efficiency of these tools (McEwin 2000: 737). On the scant attention that politics has devoted to the adoption of these systems, see Sugarman (1985: 627).

160   The volume of legal scholarship on compensation schemes shrank progressively in the 1980s; some of the last significant contributions are contained in volume no. 73 of the *California Law Review* (1985), reporting the papers discussed at the symposium "Alternative Compensation Schemes and Tort Theory." Nowadays, the topic seems to get scant consideration by academics, except for some contributions on the recent September 11 Victim Compensation Fund.

161   An interesting analysis concerning the influence of the social security model on liability issues and the role of the state is developed by François Ewald (1986).

create a self-reinforcing mechanism for the production of no-fault compensation schemes, which contributes to an explanation for their wide diffusion. Hence, it is not surprising to find examples ranging from plans for indemnifying the victims of crimes[162] to compensation for injuries suffered because of road accidents due to wild animals (Guarda 2004). The most important and recent examples relate to the no-fault schemes provided for traffic accidents and for HIV-contaminated patients (Ponzanelli 2001a; Fairgrieve 2003: 151 ff.; Dute, Faure, Koziol 2004).

Japan has implemented many compensation plans in the years following World War II; these plans resemble those described with regard to the European countries. There are areas of the law, such as product liability, where the adoption of these schemes has been wider than in the case of Japan's European counterparts. Here, compensation plans exist both for specific emergencies, such as in the case of the HIV-contaminated patients, but also for the adverse effects deriving from entire categories of products, such as pharmaceuticals (Tejima 1993), or products whose safety has been certified by a government body (Ramseyer 1996). Moreover, the Japanese experience shows that indemnification schemes can be used by the bureaucracy to channel and control issues of potential social conflict. In this sense, the plans are part of the broader pattern of action taken by government bodies to address the requests of social change in a way that is not too disruptive with respect to the traditional set of values and principles characterizing the Japanese order of life.[163]

The BSE Case: Government Liability, Criminal Law, and No-Fault Compensation Plans

The analysis conducted so far leaves us with many options, but also with a wide array of legal problems and uncertainties. It becomes particularly interesting to investigate whether and, if so, how the relatives of the vCJD victims have decided to act to obtain some compensation for their terrible losses. The investigation will

---

162   Art. 706-3 of the French criminal procedure code. For a survey of the compensation plans implemented in France to circumvent potential government liability, see Rivero, Waline 2006: 437 ff.

163   Frank Upham (1987) has analyzed the role of bureaucracy in channeling issues of social change. The author, starting from the premise that litigation can be a means of expressing requests for social reform, points to the fact that Japanese bureaucracies have preferred keeping such requests out of the courts wherever possible. The fear was that litigating the cases could have had disruptive effects on society; at the same time, bureaucracies were aware that this solution would have allowed them to channel the requests in the desired directions. Compensation plans can be considered, thus, a further tool to keep cases away from the courts.

only concern Europe since, as far as we know, no initiative has been taken in non-European countries.[164]

The legal hurdles underlined previously are clearly reflected in the varying paths that the victims' relatives have followed. No tort suit has been commenced against the producers of BSE-tainted meat. The causation problem has discouraged any attempt to go in this direction. In addition, the fact that most of the victims contracted vCJD before 1999 precluded the possibility of applying the more pro-consumer amendment extending the strict liability regime to primary agricultural products. The bottom line, in this sense, is that the possibility of an action against specific individuals was soon discarded.

On the other hand, victims' families have tried to make public bodies responsible for what has happened. The impossibility of singling out individuals liable for the epidemic's spread, along with the scandals which have characterized politicians' management of the crisis, has heavily influenced the choice to look to public authorities as the target of possible initiatives. As we will see, the very nature of the risk represented by BSE/vCJD has contributed to forming this preference: the collective dimension of the BSE/vCJD risk, with respect to which causation is one of its legal manifestations, has made it natural to turn to the government to provide some remedy.

In France, the family of one of the victims asked the authorities to investigate the criminal responsibilities of the French, British and European Union governments for having failed to adopt measures to avoid the spread of the human variant of BSE (Moya 2001; McAteer 2001). The demand was aimed at identifying the officials who could be held liable for this failure. But such investigations never gave rise to a criminal charge naming specific persons. Relatives of a victim in Spain tried a different solution. They claimed compensation from the government under a law providing for indemnity where citizens have incurred damages as a consequence of the activity of public bodies (Moya 2001).[165] The claim is for damages incurred by the vCJD victim and her relatives, arising from the management of the mad cow crisis by the Spanish authorities. Two elements must be highlighted. First, the claim is addressed to the same public body which is being asked to pay the indemnity. In other words, the claimants do not go through the courts, but seek

---

164   In the US, no case of vCJD has been registered so far, at least arising from the consumption of domestic cattle. A few cases of the disease have been reported among hunters who consumed elk meat (Stapleton 2003: 132). In Japan, only one case of vCJD has been ascertained.

165   Spain experienced another scandal relating to food safety in the 1980s, which has deeply influenced its legal landscape. It is the so-called "*caso de la Colza*," which concerned an oil, processed with a noxious chemical component, which was distributed for human consumption. As a result of the contamination, hundreds of people died and thousands suffered injury (Montañés 2005).

compensation by following an entirely administrative circuit.[166] Second, the prospective indemnification leaves aside an assessment of the negligent character of the actions taken by the public body in dealing with the emergency. Claimants must prove the loss suffered and the causal link between such loss and the activity of the public body.[167]

The most interesting case to be analyzed concerns Britain. It is in this country that the epidemic originated and was concentrated; it was here that most of the casualties occurred. No wonder, then, that this country has created a trust fund to finance a no-fault compensation scheme (Melville 2004; Boggio 2005). A mix of political, efficiency and fairness considerations have led the government to enact a plan capable of providing prompt and nearly full compensation for the families of the vCJD victims (Boggio 2005: 25–6). The expediency of this action was already contained in the Phillips' Report which, although it did not expressly mention no-fault compensation, suggested the need to provide relief to the victims (Phillips of Worth Matravers 2000: vol. I: *Findings and conclusion,* xxix).[168] Even if the scheme does not bar the possibility of suing in tort, the generosity of the compensation provided by the plan, together with the costs and uncertainties of litigation, have put the conditions in place to halt the proceedings which were commenced in 1996 (Boggio 2005: 19 ff.). The vCJD Trust Fund is now the only route taken by the families of mad cow disease victims to obtain compensation in Britain.

---

166 It should be added that the claimants can turn to the (administrative) courts in cases in which their claim is dismissed (Moya 2001).

167 Art. 6, Real Decreto no. 429/1993, March 26, 1993.

168 The idea that the victims of vCJD deserve some kind of compensation can also be inferred from the grave accusations leveled at the British government in the Report. The exposure of the mismanagement of the BSE crisis by the British institutions implied the need to redress the wrongs suffered by the victims of such maladministration.

Chapter 4

Conclusions

Comparison, then, should aspire less to prescribe policy solutions than to explain outcomes; it should offer interpretative criticism rather than clinical diagnosis, or *Verstehen* (understanding) rather than *Erklärung* (causal explanation).

S. Jasanoff, *Designs on Nature*, Princeton, 2005, 291

Risk, Regulation, and Compensation

The analysis developed so far allows some conclusions to be drawn regarding the interaction between risk, regulation and compensation. The manufacturing and distribution of food have always posed risks for public health: symmetrically, legal systems have reacted to such risks by implementing different tools to counteract them. Regulation is one of the tools which states have always used to cope with the problems raised by the manufacture of defective foodstuffs. On the other hand, the overview of liability for defective foodstuffs has highlighted that the use of compensation for providing relief to the victims and, at the same time, discouraging producers and sellers from marketing noxious aliments is well established.

But something has changed in today's framework of reference. Indeed, the risks traditionally experienced in the food sector are quantitatively and qualitatively different from the risks existing in the present era of food production. Quantitatively, since the so-called globalization of the market has brought about a change of status, from a local risk to a (potentially) world-wide risk. This effect is magnified by the fact that globalization concerns not only the final products, but also feed and raw materials. The consequence is that the sources of contamination can spread faster and wider than in the past.

Risks are also qualitatively different. First, enhanced scientific knowledge implies a better understanding of the dangers that the production of food can pose. We think that food risks are more numerous or terrible nowadays than in the past, in part because we are better equipped to comprehend them. At the same time, we tend to rely more on technology to reduce this qualitative dimension of risk. Second, and paradoxically with respect to the preceding point, the technologies used to reduce the traditional risks posed by foodstuffs can create new risks. New risks are usually more complex than the original, since the number of variables involved increases progressively when we employ new technology. Their greater complexity requires considerable financial investment in the R&D sector and a strong scientific awareness on the part of the industries involved. Third, the globalization of risk does not always mean easier access to information; indeed, it can determine the opposite effect, namely the dissemination of information on a global scale, making it time-consuming or difficult to gather data.

This is also the case regarding scientific information. While the risks created by the distribution of animal feeds, as seen in this case study, spread rapidly around the world because of market forces, the dissemination of the information linking the animal feed to the occurrence of BSE might not have been able to circulate as quickly. In other words, the dynamics of globalization pose a world-wide risk, but are not able to provide so prompt an antidote for the new threat. The time-lag between the spread of the risk and the spread of the information is often at the origin of the emergence of a public health crisis.

This is a problem affecting the responses prepared both at the regulatory level and by the industry. With regard to regulation, states are not always in the best position to notice the first signs of an oncoming crisis and to fully appreciate the real dynamics behind it; indeed, they often need cooperation from the industry, which might be unable or reluctant to offer it. Second, economic interests, political pressures and institutional deficiencies can slow down the gathering of information; BSE provides a classic example in this regard.

On the industry's side, the fragmentation of the producers' institutional and economic organization can constitute further difficulties in gathering the relevant information. Again, the BSE case illustrates this well. The division between animal feed manufacturers, cattle raisers and slaughterhouses has hindered the production and/or collection of data. All were in some measure involved in the spread of the risk, but unrelated to its creation. Being foreign to the production of the risk, the different industries did not consider an investigation necessary, to confirm its existence or discover its nature. Furthermore, it should be added that, at least in the case of the cattle raisers, the paucity of financial resources and the lack of scientific background have prevented research activities relating to BSE. The same rationale which hampers the application of strict liability thus provides a key to understanding how the fragmentation at the production level also involves fragmentation at the information level.

Before commenting briefly on the interaction between risk, regulation and compensation, a point which might raise doubts should be clarified. Regulation and compensation are products resulting from the choices made by two different institutional bodies, namely, the legislators and the courts. The reader might wonder whether my remarks apply to the former or the latter. They apply to both. In the first place, legislators and courts participate, in differing ways and varying degrees, in the collective economic, cultural and political dimensions to which I will shortly refer. Their choices, whether to regulate and/or to compensate, are influenced by the cultural and political environment within which they operate and largely reflect the body of values characterizing the society to which they belong. I am aware of the fact that both legislators and courts can sometimes express competing views, making reference to rival sets of values. My answer reiterates the argument I offered in Chapter 1: any society has a predominant set of values which coexists with other competing values. Most of the choices made by legislators and the courts conform to this predominant view, but sometimes it may happen that "non-orthodox" decisions are taken.

Second, the institutional division between legislators, who make regulations, and courts, which award compensation, does not fit the realities of any legal system. The judges' decisions, even if aimed primarily at resolving specific disputes which have arisen in the past, also have a regulatory impact, capable of conditioning individuals' future conduct. On the other hand, in Chapter 3, I have cited examples of no-fault compensation plans where administrative bodies have awarded compensation to the victims of particular events. The parallelism between legislators-regulation and judges-compensation is therefore blurred, and does not reflect the complexities characterizing the legal systems.

The Collective Dimension

The first comment which arises from contemplating the dynamic between risk, regulation and compensation in the BSE context relates to the nature of the risk. It has a collective dimension which impedes any attempt to single out specific subjects responsible for the loss incurred by the vCJD victims and their families (Jonas 1984). The collective dimension has a distorting influence on the compensation side of the triangular dynamic. If liability cannot be pinned on the producers who distributed the tainted meat (or feed) because of the causation problem, if the entities who should have performed research or data collection activities cannot be identified, if any potential defendant can advance the defense that someone else created the risk, then turning to public authorities to obtain some relief becomes the only viable alternative.

In my view, this is not just an option available to desperate families, unable to discover anyone who is liable for the terrible losses suffered, but it amounts to an implicit recognition of the collective nature of the risk. Its very nature requires more proactive intervention by the governments, which are often the bodies with sufficient resources and coordination capacity to deal with the new risks. But, on the other hand, it places the burden on governments to adopt an institutional structure capable of overcoming the deficiencies mentioned before, that can hamper the smooth operation of their regulatory functions. If governments fail to carry out their duties in this regard, the question of their liability may arise. We can call this feature the collective dimension of the interaction between risk, regulation and compensation.

The Economic Dimension

The risk–regulation–compensation dynamic also possesses an economic dimension. The preceding section concluded with the statement that, if the government fails to perform its duties of regulation and control (which, in their turn, derive from the collective nature of the risk), it can be asked to provide compensation. But both regulation and compensation involve costs, and in both cases, these costs become collective costs. On the other hand, the choice of holding only the state liable dramatically reduces the responsibilities placed on the shoulders of the private producers. This may bring about a marked reduction in the incentives for producers to refrain from carrying out dangerous activities.

Such consequences can be seen as the dark side of the collective nature of the risk. Indeed, a tension exists between the expediency of compensating the victims according to considerations of justice and fairness, together with the desire to penalize the government for having disregarded its duties, and the consequential financial burden and disincentives that such an option involves. The second remark concerns precisely this conflict and the choice that every legal system must make in this regard. In my view, the conflict is resolved through cultural evaluations that make it acceptable for the victim to bear the loss, or to shift it onto the government (and, eventually, on the pockets of the citizens). Additionally, shifting liability to the government has also a symbolic meaning, implying the stigma of blame for not having protected citizens' interests.

The Cultural Dimension

The tension I have referred to is preparatory to a third observation: the cultural dimension of the interaction between risk, regulation and compensation. First, regulation and compensation can both be thought of as variables which depend on cultural perceptions of risks. States do not regulate every single risk present in the physical world, just as individuals are not compensated for any risk that materializes. The distinction between risks which can be regulated/compensated for and those which cannot is based, at least in part, on the cultural order we want to preserve.

Second, a different philosophy characterizes the concept of compensation in Europe and Japan, on the one hand, and the US, on the other. While in the European and Japanese systems, compensation is also perceived as an instrument of social security, the approach followed in the US is more individualistic. The European and Japanese systems reject the idea that compensation can replace social welfare initiatives: this is clearly demonstrated by the reluctance to adopt no-fault compensation plans. This different conception influences the way in which the tension between compensation and no compensation is resolved in contexts of collective risks. Facing the inability to identify a single subject to be made liable for the damage, the US tends to leave the losses where they fall, while Europe and Japan are more prone to find solutions to socialize the collective risk.

But this is only one aspect of the cultural dimension. We should not neglect the fact that even in countries like the US, where a more individualistic philosophy seems to hamper initiatives for the socialization of collective risks, there are examples in which no-fault compensation plans have been adopted. This is the case of the September 11 Victim Compensation Fund. Conversely, in Europe and Japan, we have examples of collective risks which have not been compensated. Why is it deemed acceptable to socialize the collective risk in some cases and not in others? The answer can be found in the cultural perception of risks. Compensation is acceptable particularly in relation to risks that are perceived to pose serious threats to the set of values characterizing a given society. As we have seen in Chapter 1, we tend to magnify the risks that run against the values we think should shape our society or, stated in other terms, that are thought to undermine some of the pillars of our society.

When the risks materialize and cause damage, we tend to empathize with the victims, representing them as martyr-figures who have paid a heavy price in relation to risks which are in the forefront of our minds. It is considered fairer to compensate the victims of these risks than the victims of other risks which are perceived as negligible. Similarly, we think it necessary to enact burdensome regulations to minimize those risks deemed unbearable by our societies, while other risks go almost totally unregulated. This may be the case for terrorism in the US, or food safety in Europe and Japan. The influence that culture has on the regulatory and compensatory contexts finds expression in the idea of fairness, which is both the representation of the empathy we feel as a society toward the victims and the basis for the choice of regulation/compensation.

The Political Dimension

The idea of fairness offers me the chance to introduce a final remark on the political dimension of the interaction between risk, regulation and compensation. Political elites tend to react promptly to risks which are magnified by the societies in which they operate. The result is the enactment of numerous laws, regulations and decisions to reduce or nullify those risks. Shortly after the announcement by the British Secretary of State for Health about the link between BSE and vCJD, when the number of fatalities was not yet predictable, questions were raised as to how to compensate the victims. Despite the low number of casualties, especially in comparison to those caused by other diseases, both the European Parliament and the British government have taken initiatives to compensate those affected by vCJD: the former by amending the Product Liability Directive, the latter by setting up the vCJD Trust Fund. As a result of recent food scandals, including the BSE affair, discussions on the expansion of the Product Liability Law to unprocessed agricultural products are also ongoing in Japan.

The reforms which have concerned the *ex ante* system of food safety controls have been both radical and impressive in Europe and Japan. Nothing comparable has happened in the US. Although the number of fatalities for vCJD in the US is higher than in Japan or Italy, measures to counteract the spread of the disease or to compensate the victims have not been a top priority in the political agenda of that country. The risks posed by BSE were not so alarming for American society as they were for its European and Japanese counterparts; consequently, political elites reacted differently in the individual legal systems.

The political dimension can be considered a sort of catalyst for the three observations I made previously. The collective nature of the risks, the cultural perception of them, the balancing of costs and benefits – all these elements find their own place in the political circuit and can lead to public action (or lack of it). The interaction between the vCJD risk and regulation provides an illustration of this type of dynamic. It points also to the importance of building a political circuit in which all the stakeholders can express their views and interact with the scientific and technical bodies which must keep on playing a fundamental role in the regulatory process (Tallacchini 2004).

But the political dimension I am referring to is also a remainder of the hurdles that the political will to compensate must overcome with respect to the legal institutions and norms that traditionally imbue the compensation system. In this sense, I do not find the European choice of extending strict liability to unprocessed agricultural products convincing. The strategy of claiming compensation from the government, through legal action or schemes of indemnification, is a preliminary sign confirming the validity of my argument. The emotional reaction by political elites to highly perceived risks can, therefore, set up a situation of conflict with the solutions and institutions existing in the legal systems.

Comparative Law and Cultural Context

The analysis I have conducted so far also offers us a methodological *caveat*. As mentioned in Chapter 1, comparative scholars have often paid scarce attention to the role that culture plays in explaining the genesis and content of many legal reforms. On the contrary, I believe that the cultural context is a crucial factor in understanding the process of legal change, since it is able to determine the acceptability of a norm in a given society. At the same time, we should avoid any oversimplification by which culture is the chief element determining the occurrence of any legal reform. Things are far more complicated than that. An extremely complex web of interactions between culture and other (political, economic, institutional, scientific) factors takes place within any legal system; only by studying the structure of this interrelationship can we have a glimpse of the realities behind the process of legal change.

Nonetheless, the case study I have presented on the reforms enacted in the wake of the mad cow crisis shows how a depiction which excludes the cultural element is unsatisfactory, as it cannot reproduce all the different tones which make the picture complex and fascinating. The European and Japanese socio-anthropological attention paid to the contraposition between "natural" and "industrial" foodstuffs has created an attitude of suspicion towards the use of technology in food production which, in its turn, has heavily conditioned the content of the reforms adopted from the end of the 1990s to counteract the spread of BSE. In the US, on the contrary, there is a more open attitude to using technology in the manufacture of foodstuffs and a more "relaxed" regulation of these aspects of food law. Here, therefore, the reaction to the BSE menace has been more lenient than in the other two systems considered. Overlooking the existence of these differences would have meant missing something which has played an important role in the post-BSE changes.

In addition, recent advances in psychology, cognitive sciences and sociology enrich legal discourse, offering valuable theories and tools to improve our understanding of the mechanisms through which culture influences legal change. The beneficial symbiosis that can take place between law and these sciences is further evidence of the importance of cross-fertilizing different branches of human knowledge and, on the other hand, of the risks in making exclusive reference to a strictly legal phraseology. It also provides a valuable reservoir of stimuli, ideas and challenges for exploring old fields with new eyes.

The usefulness of the methodological *caveat* I am stressing in these pages is not limited just to a better theoretical understanding of the origin and contents of the legal norms we study. I am convinced it has also some practical implications worth mentioning. A careful analysis of the cultural environment within which new norms, copied from or inspired by other legal systems, must operate could facilitate their implementation and improve their efficacy. On the contrary, a transplant of norms irrespective of the cultural context in which they must operate carries the risk that such norms will at best not work properly or at worst be rejected. If comparative law aspires to become a useful support both for planning new institutional scenarios and for making them operative, it has necessarily to deal with the values that characterize the society which will adopt the new institutions. This implies that the functionalist method, which can be considered predominant nowadays, must be tempered with a cultural analysis, making a deeper understanding of the mechanisms governing legal change possible.

The idea that culture represents a crucial factor also introduces new problems, which deserve further exploration. Here I will briefly mention only three issues which could represent three whole new fields of analysis. A preliminary question concerns how institutional constraints influence (and are influenced by) cultural factors. Indeed, there might be institutional arrangements that facilitate the emergence of such factors, while other arrangements might suffocate them. On the other hand, the adoption itself of arrangements stimulating or restraining the appearance of cultural elements might be a political choice, deemed appropriate in some contexts but not in others. A second problem relates to the possibility of predicting the direction that legal change will take. The complex web of interactions taking place between culture and other factors makes it currently difficult, if not impossible, to forecast whether a legal change will happen, which form it will take, what the final result will be. Nonetheless, advances in cognitive sciences and the refining of predictive models such as the Social Amplification of Risk Framework could, in the not-too-distant future, bring what is now impossible to fruition. Legal scholars could provide an important contribution to identifying the institutional and factual conditions facilitating the process of legal change.

The third problem I wish to mention regards the possibility of applying the cultural paradigm of analysis in areas other than food safety or, more in general, risk perception. The answer depends on the fields we want to study. I do not think that the method I am proposing can be used indiscriminately. There are areas where its use is more promising, since there are historical, religious, social factors that have determined a deep cultural background. Applying a cultural explanation here can provide valuable insights and enrich our understanding of legal norms. But there are also areas where the cultural background is thin and has barely influenced the contents of legal norms; in such contexts, the risk is that a cultural paradigm can add little to our knowledge.

Despite these crucial problems and the many precautions we must take in handling such a tricky concept as culture, the point I want to stress is that legal change does reflect cultural values. In doing so, I cannot do better than draw on the acute observation that Sheila Jasanoff has made with reference to the biotechnology realm, but that can also be aptly extended to the reforms adopted in the wake of the mad cow crisis:

> To make sense of the resulting national settlements, one must look not only at the discoveries and commodities that materialize out of research laboratories and industrial facilities; one must equally take into account the scripts for human development and collective choice that emanate from a nation's political and social institutions, and from its citizens. (Jasanoff 2005: 290)

Bibliography

Aa. Vv. 1990. *Symposium on the International Protection of Geographical Indications*. Geneva: World Intellectual Property Organization.

—— 1996. "An explanation of Japan's product liability law." *Pacific Rim Law and Policy Journal* 5, 299–329.

—— 2002. *4 Rapporto sull'Obesità in Italia: 2002*. Milano: Angeli.

—— 2003. "La sicurezza alimentare nell'Unione Europea. Commentario a cura dell'Istituto di diritto agrario internazionale e comparato (IDAIC)." *Le Nuove Leggi Civili Commentate*, 1–2, 114–484.

Abromeit, H. 1998. *Democracy in Europe. Legitimising Politics in a Non-State Polity*. New York: Berghahn Books.

Adler, M. 2003. "Risk, death and harm: the normative foundations of risk regulation," *Minnesota Law Review*, 87, 1293–445.

—— 2004, "Fear assessment: cost-benefit analysis and the pricing of fear and anxiety," *Chicago-Kent Law Review*, 79, 977–1053.

—— Posner E. 2006. *New Foundations of Cost-Benefit Analysis*. Cambridge, MA: Harvard University Press.

Aime, M. 2008. *Il Primo Libro di Antropologia*. Torino: Einaudi.

Albisinni, F. 2003a. "L'informazione del consumatore e la tutela della salute," in *Trattato Breve di Diritto Agrario Italiano e Comunitario*, edited by L. Costato. Padova: Cedam, 631–48.

—— 2003b. "Commento all'art. 21, *Le nuove leggi civili commentate*, 1–2, 284–9.

Alemanno, A. 2008. "The European Food Safety Authority at five." Social Science Research Network. Accepted Paper Series [Online]. Available at: <http://papers.ssrn.com/sol3/papers.cfm?abstract_id=1095703> [accessed: June 15, 2009].

Alpa, G., Bessone, M. 1999. *La Responsabilità del Produttore*. Milano: Giuffrè.

Ambrosoli, M. 2000. "Responsabilità della CE e teoria dell'illecito extracontrattuale." *Rivista di diritto privato*, 3, 528–50.

Ames, J. 1888. "The history of assumpsit." *Harvard Law Review*, 2, 1–19.

Ansell, C., Maxwell, R., Sicurelli, D. 2006. "Protesting food: NGOs and political mobilization in Europe," in *What's the Beef? The Contested Governance of European Food Safety*, edited by C. Ansell, D. Vogel. Cambridge, MA: MIT Press, 97–122.

Antle, J. 1995. *Choice and Efficiency in Food Safety Policy*. Washington, DC: AEI Press.

Arcuri, A. 2005. "The post-discriminatory era of the WTO: toward world-wide harmonization of risk law?" Social Science Research Network. Working Paper Series [Online]. Available at: <http://ssrn.com/abstract=974981> [accessed: June 15, 2009].

Arrowsmith, S. 1992. *Civil Liability and Public Authorities.* Winteringham: Earlsgate Press.

Assumma, B. 1987. "Avvelenamento, adulterazione o contraffazione in danno della salute pubblica." *Digesto delle Discipline Penalistiche.* Torino: Utet, I, 391–8.

Atiyah, P. 1979. *The Rise and Fall of Freedom of Contract.* Oxford: Clarendon.

Aughenbaugh, L. 1994. "The demise of the foreign-natural test in North Carolina." *Campbell Law Review,* 16, 275–302.

Babuscio, T. 2005, *Alimenti Sicuri e Diritto.* Milano: Giuffrè.

Bailey, S. 2006. "Public authority liability in negligence: the continued search for coherence." *Legal Studies,* 26(2), 155–84.

Baker, J., Milsom, S. 1986. *Sources of English Legal History.* London: Butterworths.

Baldwin, R., Wyplosz, C. 2004. *The Economics of European Integration.* London: McGraw-Hill.

Basili, M., Franzini, M. 2004. "Institutions and the precautionary principle: the case of mad cow disease," *Risk, Decision and Policy,* 9, 9–21.

Beck, U. 1992, *Risk Society: Towards a New Modernity,* London: Sage.

—— 1995. *Ecological Politics in an Age of Risk. Cambridge*: Polity Press.

—— 2008. *Conditio Humana. Il Rischio nell'Età Globale,* Bari: Laterza.

Becker, G. 1983. "A theory of competition among pressure groups for political influence." *Quarterly Journal of Economics,* 98, 371–400.

Bell, J. 2005. "La responsabilità del governo: alcune riflessioni comparate," in *Verso un'Amministrazione Responsabile,* edited by F. Astone et al. Milano: Giuffrè, 27–51.

Bellantuono, G. 2000. *I Contratti Incompleti nel Diritto e nell'Economia.* Padova: Cedam.

Benforado, A., Hanson, J., Yosifon, D. 2004. "Broken scales: obesity and justice in America." *Emory Law Journal,* 53, 1645–806.

Bergström, C. 2005. *Comitology: Delegation of Powers in the European Union and the Committee System.* Oxford: Oxford University Press.

Berlowitz, G. 2006. "Food safety vs. promotion of industry: can the USDA protect the Americans from bovine spongiform encephalopathy?" *University of Illinois Law Review,* 2006, 625–58.

Bernardi, A. 2003. "La responsabilità da prodotto nel sistema italiano: profili sanzionatori." *Rivista Trimestrale di Diritto Penale dell'Economia,* 1–2, 1–45.

—— 2006. "Società multiculturale e 'reati culturali' Spunti per una riflessione," in *Studi in Onore di Giorgio Marinucci,* edited by E. Dolcini, C. Paliero Milano: Giuffrè, I, 45–98.

Boggio, A. 2005. "The compensation of the victims of the Creutzfeldt-Jakob disease in the United Kingdom." Social Science Research Network. Working Paper Series [Online]. Available at <http://papers.ssrn.com/sol3/papers.cfm?abstract_id=681086> [accessed: June 15, 2009].

Bona, M. 2004. "Prescrizione e dies a quo nel danno alla persona: quale modello?" *Responsabilità Civile e Previdenza*, 2, 574–636.

Bonny, S. 2003. "Why are most Europeans opposed to GMOs? Factors explaining rejection in France and Europe." *Electronic Journal of Biotechnology* [Online], 6, 50–71. Available at: <http://www.ejbiotechnology.info/content/vol6/issue1/full/4/bip/index.html> [accessed: June 15, 2009].

Borchard, E. 1926. "Government responsibility in tort." *Yale Law Journal*, 36, 1–41.

Borghetti, J. 2004. *La Responsabilité du Fait des Produits: Étude de Droit Comparé*, Paris: Libraire générale de droit et de jurisprudence.

Borghi, P. 2004. *L'Agricoltura nel Trattato di Marrakech. Prodotti Agricoli e Alimentari nel Diritto del Commercio Internazionale*. Milano: Giuffrè.

Boyce, B. 1993. "The democratic deficit of the European Community." *Parliamentary Affairs*, 46, 458–77.

Brazier, M. 1988. *Street on Torts*, London: Butterworths.

Breakwell, G., Barnett, J. 2001. "The impact of social amplification of risk on risk communication." Health and Safety Executive [Online], Contract Research Report 322/2001. Available at <http://www.hse.gov.uk/research/crr_pdf/2001/crr01332.pdf> [accessed: June 15, 2009].

Brent, R. 2006. *Applied Cost-Benefit Analysis*. Cheltenham: Edward Elgar Publisher.

Browne, W. 1988. *Private Interests, Public Policy, and American Agriculture*, Lawrence: University Press of Kansas.

Bullock, R. 1997. "Nokyo: a short cultural history." Japan Policy Research Institute, Working Paper n. 41 [Online]. Available at <http://www.jpri.org/publications/workingpapers/wp41.html> [accessed: June 15, 2009].

Burchell, G., Gordon, C., Miller, P. 1991. *The Foucault Effect: Studies in Governmentality*, London: Harvester-Wheatsheaf.

Burk D., Boczar B. 1994. "Biotechnology and tort liability: a strategic industry at risk." *University of Pittsburgh Law Review*, 55, 791–864.

Burrows, P. 1999. "Combining regulation and legal liability for the control of external costs." *International Review of Law and Economics*, 19, 227–44.

Cafaggi, F. 2005. "Gouvernance et responsabilité des régulateurs privés." European University Institute Working Paper Law n. 2005/06 [Online]. Available at <http://cadmus.iue.it/dspace/bitstream/1814/3326/1/law05-06.pdf> [accessed: June 15, 2009].

Calais-Auloy, J., Steinmetz, F. 2006. *Droit de la Consommation*. Paris: Dalloz.

Calfee, J. 2002. "Comment on Viscusi," in *Regulation through Litigation*, edited by K. Viscusi. Washington, DC: Brookings Institution Press, 52–66.

Capelli F., Silano V., Klaus B. 2006. *Nuova Disciplina del Settore Alimentare e Autorità Europea per la Sicurezza Alimentare*. Milano: Giuffrè.

Capizzano, E., Petrelli, L. 1990. "L'attuazione in Italia della Direttiva 85/374 con riferimento alla responsabilità del produttore agricolo e nella prospettiva dell'agricoltura c.d. biologica," in *Il Danno da Prodotti in Italia, Austria, Repubblica Federale di Germania, Svizzera*, edited by S. Patti, Padova: Cedam, 161–92.

Caranta, R. 1992. "La responsabilità extracontrattuale della pubblica amministrazione nel diritto inglese." *Rivista Trimestrale di Diritto Pubblico,* 2, 513–59.

—— 1993. *La Responsabilità Extracontrattuale della Pubblica Amministrazione: Sistemi e Tecniche.* Milano: Giuffrè.

Carnevali, U. 1974. *La Responsabilità del Produttore.* Milano: Giuffrè.

Carriero, G. 2008. "La responsabilità civile delle autorità di vigilanza (in difesa del comma 6 bis dell'art. 24 della legge sulla tutela del risparmio)." *Foro Italiano,* 9, V, 221–5.

Carrozza, A. 1995. "Riflessioni intorno al concetto di 'prodotto agricolo'." *Rivista di Diritto Agrario,* 4, 392–404.

Casella, A. 2001. "Product standards and international trade. Harmonization through private coalitions." *Kyklos,* 54, 243–64.

Casey, D. 1998. "Agency capture: the USDA's struggle to pass food safety regulations." *Kansas Journal of Law and Public Policy,* 7, 142–56.

Cassese, S. 2004. "Shrimps, turtles and procedure: global standards for national administrations." Institute for International Law and Justice Working Paper n. 2004/4 [Online]. Available at <http://iilj.org/publications/2004-4Cassese.asp> [accessed: June 15, 2009].

Castronovo, C. 1979. *Problema e Sistema nel Danno da Prodotti.* Milano: Giuffrè.

Caterina, R. 2005. "Paternalismo e antipaternalismo nel diritto privato." *Rivista di Diritto Civile,* 6, 771–96.

—— (ed.) 2008. *I Fondamenti Cognitivi del Diritto.* Milano: Mondadori.

Cazala, J. 2004. "Food safety and the precautionary principle: the legitimate moderation of community courts." *European Law Journal,* 10, 539–54.

Cerini, D. 1996. "Responsabilità del produttore e rischio di sviluppo: oltre la lettera della dir. 85/374/CEE." *Diritto ed Economia dell'Assicurazione,* 1, 29–59.

Chalmers, D. 2003. "'Food for thought': reconciling European risks and traditional ways of life." *The Modern Law Review,* 66(4), 532–62.

Chambers, G. 1999. "The BSE crisis and the European parliament," in *EU Committees: Social Regulation, Law and Politics,* edited by C. Joerges, E. Vos. Oxford: Hart Publishing, 95–108.

Chang, H. 2004. "Risk regulation, endogenous public concerns, and the hormones dispute: nothing to fear but fear itself?" *Southern California Law Review,* 77, 743–75.

Charnovitz, S. 2005. "International standards and the WTO." Social Science Research Network. Working Paper Series [Online]. Available at <http://ssrn.com/abstract=694346> [accessed: June 15, 2009].

Chase, O. 1997. "Some observations on the cultural dimension in civil procedure reform." *American Journal of Comparative Law,* 45, 861–70.

Checkel, J. 1999. "Norms, institutions, and national identity in contemporary Europe." *International Studies Quarterly,* 43, 83–114.

Chichester, D. 2005. "Battle of the beef, the rematch: an evaluation of the latest E.C. directive banning beef produced with growth hormones and the U.S. refusal to accept the directive as WTO compliant." *American University International Law Review*, 21, 221–76.

Claus, J. 2003. "The European Union's efforts to sidestep the WTO through its ban on GMOs: a response to Sarah Lively's paper, 'The ABCs and NTBs of GMOs'." *Northwestern Journal of International Law and Business*, 24, 173–98.

Clemens, R. 2003a. "Meat traceability in Japan." *Iowa Ag Review*, 9, 4–5.

—— 2003b. "Meat traceability and consumer assurance in Japan." Midwest Agribusiness Trade Research and Information Center Briefing Paper 03-MBP 5 [Online]. Available at <http://www.matric.iastate.edu/publications.aspx> [accessed: June 15, 2009].

Coglianese, C. 2006. "Citizen participation in rulemaking: past, present, and future." *Duke Law Journal*, 55, 943–68.

Cohen, A., Dehejia, R. 2004. "The effect of automobile insurance and accident liability on traffic fatalities." *Journal of Law and Economics*, 47, 357–93.

Cohen, J. 1997. "The Japanese product liability law: sending a pro-consumer tsunami through Japan's corporate and judicial worlds." *Fordham International Law Journal*, 21, 108–89.

Conk, G. 2000. "Is there a design defect in the restatement (third) of torts: products liability?" *Yale Law Journal*, 109, 1087–133.

—— 2002. "The true test: alternative safer designs for drugs and medical devices in a patent-constrained market." *UCLA Law Review*, 49, 737–88.

Corman, C. 1991. *Limitation of Actions*. Boston, MA: Little, Brown.

Cortell, A., Davis, J. 2000. "Understanding the domestic impact of international norms: a research agenda." *International Studies Review*, 2, 65–87.

Cotterrell, R. 2006. *Law, Culture and Society: Legal Ideas in the Mirror of Social Theory*. Aldershot: Ashgate Publishing.

Courtney, B. 2006. "Is obesity really the next tobacco? Lessons learned from tobacco for obesity litigation." *Annals of Health Law*, 15, 61–106.

Cozian, M. 1969. *L'action directe*. Paris: Libraire générale de droit et de jurisprudence.

Craig, P. 2003. *Administrative Law*. 5th edition. London: Sweet and Maxwell.

Cubeddu, M. 1990. "La responsabilità del produttore per prodotti naturali," in *Il Danno da Prodotti in Italia, Austria, Repubblica Federale di Germania, Svizzera*, edited by S. Patti. Padova: Cedam, 193–216.

Cupp, R. 1994. "Rethinking conscious design liability for prescription drugs: the restatement (third) standard versus a negligence approach." *George Washington Law Review*, 63, 76–110.

Curran, V. 1998. "Cultural immersion, difference and categories in U.S. comparative law." *American Journal of Comparative Law*, 46, 43–92.

Cwiertka, K. 2006. *Modern Japanese Cuisine: Food, Power and National Identity*. London: Reaktion Books.

D'Arrigo, R. 2006. *La Responsabilità del Produttore: Profili Dottrinali e Giurisprudenziali dell'Esperienza Italiana*. Milano: Giuffrè.

Damasio, A. 2003. *Looking for Spinoza: Joy, Sorrow and the Feeling Brain*. London: Heinemann.

Damron, E. 2006. "Reviving the market for liability theories: the 'commingled product' theory of market share liability enters the judicial lexicon." *Penn State Law Review*, 111, 505–25.

Davies, J., Levine, C. 2000. "Biotechnology's challenge to the law of torts." *McGeorge Law Review*, 32, 221–35.

Davis, C. 2003. *Food Fights over Free Trade. How International Institutions Promote Agricultural Trade Liberalization*. Princeton, NJ: Princeton University Press.

Deakin, S., Johnston, A., Markesinis, B. 2003. *Markesinis and Deakin's Tort Law*. Oxford: Clarendon.

de Figueiredo, J. 2006. "E-rulemaking: bringing data to theory at the federal communications commission." *Duke Law Journal*, 55, 969–93.

de Gorter, H., Swinnen, J. 2002. "Political economy of agricultural policy," in *Handbook of Agricultural Economics*, edited by B. Gardner, G. Rausser. Amsterdam: Elsevier, Vol. 2, Part 2, 1893–943.

della Cananea, G., Sandulli, A. 2005. "La responsabilità dell'amministrazione per omessa vigilanza sugli operatori finanziari: Italia e Regno Unito," in *Verso un'Amministrazione Responsabile*, edited by F. Astone et al. Milano: Giuffrè, 53–71.

Dickerson, R. 1951. *Products Liability and the Food Consumer*. Boston, MA: Little, Brown.

Dierson, F., Dunn, C. 1955. *Product Liability Cases*. Chicago, IL: Commerce Clearing House.

Douglas, M. 1986. *Risk Acceptability According to Social Sciences*. London: Routledge and Kegan Paul.

—— 1992. *Risk and Blame: Essays in Cultural Theory*. London: Routledge.

—— Wildavsky, A. 1982. *Risk and Culture. An Essay on the Selection of Technological and Environmental Dangers*. Berkeley: University of California Press.

Draper, J. 2005. "Liability for injury or death allegedly caused by food product containing object related to, but not intended to be present in, product." *American Law Reports* 5, 2, 189.

Dute J., Faure, M., Koziol, H. (eds) 2004. *No-Fault Compensation in the Health Care Sector*. Wien: Springer.

Dynan, K. 2000. "Habit formation in consumer preferences: evidence from panel data." *American Economic Review*, 90, 391–406.

Echols, M. 2001. *Food Safety and the WTO. The Interplay of Culture, Science and Technology*. London: Kluwer Law International.

Edwards, W., von Winterfeldt, D. 1986. "Cognitive illusions and their implications for the law." *Southern California Law Review*, 59, 225–75.

Eisenberg, M. 1995. "The limits of cognition and the limits of contract." *Stanford Law Review*, 47, 211–59.

Ellickson, R. 1989. "Bringing culture and human frailty to rational actors: a critique of classical law and economics." *Chicago-Kent Law Review*, 65, 23–55.

Elliott, M., Heath, A. 2000. "The failure of CAP reform: a public choice analysis." *Economic Affairs*, 20, 42–8.

Elster, J. 1999. *Alchemies of the Mind: Rationality and the Emotions*, Cambridge: Cambridge University Press.

Epstein, D., O'Halloran, S. 1995. "A theory of strategic oversight: congress, lobbyists, and the bureaucracy." *Journal of Law, Economics, and Organization*, 11, 227–55.

Epstein, R. 1985. "Products liability as an insurance market." *Journal of Legal Studies*, 14, 645–69.

Epstein, S. 1994. "Integration of the cognitive and psychodynamic unconscious." *American Psychologist*, 49, 709–24.

Ewald, F. 1986. *L'Etat Providence*, Paris: Grasset.

Ewald, W. 1995a. "Comparative jurisprudence (I): what was it like to try a rat?" *University of Pennsylvania Law Review*, 143, 1889–990.

—— 1995b. "Comparative jurisprudence (II): the logic of legal transplants." *American Journal of Comparative Law*, 43, 489–510.

Fairgrieve, D. 2003. *State Liability in Tort. A Comparative Law Study*. Oxford: Oxford University Press.

—— (ed.) 2005. *Product Liability in Comparative Perspective*. Cambridge: Cambridge University Press.

Faure, M. 2002. "Comments on paper by Marcel Boyer and Donatella Porrini," in *An Introduction to the Law and Economics of Environmental Policy: Issues in Institutional Design*, edited by R. Zerbe, T. Swanson. Antwerp: North Holland, 269–80.

—— 2004a. "Economic observations concerning optimal prevention and compensation of damage caused by medical malpractice," in *No-Fault Compensation in the Health Care Sector*, edited by J. Dute, M. Faure, H. Koziol, Wien: Springer, 5–87.

—— 2004b. "Financial Compensation in Case of Catastrophes: a European Law and Economics Perspective." [Online: METRO Institute]. Available at <http://www.hertig.ethz.ch/LE_2004_files/Papers/Faure_Financial_Compensation_Catastrophes.pdf> [accessed: June 15, 2009].

—— 2007. "Insurability of damage caused by climate change: a commentary." *University of Pennsylvania Law Review*, 155, 1875–99.

Feigenson, N., Bailis, D., Klein, W. 2004. "Perception of terrorism and disease risks: a cross-national comparison." *Missouri Law Review*, 69, 991–1012.

Feldman, E., 1999. "HIV and blood in Japan. Transforming private conflict into public scandal," in *Blood Feuds. AIDS, Blood, and the Politics of Medical Disaster*, edited by R. Bayer, E. Feldman. New York: Oxford University Press, 60–93.

——— 2006. "The culture of legal change: a case study of tobacco control in twenty-first century Japan." *Michigan Journal of International Law*, 27, 743–821.

——— Bayer, R. (eds) 1999. *Blood Feuds: AIDS, Blood, and the Politics of Medical Disaster*, New York: Oxford University Press.

Fennell, R. 1997. *The Common Agricultural Policy. Continuity and Change.* Oxford: Clarendon.

Ferrero, E. 1989. "Il prodotto, in *La Responsabilità del Produttore*, edited by G. Alpa, M. Bin, P. Cendon. Padova: Cedam, 39–56.

Finucane, M., Alhakami, A., Slovic, P., Johnson, S. 2000. "The affect heuristic in judgments of risks and benefits." *Journal of Behavioral Decision Making*, 13, 1–17.

Fischer, D. 1981. "Products liability – an analysis of market share liability." *Vanderbilt Law Review*, 34, 1623–50.

Fishback, P., Kantor, S. 2000. *A Prelude To the Welfare State: The Origins of Workers' Compensation.* Chicago, IL: University of Chicago Press.

Fisher, B. 2006. "Community-based efforts at reducing America's childhood obesity epidemic: federal lawmakers must weigh in." *DePaul Law Review*, 55, 711–43.

Fleming, J. 1957. "General products – Should manufacturers be liable without negligence?" *Tennessee Law Review*, 24, 923–7.

——— 1985. *An Introduction to the Law of Torts.* Oxford: Clarendon.

Flogaitis, S. 2002. "State extra-contractual liability in France, England and Greece," in *Tort Liability of Public Authorities in Comparative Perspective*, edited by D. Fairgrieve, M. Andenas, J. Bell. London: British Institute of International and Comparative Law, 439–50.

Follieri, E. 2004. *La Responsabilità Civile della Pubblica Amministrazione.* Milano: Giuffrè.

Foucault, M. 1991. "Governmentality," in *The Foucault Effect: Studies in Governmentality*, edited by G. Burchell, C. Gordon, P. Miller. London: Harvester-Wheatsheaf, 87–104.

Frewer, L. 2003. "Trust, transparency, and social context: implications for social amplification of risk," in *The Social Amplification of Risk*, edited by N. Pidgeon, R. Kasperson, P. Slovic. Cambridge: Cambridge University Press, 123–37.

Galasso, G. 2002. *Il Principio di Precauzione nella Disciplina degli OGM.* Torino: Giappichelli.

Gambaro, A., Sacco, R. 2002. *Sistemi Giuridici Comparati.* Torino: Utet.

Garner, B. (ed.) 2004. *Black's Law Dictionary.* St. Paul, MN: West Group.

Gattinara, G. 2005. "La responsabilità extracontrattuale della Comunità europea per violazione delle norme OMC." *Il Diritto dell'Unione Europea*, 1, 111–58.

Gawande, K. 2005. "The structure of lobbying and protection in U.S. agriculture." Social Science Research Network. Working Paper Series [Online]. Available at <http://ssrn.com/abstract=821445> [accessed: June 15, 2009].

Geertz, C. 1983. *Local Knowledge: Further Essays in Interpretive Anthropology.* New York: Basic Books.

Geistfeld, M. 2006. "The doctrinal unity of alternative liability and market-share liability." *University of Pennsylvania Law Review*, 155, 447–501.

Gerber, D. 2001. "Sculpting the agenda of comparative law: Ernst Rabel and the facade of language," in *Rethinking the Masters of Comparative Law*, edited by A. Riles. Oxford: Hart Publishing, 190–208.

Gerhardt, M. 2005. "The limited path dependency of precedent." *University of Pennsylvania Journal of Constitutional Law*, 7, 903–1000.

Germanò, A., Rook Basile, E. 2005. "La sicurezza alimentare," in *Il Diritto Alimentare tra Comunicazione e Sicurezza dei Prodotti*, edited by A. Germanò, E. Rook Basile. Torino: Giappichelli, 223–316.

—— 2007. *Corso di Diritto Agroalimentare*. Torino: Giappichelli.

Gerstenblith, P. 1995. "United States report," in *Extinctive Prescription: On the Limitation of Actions. Reports to the 14th Congress International Academy of Comparative Law*, edited by E. Hondius. Hague: Kluwer Law International, 359–73.

Getz, D. 1994. "Illinois redefines the standard of merchantability for food products: reasonable expectations." *Southern Illinois University Law Journal,* 18, 637–53.

Gifford, G., Pasicolan, P. 2006. "Market share liability beyond DES cases: the solution to the causation dilemma in lead paint litigation?" *South Carolina Law Review*, 58, 115–59.

Gilovich, T., Griffin, D., Kahneman, D. (eds) 2002. *Heuristics and Biases: The Psychology of Intuitive Judgment*. Cambridge: Cambridge University Press.

Giuffrida, M. 2003. *I Nuovi Limiti ai Poteri dell'Imprenditore Agricolo. Riflessioni in Tema di Responsabilità*. Milano: Giuffrè.

Goldman, B. 1992. "Can the king do no wrong? A new look at the discretionary function exception to the federal tort claims act." *Georgia Law Review*, 26, 837–60.

Goodhart, M. 2007. "Europe's democratic deficits through the looking glass: the European Union as a challenge for democracy." *Perspectives on Politics*, 5, 567–84.

Goodman, R., Jinks, D. 2003. "Toward an institutional theory of sovereignty." *Stanford Law Review*, 55, 1749–88.

Gradoni, L. 2003a. "Commento all'art. 6." *Le Nuove Leggi Civili Commentate*, n.1–2, 198–203.

—— 2003b. "Commento all'art. 7." *Le Nuove Leggi Civili Commentate*, n.1–2, 204–17.

Graziadei, M. 1999. "Il diritto comparato, la storia del diritto e l'olismo nello studio delle culture giuridiche." *Rivista Critica del Diritto Privato*, 3, 337–51.

—— 2003. "The functionalist heritage," in *Comparative Legal Studies: Traditions and Transitions*, edited by P. Legrand, R. Mundey. Cambridge:, 100–127.

—— 2006. "Comparative law as the study of transplants and receptions," in *The Oxford Handbook of Comparative Law*, edited by M. Reimann, R. Zimmermann. Oxford: Oxford University Press, 441–75.

Green, M. 1988. "The paradox of statutes of limitations in toxic substances litigation." *California Law Review*, 76, 965–1014.

Gresser, J., Fujikura, K., Morishima, A. 1981. *Environmental Law in Japan*. Cambridge, MA: MIT Press.

Griffith, S. 1999. "If you shuck enough oysters, you will find a pearl." *Loyola Law Review*, 44, 811–24.

Grignon, C. 1988. "Les enquêtes sur la consommation et la sociologie des goûts." *Revue économique*, 15–32.

Gruber-Magitot, S. 1978. *L'action du consommateur contre le fabricant d'un object affecté par un vice caché*. Paris: Presses Universitaires de France.

Guarda, P. 2004. "Automobilisti danneggiati dalla fauna selvatica: regole di responsabilità e piani di indennizzo no-fault." *Danno e Responsabilità*, 1181–92.

Guiher, J., Morris, S. 1946. "Handling food products liability cases." *Food Drug Cosmetic Law Quarterly*, 1, 109–31.

Guzman, A. 2004. "Food fears: health and safety at the WTO." *Virginia Journal of International Law*, 45, 1–39.

Hackman, A. 1997. "The discretionary function exception to the federal tort claims act: how much is enough?" *Campbell Law Review*, 19, 411–46.

Haines, P., Guilkey, D., Popkin, B. 1988. "Modeling food consumption decisions as a two-step process." *American Journal of Agricultural Economics*, 70, 543–52.

Haley, J. 1991. *Authority without Power: Law and the Japanese Paradox*. Oxford: Oxford University Press.

Hansen, J. 1991. *Gaining Access: Congress and the Farm Lobby, 1919–81*. Chicago, IL: University of Chicago Press.

Hanson, J., Kysar, D. 1999a. "Taking behavioralism seriously: the problem of market manipulation." *New York University Law Review*, 74, 630–749.

—— Kysar, D. 1999b. "Taking behavioralism seriously: some evidence of market manipulation." *Harvard Law Review*, 112, 1420-1572.

—— Yosifon, D. 2003. "The situation: an introduction to the situational character, critical realism, power economics, and deep capture." *University of Pennsylvania Law Review*, 152, 129–346.

Harris, G. 2009. "President promises to bolster food safety." *The New York Times* [Online]. March 14. Available at <http://www.nytimes.com/2009/03/15/us/politics/15address.html?ref=politics> [accessed: June 15, 2009].

—— Martin, A. 2009. "Pistachio recall signals tough stance on safety." *The New York Times* [Online]. April 6. Available at <http://www.nytimes.com/2009/04/07/health/policy/07food.html?hp> [accessed: June 15, 2009].

Harris, R., Milkis, S. 1996. *The Politics of Regulatory Change: A Tale of Two Agencies*. Oxford: Oxford University Press.

Hathaway, O. 2001. "Path dependence in the law: the course and pattern of legal change in a common law system." *Iowa Law Review*, 86, 601–65.

Heinz, J., Laumann, E., Nelson, R., Salisbury, R. 1993. *The Hollow Core: Private Interests in National Policy Making*. Cambridge, MA: Harvard University Press.

Henderson, D. 1965. *Conciliation and Japanese Law, Tokugawa and Modern*. Seattle: University of Washington Press.

Henderson, J., Twerski, A. 2001. "Drug designs are different." *Yale Law Journal*, 111, 151–81.

—— 2004. *Products Liability. Problems and Process*. New York: Aspen Publishers.

Henrich, J. (rapporteur) 2002. "Group report: what is the role of culture in bounded rationality?," in *Bounded Rationality. The Adaptive Toolbox*, edited by G. Gigerenzer, R. Selten. Cambridge, MA: MIT Press, 343–59.

Henshall, K. 2004. *A History of Japan: From Stone Age to Superpower*. London: Macmillan.

Heuston, R. 1977. *Salmond on the Law of Torts*. London: Sweet and Maxwell.

Hinderliter, J. 2006. "From farm to table: how this little piggy was dragged through the market." *University of San Francisco Law Review*, 40, 739–67.

Hirata, K. 2004a. "Beached whales: examining Japan's rejection of an international norm." *Social Science Japan Journal*, 7, 177–97.

—— 2004b. "Civil society and Japan's dysfunctional democracy." *Journal of Developing Societies*, 20, 107–24.

Hiriart, Y., Martimort, D., Pouyet, J. 2004. "On the optimal use of ex ante regulation and ex post liability." *Economics Letter*, 84, 231–5.

Hodges, C. 1998. "Developments risks: unanswered questions." *Modern Law Review*, 61, 560–70.

Hogan, J., Colonna, T. 1998. "Products liability implications of reprocessing and reuse of single-use medical devices." *Food and Drug Law Journal*, 53, 385–402.

Hondius, E. (ed.) 1995. *Extinctive Prescription: On the Limitation of Actions. Reports to the 14th Congress International Academy of Comparative Law*. The Hague: Kluwer Law International.

Houston, C. 2006. "From the Farm to the Factory: An Overview of the American and European Approaches to Regulation of the Beef Industry" [Online: Agricultural Law Research Article]. Available at <http://www.nationalaglawcenter.org/assets/articles/houston_farmtofactory.pdf> [accessed: June 15, 2009].

Howarth, R. 2000. "The CAP: history and attempts at reform." *Economic Affairs*, 20(2), 4–10.

Howells, G., Mildred, M. 2002. "Infected Blood: Defect and Discoverability. A First Exposition of the EC Product Liability Directive." *Modern Law Review*, 65, 95–106.

Huehnergarth, N. 2005. "Sugar High." July 17. *The New York Times* [Online]. Available at <http://www.nytimes.com/2005/07/17/opinion/nyregionopinions/17LIhuehnergarth.html?pagewanted=print> [accessed: June 15, 2009].

Hughes, D. 1995. "Animal welfare: the consumer and the food industry." *British Food Journal*, 97(10), 3–7.

Hugill, P., Dickson, B. (eds) 1988. *The Transfer and Transformation of Ideas and Material Culture*. College Station: Texas A&M University Press.

Hutt, P., Merrill, R., Grossman, L. 2007. *Food and Drug Law: Cases and Materials*. New York: Foundation Press.

Ingersent, K., Rayner, A., Hine, R. (eds) 1998. *The Reform of the Common Agricultural Policy*. New York: St. Martin's Press.

Izzo, U. 1999. "La responsabilità dello stato per il contagio da HIV ed epatite di emofilici e politrasfusi: i limiti della responsabilità civile." *Danno e Responsabilità*, 2, 220–33.

—— 2004. *La Precauzione nella Responsabilità Civile. Analisi di un Concetto sul Tema del Danno da Contagio per Via Trasfusionale*. Padova: Cedam.

—— 2004. "Rigenerazione di dispositivi medici e responsabilità. Verso nuovi equilibri fra tecnologia, medicina e diritto." *Danno e responsabilità*, 7, 769–72.

Jackson, C. 1970. *Food and Drug Legislation in the New Deal*. Princeton, NJ: Princeton University Press.

Jaffe, L. 1963. "Suits against governments and officers: sovereign immunity." *Harvard Law Review*, 77, 1–39.

Jarvis, J. 1993. "The discretionary function exception and the failure to warn of environmental hazards: taking the 'protection' out of environmental protection agency." *Cornell Law Review*, 78, 543–73.

Jasanoff, S. 2005. *Designs on Nature. Science and Democracy in Europe and the United States*. Princeton, NJ: Princeton University Press.

Joerges, C., Vos, E. (eds) 1999. *EU Committees: Social Regulation, Law and Politics*. Oxford: Hart Publishing.

Johnson, B. 2004. "The supreme beef case: an opportunity to rethink federal food safety regulation." *Loyola Consumer Law Review*, 16, 159–74.

Jolls, C., Sunstein, C., Thaler, R. 1998. "A behavioral approach to law and economics." *Stanford Law Review*, 50, 1471–550.

Jonas, H. 1984. *The Imperative of Responsibility: In Search of an Ethics for the Technological Age*. Chicago, IL: University of Chicago Press.

Jörgens, H. 2005. "Governance by diffusion – Implementing global norms through cross-national imitations and learning." Social Science Research Network. Accepted Paper Series [Online]. Available at <http://ssrn.com/abstract=652942> [accessed: June 15, 2009].

Jussaume, R., Judson, D. 1992. "Public perceptions about food safety in the United States and Japan." *Rural Sociology*, 57(2), 235–49.

Justice, G. 2004. "Swift Response to News of Mad Cow, Years in the Making." *The New York Times* [Online]. January 1. Available at <http://www.nytimes.com/2004/01/01/us/swift-response-to-news-of-mad-cow-years-in-the-making.html?pagewanted=all> [accessed: June 15, 2009].

Kahan, D. 2008. "Two conceptions of emotion in risk regulation." *University of Pennsylvania Law Review*, 156, 741–66.

—— Slovic, P., Braman, D., Gastil, J. 2006. "Fear of democracy: a cultural evaluation of Sunstein on risk." *Harvard Law Review*, 119, 1071–109.

—— Slovic, P., Braman, D., Gastil, J., Cohen, G. 2007. "Affect, values, and nanotechnology risk perceptions: an experimental investigation." Social Science Research Network. Working Paper Series [Online]. Available at <http://ssrn.com/abstract=968652> [accessed: June 15, 2009].

Kahneman, D., Slovic, P., Tversky, A. (eds) 1986. *Judgment under Uncertainty: Heuristics and Biases*. Cambridge: Cambridge University Press.

Kahn-Freund, O. 1974. "On uses and misuses of comparative law." *Modern Law Review*, 37, 1–27.

Kaminski, L. 1952. "Application of discretionary function exception of federal tort claims Act." *Marquette Law Review*, 36, 88–96.

Kanayama, N. 1995. "Japan Report," in *Extinctive Prescription: On the Limitation of Actions. Reports to the 14th Congress International Academy of Comparative Law*, edited by E. Hondius. Hague: Kluwer Law International, 231–48.

Kanazawa, M., Yoshiike, N., Osaka, T., Numba, Y., Zimmet, P., Inoue, S. 2002. "Criteria and classification of obesity in Japan and Asia-Oceania." *Asia Pacific Journal of Clinical Nutrition*, 11 (Suppl. 7), 732–37.

Kasperson, J., Kasperson, R., Pidgeon, N., Slovic, P. 2003. "The social amplification of risk: assessing fifteen years of research and theory," in *The Social Amplification of Risk*, edited by N. Pidgeon, R. Kasperson, P. Slovic. Cambridge: Cambridge University Press, 13–46.

Kershen, D. 2003. "Innovations in biotechnology – Public perceptions and cultural attitudes. An American's viewpoint." *Global Jurist Topics*, 3, 1–22.

Kitagawa, Z. (ed.) 2006. *Doing Business in Japan*. Volume 5. New York: Matthew Bender.

Kjærnes, U., Dulsrud, A., Poppe, C. 2006. "Contestation over food safety: the significance of consumer trust," in *What's the Beef? The Contested Governance of European Food Safety*, edited by C. Ansell, D. Vogel. Cambridge, MA: MIT Press, 61–79.

Klein, C., Huang, L. 2008. "Cultural norms as a source of law: the example of bottled water." Social Science Research Network. Accepted Paper Series [Online]. Available at <http://ssrn.com/abstract=1287269> [accessed: June 15, 2009].

Koh, H. 2005. "How to influence states: internalization through socialization." *Duke Law Journal*, 54, 975–82.

Kolstad, C., Ulen, T., Johnson, G. 1990. "Ex post liability for harm vs. ex ante safety regulation: substitutes or complements?" *American Economic Review*, 80(4), 888–901.

Korobkin, R. 1998. "The status quo bias and contract default rules." *Cornell Law Review*, 83, 608–87.

—— 2003. "The endowment effect and legal analysis." *Northwestern University Law Review*, 97, 1227–93.

—— Ulen, T. 2000. "Law and behavioral science: removing the rationality assumption from law and economics." *California Law Review*, 88, 1051–144.

Krapohl, S., Zurek, K. 2006. "The perils of committee governance: intergovernmental bargaining during the BSE scandal in the European Union." European Integration Online Papers, 10(2) [Online]. Available at <http://eiop. or.at/eiop/texte/2006-002a.htm> [accessed: June 15, 2009].

Kunreuther, H., Freeman, P. 2001. "Insurability, environmental risks and the law," in *The Law and Economics of the Environment*, edited by A. Heyes. Cheltenham: Edward Elgar Publishing, 302–18.

—— Michel-Kerjan, E. 2007. "Climate change, insurability of large-scale disasters, and the emerging liability challenge." *University of Pennsylvania Law Review*, 155, 1795–842.

Kuran, T., Sunstein, C. 1999. "Availability cascades and risk regulation." *Stanford Law Review*, 51, 683–768.

Lassiter, S. 1997. "From hoof to hamburger: the fiction of a safe meat supply." *Willamette Law Review*, 33, 411–65.

Lawson, G. 1991. "Food quality: the legal controls." *New Law Journal*, 141, 1102–04.

Lazari, A. 2005. *Modelli e Paradigmi della Responsabilità dello Stato*. Torino: Giappichelli.

Lazzaro, A. 2003. "La sicurezza alimentare e la responsabilità." *Rivista di Diritto Agrario*, 4, 450–97.

Leff, A. 1974. "Economic analysis of law: some realism about nominalism." *Virginia Law Review*, 60, 451–82.

Legrand, P. 1999. *Fragments on Law-as-Culture*. Deventer: Tjeenk Willink.

—— 2003. "The same and the different," in *Comparative Legal Studies: Traditions and Transitions*, edited by P. Legrand, R. Mundey. Cambridge: Cambridge University Press, 240–311.

Leiter, B. 2005. "American legal realism," in *The Blackwell Guide to the Philosophy of Law and Legal Theory*, edited by M. Golding, W. Edmundson. Malden: Blackwell, 50–66.

Le Tourneau, P. 2001. *La Responsabilité des Vendeurs et Fabricants*. Paris: Dalloz.

—— 2004. *Droit de la Responsabilité et des Contrats*. Paris: Dalloz.

Levine, K. 2003. "Negotiating the boundaries of crime and culture: a sociolegal perspective on cultural defense strategies." *Law and Social Inquiry*, 28, 39–86.

Levy, A. 1987. *Solving Statute of Limitations Problems*. New York: Kluwer Law Book Publishers.

Liao, Y., White, M. 2002. "No-fault for motor vehicles: an economic analysis." *American Law and Economics Review*, 4(2), 258–94.

Licht, A. 2001. "The mother of all path dependencies. Toward a cross-cultural theory of corporate governance systems." *Delaware Journal of Corporate Law*, 26, 147–205.

Liebowitz, S., Margolis, S. 1995. "Path dependence, lock-in, and history." *Journal of Law Economics and Organization*, 11(1), 205–26.

Livermore, M. 2006. "Authority and legitimacy in global governance: deliberation, institutional differentiation, and the *Codex Alimentarius*." *New York University Law Review*, 81, 766–801.

Lledo, P.M. 2001. *Malati di Cibo. Storia della Mucca Pazza*. Milano: Cortina.

Löfstedt, R. 2003. "The swing of the regulatory pendulum in Europe: from precautionary principle to (regulatory) impact analysis." Social Science Research Network. Working Paper Series [Online]. Available at <http://ssrn.com/abstract=519563> [accessed: June 15, 2009].

Longworth, J. 1983. *Beef in Japan. Politics, Production, Marketing and Trade*. St. Lucia: University of Queensland Press.

Losavio, C. 2004. "La riforma della normativa comunitaria in materia di igiene dei prodotti alimentari: il c.d. 'pacchetto igiene'." *Diritto e Giurisprudenza Agraria, Alimentare e dell'Ambiente*, 679–82.

—— 2007. *Il Consumatore di Alimenti nell'Unione Europea e il Suo Diritto ad Essere Informato*. Milano: Giuffrè.

Luhmann, N. 1993. *Risk: A Sociological Theory*. Berlin: Walter de Gruyter and Co.

Lupton, D. 1996. *Food, the Body and the Self*. London: Sage.

—— 1999. *Risk*. London: Routledge.

Lyon, J. 1998. "Coordinated food systems and accountability mechanisms for food safety: a law and economics approach." *Food and Drug Law Journal*, 53, 729–76.

Machado, K. 2003. "'Unfit for human consumption': why American beef is making us sick." *Albany Law Journal of Science and Technology*, 13, 801–34.

Maclachlan, P. 1999. "Protecting producers from consumer protection: the politics of products liability reform in Japan." *Social Science Japan Journal*, 2(2), 249–66.

—— 2002. *Consumer Politics in Postwar Japan. The Institutional Boundaries of Citizen Activism*. New York: Columbia University Press.

—— 2006. "Global trends vs. local traditions: genetically modified foods and contemporary consumerism in the United States, Japan, and Britain," in *The Ambivalent Consumer. Questioning Consumption in East Asia and the West*, edited by S. Garon, P. Maclachlan. Ithaca, NY: Cornell University Press, 236–59.

Malone, W. 1941. "*Res ipsa loquitur* and proof by inference – A discussion of the Louisiana cases." *Louisiana Law Review*, 4, 70–78.

Mandel, G., Gathii, J. 2006. "Cost-benefit analysis versus the precautionary principle: beyond Cass Sunstein's laws of fear." *University of Illinois Law Review*, 2006, 1037–79.

Maney, A., Bykerk, L. 1994. *Consumer Politics: Protecting Public Interests on Capitol Hill.* Westport, CT: Greenwood Press.

Manoukian, N. 1994. "The federal government's inspection and labeling of meat and poultry products: is it sufficient to protect the public's health, safety and welfare." *Western State University Law Review*, 21, 563–77.

Marcuse, A. 1996. "Why Japan's New Products Liability Isn't." *Pacific Rim Law and Policy Journal*, 5, 365–98.

Mariner, W. 1986. "Compensation programs for vaccine-related injury abroad: a comparative analysis." *Saint Louis University Law Journal*, 31, 599–654.

Marini, L. 2004. *Il Principio di Precauzione nel Diritto Internazionale e Comunitario: Disciplina del Commercio di Organismi Geneticamente Modificati e Profili di Sicurezza Alimentare.* Padova: Cedam.

Markesinis, B. 1997. *Foreign Law and Comparative Methodology. A Subject and a Thesis.* Oxford: Hart Publishing.

—— 2001. *Always on the Same Path: Essays on Foreign Law and Comparative Methodology.* Oxford: Hart Publishing.

—— 2003. *Comparative Law in the Courtroom and Classroom: The Story of the Last Thirty-Five Years.* Oxford: Hart Publishing.

—— Unberath, H. 2002. *The German Law of Torts. A Comparative Treatise.* Oxford: Hart Publishing.

Martin, J. 2002. *Nader: Crusader, Spoiler, Icon.* Cambridge: Basic Books.

Martorana, C. 1992. "La responsabilità per prodotti agricoli difettosi." *Rivista di Diritto Agrario*, 3, 400–25.

Matsutani, M., Martin, A. 2008. "Food Maker Pulls 'Konnyaku' Sweets." *The Japan Times* [Online]. October 9. Available at <http://search.japantimes.co.jp/cgi-bin/nn20081009a3.html> [accessed: June 15, 2009].

Mattei, U. 2003. "A theory of imperial law: a study on U.S. hegemony and the Latin resistance." *Global Jurist Frontiers*, 3(2), 1–61.

Mazzo, M. 2007. *La Responsabilità del Produttore Agricolo.* Milano: Giuffrè.

McAteer, N. 2001. "Continuing Spectre of BSE Overshadowed by Foot and Mouth Crisis" [Online: Allens Arthur Robinson. Focus on Product Liability]. Available at <http://www.aar.com.au/pubs/prod/fopljul01.htm> [accessed: June 15, 2009].

McDonald, M. 2004. "International trade law and the U.S.-EU GMO debate: can Africa weather this storm?" *Georgia Journal of International and Comparative Law*, 32, 501–38.

McEwin, I. 2000. "No-fault compensation systems," in *Encyclopaedia of Law and Economics*, edited by B. Bouckaert, G. De Geest. Chelthenam: Edward Elgar, 735–63.

McGarity, T. 2005. "Federal regulation of mad cow disease risks." *Administrative Law Review*, 57, 289–410.

McKinley, J. 2007. "San Francisco's Mayor Proposes Fee on Sales of Sugary Soft Drinks." December 18. *The New York Times* [Online]. Available at <http://www.nytimes.com/2007/12/18/us/18soda.html> [accessed: June 15, 2009].

McMenamin, J., Tiglio, A. 2006. "Not the next tobacco: defenses to obesity claims." *Food and Drug Law Journal*, 61, 445–518.

Medina Ortega, M. 1997 (Rapporteur). "Report on alleged contraventions or maladministration in the implementation of Community law in relation to BSE, without prejudice to the jurisdiction of the Community and national courts." (A4-0020/97/A), Strasbourg: Temporary committee of inquiry into BSE. European Parliament, February 7, 1997 [Online]. Available at <http://www.europarl.europa.eu/conferences/19981130/bse/a4002097_en.htm> [accessed: June 15, 2009].

Melchinger, G. 1997. "For the collective benefit: why Japan's new strict product liability law is 'strictly business'." *University of Hawaii Law Review*, 19, 879–940.

Melick, H. 1936. *The Sale of Food and Drink at Common Law and under the Uniform Sale Act*. New York: Prentice-Hall.

Melville, J. 2004. "Setting up the vCJD Trust – Operations and Lessons for the Future" [Online: The vCJD Trust]. Available at <http://www.cjdtrust.co.uk/pdfs.docs/settingupatrust.pdf> [accessed: June 15, 2009].

Mercurio, O. 2007. "Osservazioni sulla sicurezza alimentare, prodotti agricoli e responsabilità civile." *Diritto e Giurisprudenza Agraria, Alimentare e dell'Ambiente*, 7–8, 433–43.

Merrill, R., Francer, J. 2000. "Organizing federal food safety regulation." *Seton Hall Law Review*, 31, 61–173.

Michaels, R. 2006. "The functional method of comparative law," in *The Oxford Handbook of Comparative Law*, edited by M. Reimann, R. Zimmermann. Oxford: Oxford University Press, 339–82.

Milhaupt, C., Ramseyer, M., West, M. 2006. *The Japanese Legal System. Cases, Codes, and Commentary*. New York: Foundation Press.

Mintener, B. 1950. "Product liability law." *Food Drug Cosmetic Law Journal*, 5, 168–74.

Mitchell, G. 2005. "Libertarian paternalism is an oxymoron." *Northwestern University Law Review*, 99, 1245–77.

Miwa, Y., Ramseyer, M. 2004. "Deregulation and market response in contemporary Japan: administrative guidance, keiretsu, and main banks." Social Science research Network. Working Paper Series [Online]. Available at <http://ssrn.com/abstract=593527> [accessed: June 15, 2009].

Monateri, P.G. 1989. *Cumulo di Responsabilità Contrattuale e Extracontrattuale (Analisi Comparata di un Problema)*. Padova: Cedam.

—— 1998. *La Responsabilità Civile*. Torino: Utet.

—— 1999. "'Cunning passages'. Comparazione e ideologia nei rapporti tra diritto e linguaggio." *Rivista Critica del Diritto Privato*, 3, 353–66.

—— 2003. "The weak law: contaminations and legal cultures." *Transnational Law and Contemporary Problems*, 13, 575–92.

Montañés, T. 2005. "Incidencia dogmática de la jurisprudencia del caso de la colza y otros casos en materia de productos defectuosos," in *Responsabilidad Penal por Defectos en Productos Destinados a los Consumidores*, edited by J. Boix Reig, A. Bernardi, R. Cristóbal. Madrid: 115–32.

Moreau, J. 1986. *La responsabilité administrative*. Paris: Presses Universitaires de France.

Morrall, J. 1986. "A review of the record." *Regulation*, 10, 25–4.

—— 2003. "Saving lives: a review of the record." *Journal of Risk and Uncertainty*, 27, 221–37.

Moya, J. 2001. "¿Come Reclamar por el Contagio Humano del Mal de las Vacas Locas?" [Online]. Available at <http://www.consumaseguridad.com/normativa-legal/2001/06/21/257.php> [accessed: June 15, 2009].

Mulgan, A. 2005. "Where tradition meets change: Japan's agricultural politics in transition." *Journal of Japanese Studies*, 31, 261–98.

Neal, J. 2006. "Childhood obesity prevention: is recent legislation enough?" *Journal of Juvenile Law*, 27, 108–22.

Nelken, D. 2006. "Signaling conformity: changing norms in Japan and China." *Michigan Journal of International Law*, 27, 933–72.

—— 2007. "Defining and using the concept of legal culture," in *Comparative Law. A Handbook*, edited by E. Örücü, D. Nelken. Oxford: Hart Publishing, 109–32.

—— Feest, J. (eds) 2001. *Adapting Legal Cultures*. Oxford: Hart Publishing.

Neresini, F., Bucchi, M., Pellegrini, G. 2002. "Biotecnologie fra Innovazione e Responsabilità" [Online: report finale, Fondazione Bassetti]. Available at <http://www.fondazionebassetti.org/0due/docs/fgb-poster-sintesi.htm> [accessed: June 15, 2009].

Nestle, M. 2003. *Safe Food. Bacteria, Biotechnology, and Bioterrorism*. Berkeley: University of California Press.

—— 2007. *Food Politics. How the Food Industry Influences Nutrition and Health*. Berkeley: University of California Press.

Nicholas, B. 1982. *The French Law of Contract*. London: Clarendon Press.

Nicolini, G. 2005. *Immissione in Commercio del Prodotto Agro-alimentare*. Torino: Giappichelli.

—— 2006. *Danni da Prodotti Agroalimentari Difettosi. Responsabilità del Produttore*. Milano: Giuffrè.

Niskanen, W. 1994. *Bureaucracy and Public Economics*. Brookfield: Edward Elgar Publishing.

Nolan, D. 2007. "Government liability," in *The Law of Tort*, edited by K. Oliphant. 2nd edition. London: Lexis Nexis Butterworths, 885–944.

Nottage, L. 2000a. "The present and future of product liability dispute resolution in Japan." *William Mitchell Law Review*, 27, 215–35.

—— 2000b. "New concerns and challenges for product safety in Japan." *Australian Product Liability Reporter*, 11(8), 101–12.

—— 2003. "Mad cows and Japanese consumers." *Australian Product Liability Reporter*, 14(9), 125–36.

—— 2004. *Product Safety and Liability Law in Japan: From Minamata to Mad Cows.* New York: Routledge.

Nussbaum, M. 2003. *Upheavals of Thought: The Intelligence of Emotions.* Cambridge: Cambridge University Press.

O'Connor, B. 2004. *The Law of Geographical Indications.* London: Cameron May.

Odeshoo, J. 2005. "No brainer? The USDA's regulatory response to the discovery of 'mad cow' disease in the United States." *Stanford Law and Policy Review,* 16, 277–315.

Olszak, N. 2001. *Droit des Appellations d'Origine et Indications de Provenance.* Paris: Techniques and documentation.

O'Reilly, J. 2004. "Are we cutting the GRAS? Food safety perceptions are diminished by dysfunctional bureaucratic silos." *Food Drug Law Journal,* 59, 417–26.

Oter, R. 1993. "A bone to pick with Mexicali Rose v. Superior Court: liability of California restaurants for injuries caused by substances in food." *Loyola of Los Angeles Law Review,* 27, 397–433.

Ottley, Y., Ottley, B. 1984. "Product liability law in Japan: an introduction to a developing area of law." *Georgia Journal of International and Comparative Law,* 14, 29–59.

Owen, D. 1985. "The intellectual development of modern products liability law: a comment on Priest's view of the cathedral's foundations." *Journal of Legal Studies,* 14, 529–33.

—— 2005. *Products Liability Law.* St. Paul, MN: West Group.

Pacileo, V. 2003a. "Autocontrollo igienico-sanitario nell'impresa alimentare e modelli di organizzazione aziendale: un confronto possibile tra D. Lg. n. 155/97 e D. Lg. n. 231/01." *Cassazione Penale,* 7–8, 2494–501.

—— 2003b. *Il Diritto degli Alimenti. Profili Civili, Penali ed Amministrativi.* Padova: Cedam.

Palmieri, A. 2001. "Responsabilità per omessa o insufficiente vigilanza: si affievolisce l'immunità della pubblica amministrazione." *Foro Italiano,* 4(I), 1141–50.

Pardolesi, R. 2006. "Il principio di precauzione a confronto con lo strumentario dell'analisi economica del diritto," in *Gli Strumenti della Precauzione: Nuovi Rischi, Assicurazione e Responsabilità,* edited by G. Comandè. Milano: Giuffrè, 13–21.

—— Ponzanelli, G. (eds) 1989. "La responsabilità per danno da prodotti." *Le Nuove Leggi Civili Commentate,* 3, 497–652.

Patti, S. (ed.) 1990. *Il Danno da Prodotti in Italia, Austria, Repubblica Federale di Germania, Svizzera.* Padova: Cedam.

Pedler, R. (ed.) 2002. *European Union Lobbying. Changes in the Arena.* New York: Palgrave.

Pennisi, G., Scandizzo, P. 2003. *Valutare l'Incertezza: L'Analisi Costi Benefici nel XXI Secolo.* Torino: Giappichelli.

Perkins, J. 1919. "Unwholesome food as source of liability." *Iowa Law Bulletin*, 5, 86–111.

Pesce, G. 2005. "L'attività di vigilanza e controllo," in *La Responsabilità Civile della Pubblica Amministrazione*, edited by F. Caringella, M. Protto. Bologna: Zanichelli, 1153–215.

Petersen, A. 2004. "Status of Food Traceability in the European Union (EU) and United States of America (US), with Special Emphasis on Seafood and Fishery Products" [Online]. Available at <http://www.seafoodlab.cmast.ncsu.edu/documents/Traceability%20of%20seafood%20products%20in%20EU%20and%20USA.pdf> [accessed: June 15, 2009].

Phillips, A. 2003. "When culture means gender: issues of cultural defence in the British courts." *Modern Law Review*, 66(4), 510–31.

Phillips of Worth Matravers, N. (Chairman) 2000. "Report to an Order of the Honourable the House of Commons dated October 2000 for the Report, evidence and supporting papers of the Inquiry into the emergence and identification of Bovine Spongiform Encephalopathy (BSE) and variant Creutzfeldt-Jakob Disease (vCJD) and the action taken in response to it up to 20 March 1996" [Online]. Available at <http://www.bseinquiry.gov.uk> [accessed: June 15, 2009].

Piccinino, R. 1988. *Diritto Penale Alimentare (Dottrina e Giurisprudenza)*. Torino: Utet.

Pidgeon, N., Kasperson, R., Slovic, P. (eds) 2003. *The Social Amplification of Risk*. Cambridge: Cambridge University Press.

Piergallini, C. 2004. *Danno da Prodotto e Responsabilità Penale*. Milano: Giuffrè.

Pittman, H. 2005. "Market Concentration, Horizontal Consolidation, and Vertical Integration in the Hog and Cattle Industries: Taking Stock of the Road Ahead" [Online: Agricultural Law Research Article]. Available at <http://www.nationalaglawcenter.org/research/#marketconcentration> [accessed: June 15, 2009].

Poli, S. 2004. "The European community and the adoption of international food standards within the *Codex Alimentarius* Commission." *European Law Journal*, 10(5), 613–30.

Pontier, J. 1992. "Sida et responsabilité: problèmes de droit public." *Revue francaise de droit administratif*, 3, 533–45.

Ponzanelli, G. 1992. *La Responsabilità Civile. Profili di Diritto Comparato*. Bologna: Mulino.

—— 1997. "Regno Unito, corte di giustizia ed eccezione dello 'state of the art'." *Foro Italiano*, 10(IV), 388–92.

—— 2001a. "Responsabilità civile e sicurezza sociale: un decennio 'tribolato'." *Foro Italiano*, 1(I), 6–10.

—— 2001b. "Estensione della responsabilità oggettiva anche all'agricoltore, all'allevatore, al pescatore e al cacciatore." *Danno e Responsabilità*, 8–9, 792–3.

Porat, A., Stein, A. 2001. *Tort Liability under Uncertainty*. Oxford: Oxford University Press.

Poto, M. 2007. "Illecito comunitario e responsabilità extracontrattuale della Commissione Europea." *Responsabilità civile e previdenza*, 10, 2051–7.

Prati, L., Massimino, F. 2001. "Organismi geneticamente modificati, danno alla salute e danno ambientale." *Danno e responsabilità*, 4, 337–48.

Priest, G. 1985. "The invention of enterprise liability: a critical history of the intellectual foundations of modern tort law." *Journal of Legal Studies*, 14, 461–527.

—— 1989. "Strict products liability: the original intent." *Cardozo Law Review*, 10, 2301–27.

Prosperi, O. 2003. "Sicurezza alimentare e responsabilità civile." *Rivista di diritto agrario*, 3, 351–78.

Prosser, W. 1948. "*Res ipsa loquitur* in California." *California Law Review*, 37, 183–234.

—— 1960. "The assault upon the citadel (strict liability to the consumer)." *Yale Law Journal*, 69, 1099–148.

Rabin, R. 1993. "Some thoughts on the efficacy of a mass toxics administrative compensation scheme." *Maryland Law Review*, 52, 951–82.

—— 2002. "Indeterminate future harm in the context of September 11." Social Science Research Network. Accepted Paper Series [Online]. Available at <http://ssrn.com/abstract_id=312025> [accessed: June 15, 2009].

Rampton, S., Stauber, J. 2004. *Mad Cow U.S.A.* Monroe, ME: Common Courage Press.

Ramseyer, M. 1996. "Law, economics, and norms: products liability through private ordering: notes on a Japanese experiment." *University of Pennsylvania Law Review*, 144, 1823–39.

Regier, C. 1933. "The struggle for federal food and drugs legislation." *Law and Contemporary Problems*, 1, 3–15.

Reimann, M. 2003a. "Product liability in a global context: the hollow victory of the European model." *European Review of Private Law*, 11, 128–54.

—— 2003b. "Liability for defective products at the beginning of the twenty-first century: emergence of a worldwide standard?" *American Journal of Comparative Law*, 51, 751–838.

Rich, S. 2006. "Using Cell Phones for Food Traceability." [Online]. Available at <http://www.worldchanging.com/archives/005403.html> [accessed: June 15, 2009].

Rickard, S. 2000. "The CAP: whence it came, where it should go." *Economic Affairs*, 20(2), 27–33.

Ritson, C., Harvey, D. (eds) 1997. *The Common Agricultural Policy*. New York: CAB International.

Rivero, J., Waline, J. 2006. *Droit Administratif*. Paris: Dalloz.

Roberts, M., O'Brien, D. 2004. "Animal Identification: Liability Exposure and Risk Management" [Online: National Agricultural Law Center]. Available at <http://www.nationalaglawcenter.org/research/#factsheet6> [accessed: June 15, 2009].

Rogers, W. 1989. *Winfield and Jolowicz on Tort*. London: Sweet and Maxwell.

Roots, R. 2001. "A muckraker's aftermath: the jungle of meat-packing regulation after a century." *William Mitchell Law Review*, 27, 2413–33.

Rose-Ackerman, S. 1991. "Tort law as a regulatory system." *American Economic Review*, 81(2), 54–8.

Rothenberg, P. 2000. "Japan's new product liability law: achieving modest success." *Law and Policy in International Business*, 31, 453–516.

Rouland, N. 1988. *Anthropologie Juridique*. Paris: Presses Universitaires de France.

Sacco, R. 1989. "Crittotipo," in *Digesto delle Discipline Privatistiche (Sezione Civile)*. Torino: Utet, V, 39–40.

―― 1991a. "Legal formants: a dynamic approach to comparative law I." *American Journal of Comparative Law*, 39, 1–34.

―― 1991b. "Legal formants: a dynamic approach to comparative law II." *American Journal of Comparative Law*, 39, 343–401.

―― 1992a. *Che Cos'E' il Diritto Comparato*. Milano: Giuffrè.

―― 1992b. *Introduzione al Diritto Comparato*. Torino: Utet.

―― 2007. *Antropologia Giuridica. Contributo ad una Macrostoria del Diritto*. Bologna: Mulino.

Sansom, G. 1963. *A History of Japan: 1615–1867*. Stanford, CA: Stanford University Press.

Santonastaso, F. 2005. "Principio di 'precauzione' e responsabilità d'impresa: rischio tecnologico e attività pericolosa 'per sua natura'. Prime riflessioni su un tema di ricerca." *Contratto e Impresa. Europa*, 1, 21–105.

Scharff, R., Parisi, F. 2006. "The role of status quo bias and bayesian learning in the creation of new legal rights." *Journal of Law, Economics and Policy*, 31, 25–45.

Schlosser, E. 2005. *Fast Food Nation*. New York: HarperCollins Publishers.

Schuller, D. 1998. "Pathogen reduction through 'HACCP' systems: is overhaul of the meat inspection system all it's cut out to be?" *San Joaquin Agricultural Law Review*, 8, 77–101.

Schwartz, A. 2000. "Statutory interpretation, capture and tort law: the regulatory compliance defence." *American Law and Economics Review*, 2(1), 1–57.

Schwartz, G. 1992. "The beginning and the possible end of the rise of modern American tort law." *Georgia Law Review*, 26, 601–702.

Schwartz, V., Tedesco, R. 2003. "The re-emergence of 'super strict' liability: slaying the dragon again." *University of Cincinnati Law Review*, 71, 917–36.

Scognamiglio, G. 2006. "La responsabilità civile della Consob." *Rivista di Diritto Commerciale e del Diritto Generale delle Obbligazioni*, 10–12, I, 695–726.

Seamon, R. 1997. "Causation and the discretionary function exception to the Federal Tort Claims Act." *U.C. Davis Law Review*, 30, 691–784.

Setbon, M., Raude, J., Fischler, C., Flahault, A. 2005. "Risk perception of the 'mad cow disease' in France: determinants and consequences." *Risk Analysis*, 25(4), 813–26.

Severson, K. 2006. "New York Gets Ready to Count Calories." December 13. *The New York Times* [Online]. Available at <http://www.nytimes.com/2006/12/13/dining/13calo.html. [accessed: June 15, 2009].

—— 2008. "Is a new food policy on Obama's list?" December 23. *The New York Times* [Online]. Available at <http://www.nytimes.com/2008/12/24/dining/24food.html> [accessed: June 15, 2009].

Sgarbanti, G. 2003. "La libera circolazione dei prodotti agroalimentari," in *Trattato Breve di Diritto Agrario Italiano e Comunitario*, edited by L. Costato. Padova: Cedam, 623–31.

Shavell, S. 1980. "Strict liability versus negligence." *Journal of Legal Studies*, 9(1), 1–25.

—— 1984a. "Liability for harm versus regulation of safety." *Journal of Legal Studies*, 13(2), 357–74.

—— 1984b. "A model of the optimal use of liability and safety regulation." *Rand Journal of Economics*, 15(2), 271–80.

—— 1987. *Economic Analysis of Accident Law*. Cambridge, MA: Harvard University Press.

—— 1992. "Liability and the incentive to obtain information about risk." *Journal of Legal Studies*, 21(2), 259-270.

Sien, I. 2007. "Beefing up the hormones dispute: problems in compliance and viable compromise alternatives." *Georgetown Law Journal*, 95, 565–90.

Simon, H. 1955. "A behavioral model of rational choice." *Quarterly Journal of Economics*, 69(1), 99–118.

—— 1982. *Models of Bounded Rationality*. Cambridge: MIT Press.

Simon, J. 2005. "Risk and reflexivity: what socio-legal studies add to the study of risk and the law." *Alabama Law Review*, 57, 119–39.

Simpson, J., Farris, D. 1982. *The World's Beef Business*. Ames: Iowa State University Press.

Sinclair, U. 1906. *The Jungle*. New York: Doubleday.

Slovic, P., Finucane, M., Peters, E., MacGregor, D. 2002. "Rational Actors or Rational Fools? Implications of the Affect Heuristic for Behavioral Economics" [Online]. Available at <http://www.decisionresearch.org/pdf/dr498v2.pdf> [accessed: June 15, 2009].

Smith, R. 2007. "Red Meat and Alcohol Are Major Cancer Causes." October 31. *Telegraph* [Online]. Available at <http://www.telegraph.co.uk/news/uknews/1567944/Red-meat-and-alcohol-are-major-cancer-causes.html> [accessed: June 15, 2009].

Sofsky, W. 2005. *Rischio e Sicurezza*. Torino: Einaudi.

Sollini, M. 2006. *Il Principio di Precauzione nella Disciplina Comunitaria della Sicurezza Alimentare: Profili Critico-Ricostruttivi*. Milano: Giuffrè.

Somma, A. 2005. "Tanto per cambiare ... Mutazione del diritto e mondializzazione nella riflessione comparatistica." *Politica del diritto*, 1, 105–34.

Spurlock, M. (director) 2004. *Super Size Me.*

Stapleton, J. 1994. *Product Liability*. London: Butterworth.

—— 2002. "Bugs in Anglo-American products liability." *South Carolina Law Review*, 53, 1225–61.

—— 2003. "BSE, CJD, mass infections and the 3rd US Restatement," in *International Perspectives on Consumers' Access to Justice*, edited by C. Rickett, T. Telfer. Cambridge: Cambridge University Press, 128–46.

Stella, G. 2006. "La responsabilità del produttore per danno da prodotto difettoso nel nuovo Codice del Consumo." *Responsabilità civile e previdenza*, 1589–625.

Stewart, T., Johanson, D. 1998. "The SPS Agreement of the World Trade Organization and international organizations: the roles of the *Codex Alimentarius* Commission, the International Plant Protection Convention, and the International Office of Epizootics." *Syracuse Journal of International and Commerce*, 26, 27–53.

Stiglitz, J. 2001. *Economics of the Public Sector*, 3rd edn. New York: Norton.

Street, H. 1948. "Tort liability of the state: the Federal Tort Claims Act and the Crown Proceedings Act." *Michigan Law Review*, 47, 341-368.

Sugarman, S. 1985. "Doing away with tort law." *California Law Review*, 73, 558–664.

Sunstein, C. 1997. "Behavioral Analysis of Law." *University of Chicago Law Review*, 64, 1175–95.

—— 2000. *Behavioral Law and Economics*. Cambridge: Cambridge University Press.

—— 2002a. "Probability neglect: emotions, worst cases, and law." *Yale Law Journal*, 112, 61–107.

—— 2002b. "Switching the default rule." *New York University Law Review*, 77, 106–34.

—— 2005. *Laws of Fear: Beyond the Precautionary Principle*. Cambridge: Cambridge University Press.

—— Thaler, R. 2003. "Libertarian Paternalism Is Not an Oxymoron." *University of Chicago Law Review*, 70, 1159–202.

Swinbank, A., Daugbjerg, C. 2006. "The 2003 CAP reform: accomodating WTO pressures." *Comparative European Politics*, 4(1), 47–64.

Takahara, K. 2006. "'Safe' U.S. beef gets green light to enter Japan." *The Japan Times* [Online]. July 28. Available at <http://search.japantimes.co.jp/cgi-bin/nb20060728a1.html> [accessed: June 15, 2009].

Tallacchini, M. 2004. "La costruzione giuridica dei rischi e la partecipazione del pubblico alle decisioni science-based," in *Scienza e diritto nel prisma del diritto comparato*, edited by G. Comandé, G. Ponzanelli. Torino: Giappichelli, 339–55.

Taylor, S. 1999. *L'Harmonisation Communautaire de la Responsabilité du Fait des Produits Défectueux: Étude Comparative du Droit Anglais et du Droit Français*. Paris: Libraire générale de droit et de jurisprudence.

Teeven, K. 1990. *A History of the Anglo-American Common Law of Contract*. New York: Greenwood.

Tejima, Y. 1993. "Tort and compensation in Japan: medical malpractice and adverse effects from pharmaceuticals." *Hawaii Law Review*, 15, 728–35.

Thompson, B. 2004. "The obesity agency: centralizing the nation's fight against fat." *American Journal Law and Medicine*, 30, 543–59.

Tizzano, A. 2001. "Tutela del consumatore e responsabilità civile del produttore e del distributore di alimenti in Europa e negli Stati Uniti." *Europa e diritto privato*, 3, 685–702.

Townsend, E. 2006. "Affective influences on risk perceptions of, and attitudes toward, genetically modified food." *Journal of Risk Research* 9(2), 125–39.

Trimarchi, P. 1961. *Rischio e Responsabilità Oggettiva*. Milano: Giuffrè.

Troiano, O. 1989. "Commento all'art. 2, in La responsabilità per danno da prodotti, supervised by R. Pardolesi, G. Ponzanelli." *Le Nuove Leggi Civili Commentate*, 3, 510–18.

Truswell, S. 2007. "Cardiovascular diseases and red meat." *Nutrition and Dietetics*, 64(4), 162–8.

Twining, W. 2005. "Social science and diffusion of law." *Journal of Law and Society*, 32(2), 203–40.

Uchtmann, D. 2002. "Starlink TM – A case study of agricultural biotechnology regulation." *Drake Journal of Agriculture Law*, 7, 159–211.

Uga, K. 1999. "The state reparation law," in *Modern Trends in Tort Law. Dutch and Japanese Law Compared*, edited by E. Hondius. The Hague: Kluwer Law International, 195–201.

Upham, F. 1987. *Law and Social Change in Postwar Japan*. Cambridge, MA: Harvard University Press.

van Boom, W.H., Pinna, A. 2005. "Liability for Failure to Regulate Health and Safety Risks. Second-Guessing Policy Choice or Showing Judicial Restraint?" *European Tort Law*, 2005, 1, 2–22.

Vandall, F. 1994. "State-of-the-art, custom, and reasonable alternative design." *Suffolk Law Review*, 28, 1193–203.

van Schendelen, M. 1994. *National Public and Private EC Lobbying*. Aldershot: Dartmouth Publishing.

van Tassel, K. 2004. "The introduction of biotech foods to the tort system: creating a new duty to identify." *University of Cincinnati Law Review*, 72, 1645–705.

van Waarden, F. 2006. "Taste, traditions, transactions, and trust: the public and private regulation of food," in *What's the Beef? The Contested Governance of European Food Safety*, edited by C. Ansell, D. Vogel. Cambridge, MA: MIT Press, 35–59.

Veilleux, D. 2002. "Liability for injury or death allegedly caused by foreign substance in beverage." *American Law Reports* 4, 90, 12.

Vera, M. 2005. "Regulatory swords that slay mad cows: EU and U.K. animal feed restrictions as guides for the FDA." *Texas International Law Journal*, 40, 299–333.

Viscusi, K. 1988. "Product liability and regulation: establishing the appropriate institutional division of labor." *American Economic Review*, 2, 300–304.

—— 2002. "Tobacco: regulation and taxation through litigation," in *Regulation through Litigation*, edited by K. Viscusi. Washington, DC: Brookings Institution Press, 22–52.

Vogel, D. 1992. "Consumer protection and protectionism in Japan." *Journal of Japanese Studies*, 18(1), 119–54.

—— 2003. "The hare and the tortoise revisited: the new politics of consumer and environmental regulation in Europe." *British Journal of Political Science*, 33(4), 557–80.

Vogel, S. 1999. "When interests are not preferences: the cautionary tale of Japanese consumers." *Comparative Politics*, 31(2), 187–207.

von Hayek F. 1973. *Law, Legislation and Liberty*. Volume I: *Rules and Order*. Chicago, IL: University of Chicago Press.

von Wangenheim, G. 1999. "Production of legal rules by agencies and bureaucracies," in *Encyclopaedia of Law and Economics*, edited by B. Bouckaert, G. De Geest. Cheltenham: Edward Elgar, 559–86.

Vos, E. 1999. *Institutional Frameworks of Community Health and Safety Regulation. Committees, Agencies and Private Bodies*. Oxford: Hart Publishing.

—— 2000. "EU food safety regulation in the aftermath of the BSE crisis." *Journal of Consumer Policy*, 23(3), 227–55.

Walker, M. 2006. "Low-fat foods or big fat lies?: the role of deceptive marketing in obesity lawsuits." *Georgia State University Law Review*, 22, 689–710.

Watson, A. 1974. *Legal Transplants: An Approach to Comparative Law*. Charlottesville: University Press of Virginia.

Weissenbacher, M. 2003. *Mucca Pazza: BSE e Incremento dei Casi della Malattia di Creutzfeldt-Jakob*. Palermo: Nuova Ipsa.

Whetstone, L. 2000. "Editorial: reforming the CAP." *Economic Affairs*, 20(2), 2–3.

Whitman, J. 2004. "The two Western cultures of privacy: dignity versus liberty." *Yale Law Journal*, 113, 1151–221.

Whittaker, S. 2005. *Liability for Products: English Law, French Law, and European Harmonization*. Oxford: Oxford University Press.

Wiener, J. 2003. "Whose precaution after all? A comment on the comparison and evolution of risk regulatory systems." *Duke Journal of Comparative and International Law*, 13, 207–62.

—— Rogers, M. 2002. "Comparing precaution in the United States and Europe." *Journal of Risk Research*, 5(4), 317–49.

Wijers-Hasegawa, Y. 2006. "Japan Sets to Lift U.S. Beef Ban." *The Japan Times* [Online]. June 21. Available at <http://search.japantimes.co.jp/cgi-bin/nb20060621a1.html> [accessed: June 15, 2009].

Will, R.G., Ironside, J.W., Zeidler, M., Cousens, S.N., Estibeiro, K., Alperovitch, A., Poser, S., Pocchiari, M., Hofman, A., Smith, P.G. 1996. "A new variant of Creutzfeldt-Jakob disease in the UK." *The Lancet*, 347, 921–5.

Winickoff, D., Jasanoff, S., Busch, L., Grove-White, R., Wynne, B. 2005. "Adjudicating the GM food wars: science, risk, and democracy in world trade law." *Yale Journal of International Law*, 30, 81–123.

Wittenberg, E., Wittenberg, E. 1989. *How to Win in Washington*. Oxford: Blackwell.

Wojtan, L. 1993. "Rice: It's More Than Just a Food." *Japan Digest* [Online]. Available at <http://iis-db.stanford.edu/docs/145/digest6.pdf> [accessed: June 15, 2009].

Wolpe, B. 1990. *Lobbying Congress: How the System Works*. Washington, DC: CQ Press.

Wong, J. 2003. "Are biotech crops and conventional crops like products? An analysis under Gatt." *Duke Law and Technology Review*, 2003, 27–41.

Yasui, A. 2004. "New food control system in Japan and food analysis at NFRI." *Accreditation and Quality Assurance*, 9, 568–70.

Young, M. 1984. "Administrative guidance in the courts: a case study in doctrinal adaptation." *Law in Japan. An Annual*, 17, 120–51.

Young, N. 1996. "Japan's new product liability law: increased protection for consumers." *Loyola of Los Angeles International and Comparative Law Journal*, 18, 893–919.

Zeidler, M., Johnstone, E.C., Bamber, R.W.K., Dickens, C.M., Fisher, C.J., Francis, A.F., Goldbeck, R., Higgo, R., Johnson-Sabine, E.C., Lodge, G.J., McGarry, P., Mitchell, S., Tarlo, L., Turner, M., Ryley, P., Will, R.G. 1997. "New variant Creutzfeldt-Jakob disease: psychiatric features." *The Lancet*, 350, 908–10.

Zerbe, R., Dively, D. 1993. *Benefit-Cost Analysis: In Theory and Practice*. New York: HarperCollins College Publishers.

Zillman, D. 1995. "Protecting discretion: judicial interpretation of the discretionary function exception to the federal tort claims act." *Maine Law Review*, 47, 366–88.

Index